"Who's Gonna Cover 'Em Up?!"

"Who's Gonna Cover 'Em Up?!"
Chapel Hill Uncovered — 1950-1985

Roland Giduz

featuring

The Newsman's Notepad

with photos by the author

Foreword by James H. Shumaker
(Former Editor of *The Chapel Hill Newspaper*)

To
the On-Going Spirit of Chapel Hill
and its constancy in change

and most especially
to my wife

Published by Citizen Publishing
Box 44, Chapel Hill, NC 27514
Telephone: 919/942-2194

© Copyright 1985 by Roland Giduz. All rights reserved

Library of Congress Catalog No. 85-072908
ISBN 0-9615867-0-2

About the book

Book design by Hollie Taylor, Chapel Hill, NC

Typesetting by Universal Printing and Publishing, Chapel Hill, NC

Printed by McCain Printing, Danville, VA

Contents

Foreword

Roland Giduz is a member of that nearly extinct species, the Chapel Hill native, and of the even rarer sub-species, the native who remained in Chapel Hill. In more than half a century he has departed only temporarily and briefly in the flesh, never in spirit.

His love affair with the town has been like most love affairs of the conventional kind, running from hot to cool, from swelling pride in the beloved to mild disgust, from great expectations to quiet desperation, and from deep fulfillment to a taste of ashes.

He has seen, with greater perception and understanding than anyone I know, Chapel Hill's transformation — some would say transmogrification — from a quiet, tree-shaded village exuding old-fashioned charm and serenity to the Chapel Hill of today with its condos, congestion, and conglomeration.

Through the years he has performed the difficult feat of being a part of the town and at the same time standing apart, after a fashion, to see it for what it is, remembering the past and at odd times deploring the future.

With his writing, he has served in a way, maybe the best way, as Chapel Hill's historian, not necessarily as a recorder of those apocalyptic events and commanding figures that flood conventional histories, but as a keeper of the journal in which are set down the ordinary comings and goings, the daily doings that are the real heartbeat of any town.

What he has put down in these pieces was seen with a clear mind, an uncluttered intelligence, and with a sure sense of what matters, what has mattered, and what ought to matter, not only in Chapel Hill but in life.

And whether looking at warts or beauty marks, he has seen it all, reflected upon it, and put it down with a warm and compassionate heart.

Jim Shumaker
Chapel Hill

Preface

The inspiration for "Who's Gonna Cover 'Em Up?!" comes from the more than 2,000 Newsman's Notepad columns of observation and opinion which I wrote in a period of over 30 years for various newspapers in Chapel Hill, beginning in 1952.

I started the process of writing this book by indexing (and even cross-indexing) each newspaper column within approximately 150 different topic headings, writing each topic in chronological order on large index cards. From the five-inch stack of index cards I compiled the favorite topics — generally things that I'd enjoyed writing about the most. That accomplished, I simply started reviewing them and selecting excerpts from the newspaper columns.

To some extent the material in each chapter is in chronological order. This is natural, but not significant. My idea was to select interesting excerpts from the various columns and link them together where appropriate with transitional writing. In many cases I wrote a concluding observation from a later perspective.

Each excerpt is dated to show at its end the date of its publication, though not the newspaper in which it was published. Through the years these newspapers were, consecutively, *The Chapel Hill Weekly, The Chapel Hill News Leader, The News of Orange County,* and *The Chapel Hill Newspaper.* You will note that the style of the Newsman's Notepad column changed during this 30-year period. Opinions in the column changed, too, sometimes very quickly. Almost all of the photographs are my own and were made either for publication with the columns or for local news events.

— Finally, if you're wondering about the significance of the title of this book, read on. It will become self-evident.

— Courtesy of Jeff MacNelly

*— Reprinted by permission of
Jefferson Communications Inc., Reston,*

Acknowledgements

The indulgence of readers and friends of the Newsman's Notepad column across the years has made this book possible. These include thousands of people who truly care about Chapel Hill as I do.

Next in order, thanks is due the late Editor of the *Chapel Hill Weekly*, Louis Graves, who was my first newspaper employer in Chapel Hill and a gracious and erudite journalist; publisher Edwin J. Hamlin of *The News of Orange County* and a co-publisher with me of *The Chapel Hill News Leader; and to Chapel Hill Newspaper* Publisher Orville Campbell, for whom I was a contributing columnist.

The actual writing of the book has been greatly helped by my patient, loving, and always supportive spouse, Helen Jeter Giduz, whose thoughtful encouragement brought the manuscript to fruition during the summer of 1985.

For his professional assistance in editing I thank Jim Vickers, the very thorough and dedicated author of the 1985 book, "Chapel Hill An Illustrated History." I was privileged to edit that significant work for him, and he capably returned the courtesy. Others who helped in this same manner were Joe Jones, retired Managing Editor of *The Chapel Hill Weekly* and my superior and mentor on that newspaper many years ago; and Clarence Whitefield, a valued colleague for years both as a newspaperman and during his tenure as Director of Alumni Affairs for the University at Chapel Hill.

"Who's Gonna Cover 'Em Up?!" displays on its cover the work of a young man whom I believe to be the best political cartoonist in the country today, and whom I predict will soon be more widely recognized – John Branch of the *San Antonio Express and News* in Texas. A Chapel Hill native who says he still yearns for draughts from The Old Well, John started his budding career on *The Chapel Hill Newspaper*, as did Pulitzer Prize-winning cartoonist Jeff MacNelly (who shares my opinion of Branch), and who graciously granted permission to reprint from his "Shoe" comic strip.

Jim Shumaker, a true newspaperman's newspaperman if ever there was one, was a fellow laborer in the vineyard with me on the staff of the *Durham Morning Herald* many years ago, and later the editor to whom I submitted my column as a contributor to *The Chapel Hill Weekly* and *The Chapel Hill Newspaper*. He continues as a friend and kindred spirit in his capacity as a lecturer in journalism at UNC-Chapel Hill. I am indebted to him for the foreword to this book. Similarly, I am grateful to a life-long friend and guiding spirit of Chapel Hill and alma mater for many decades, Chancellor Emeritus Robert B. House, for his kind words on the dust jacket of this book.

To Gran Childress, an expatriate Chapel Hill soul-mate and long-time friend, and to his wife, Gayle Hancock Childress—as "The Old Mountain Two" of Asheville—I give special thanks for their inspiration in suggesting the ideal name for this book.

The keen insight of Edwin W. Tenney Jr., a Chapel Hillian to the marrow, is deeply appreciated by me for his always-available and valuable counsel.

Finally, to Jim Heavner, President of The Village Companies, I extend my heartfelt thanks for his supportive spirit, wise counsel, and warm personal friendship in this and my daily endeavors.

Introduction

The goal of this book is to give the "feel" of Chapel Hill during the second half of this 20th century to date as a dynamic community with a significant continuing heritage.

As a resident of the Southern Part of Heaven since infancy, I have known no other home – save a World War II stretch in the Army, followed by two years in Manhattan. The latter experiences were ideal for providing a perspective of Chapel Hill as a unique and lovable locale in the world. That period also helped me shed the mantle of Chapel Hill smugness, which, unless we deliberately face it down, tends to become an unfortunate and involuntary handmaiden of local personality.

Yes, we all dearly love this Southern Part of Heaven for its singular qualities of charm and the free spirit it provides and encourages within us. The danger is that we flaunt these as a cloak and shield against the outside world. That attitude ill suits us, but I see it growing around the community like weeds in a beautiful but untended garden.

"Who's Gonna Cover 'Em Up?!" is intended to foster our pride in the joy of living in Chapel Hill. It should celebrate our historic heritage as a university community which believes in alma mater's motto of "lux et libertas."

But it is specifically not intended to be a definitive statement of what Chapel Hill is all about. That is because it is basically limited by what I happened to write in the Newsman's Notepad newspaper column through these years. Most of the time those subjects were directed to specific matters of the moment.

Through it all, though, I have hoped to help Chapel Hillians to believe in our community as a human – not a super-human place – and to remember to laugh at ourselves occasionally and to smile with the rest of the world.

Chapter 1

Gracious Living in Chapel Hill (GLICH)

Admonish the kissers to be considerate enough of drivers behind them not to overdo their thing. Gracious Living in Chapel Hill would be abetted.

There are certain little somethings that make Chapel Hill a special, indeed, a better place to live than it would otherwise be. Some of them would improve the quality of life anywhere, and others are unique to the spirit of Chapel Hill. All of them I put under the heading of things that contribute to GLICH, or Gracious Living in Chapel Hill.

They don't have to be things of great import in the over-all scheme of life. In fact, to me they're "Chapel Hillier" when they're more minute. Chapel Hill is a place which ought to be concerned with the little things that add a cubit to our quality of life in the storied Southern Part of Heaven.

Two of my all-time favorite Chapel Hilly contributions to GLICH are of truly modest proportions, but they supremely qualify. First is a simple statement of empathy. I called it a "hallmark" of the expectation that human beings and their psyches in this supposed-to-be sophisticated community are due a bit more sensitivity.

This particular quality of GLICH was cited in connection with an exhibit of home-made quilts at the Chapel Hill Preservation Society's Horace Williams House. It was a simple sign. But in a New York museum, I wrote, there would be an armed guard glaring at spectators to protect the exhibit. In Washington the museum would post big bold signs warning one and all, "DON'T TOUCH!" At a state museum in Raleigh the sign would read "Please Do Not Touch." But in Chapel Hill:

... only in Chapel Hill, too, I suggest – the issue is taken up with delicate insight. Discreetly, but visibly attached to each quilt on the display is a hand-lettered card, imploring the tender sensibilities of the viewer and asking him:

"Please try not to touch." Now that's real Chapel Hilly.

(10/31/73)

GLICH was also abetted supremely and to a similar extent by the good people of the Morehead Planetarium in a very special way. There's a contradictory trend in business operations in general, I suggested. When you buy goods in greater quantity you realize a saving on the unit price, such as five cents each and three for a dime. The contradiction is that when business is best entrepreneurs often hike their prices, invoking the laws of supply and demand, or as in Chapel Hill, raising the bus fares during peak hours of patronage. On the other hand:

... Now comes along the Morehead Planetarium, lowering the admission price during the busiest period. Announcement is made through The Newspaper that ALL spectators will be admitted to the Planetarium shows on this UNC commencement week-end at the student rate – a nice saving off the regular adult ticket price.

This is scarcely a straw in the winds of general commerce, but it's a nice gesture – very Chapel Hilly.

(5/7/76)

A similarly gracious gesture that was unique to Chapel Hill was the decision of University athletic administrators several years ago to suggest to ticket holders for Carmichael Auditorium basketball games that if they didn't plan to use their tickets they lend them to somebody else who otherwise wouldn't be able to attend the always sold-out Carolina home basketball games. That, it seemed to me, was Chapel Hill's response to the oft-printed "Not Transferable" warning printed on tickets to various entertainment events.

In our automobile-oriented society there are boundless opportunities for contributing to GLICH:

... Ordinarily the human being who seats himself behind the wheel of an automobile tends to show as much compassion as the machine he's driving. But there is an unwritten rule of courtesy among a goodly number of the (UNC) campus denizens. They make it a regular practice to stop in lines of traffic to let those waiting on the side streets and driveways enter the line.

This may be a bit of foresighted self-interest for the day they'll be waiting at the side. But it is nonetheless one of those little things that contribute significantly to Gracious Living in Chapel Hill. In the City of Charleston, WV, the citizens take special pride in claiming to be the most courteous drivers in the country. It's a title Chapel Hillians should covet – and could easily capture if they but would.

(6/2/68)

The passing years since that suggestion haven't seen any significant increase in such driver courtesy, but singular examples of GLICH do live on. That is abetted by another Chapel Hill tradition, oft-cited. It is the un- written and perhaps informal policy of Chapel Hill policemen:

... The Town's bluecoats try to be firm but tractable, to go to considerable lengths to be helpful, and to warn tactfully rather than arrest, where possible. This attitude has been inherited from the complexion of the force under the late Chief W.T. Sloan and is carried on by Chief Bill Blake. And every patrolman who practices this preaching is distinctly honoring both his employer and his community at large.

(6/2/68)

Needless to say, Chief Herman Stone, who began his law enforcement tenure under Chief Sloan, sees to it that this policy is carried on, actually in a more deliberately positive way. To give Chapel Hill drivers themselves more credit as a general body politic, I cite the ploy used by a successful local realtor. When he's showing a prospective newcomer around town, he says, he'll often wait a few moments after a traffic signal turns green, then turn to the visitor as he puts his cupped hand to his ear and say "Hear that? – Nothing; nobody blowing a horn behind you!" The realtor's point is the same as mine – that such patient courtesy is Chapel Hilly, and contributes to GLICH.

A practice in this realm that Chapel Hill could honorably import from many other places, I suggested, was "Kiss and Go," a traffic policy I first noted at Raleigh-Durham Airport for quick unloading of passengers and baggage, as opposed to stationary parking:

... There are a number of crucial curb spots alongside moving traffic lanes in Chapel Hill where such signs would also be an asset to relieving congestion at busy times of the day. It could accomplish two things: (1) Give official sanction to this tender practice; and (2) Admonish the kissers to be considerate enough of drivers behind them not to overdo their thing.

Gracious Living in Chapel Hill would be enhanced.
(4/2/79)

Speaking of that Great American Dilemma, automobile parking, it has always seemed to me that parking meters, while an understandably necessary trapping of our contemporary society, are inherently un-Chapel Hilly. With the growth of off-street parking lots here, plus the innovation of free-parking suburban shopping malls, I urged that:

... our super appearance-conscious decision makers should consider this idea (removing curbside parking meters) for additional reasons: The meters are ugly, annoying, and totally un-Chapel Hilly.

The purpose of on-street parking meters, it is often forgotten, is to gain revenue — not to create additional parking, which they don't. ... They may be necessary evils, but unless they continue to serve the necessary purpose, they should be banished. Gracious Living in Chapel Hill will be greatly abetted when they are.
(8/27/72)

Parking meters are just as un-Chapel Hilly today, but their long-time legalized squatters' tenure here has brought about greater public acceptance of them. Automotive life in Chapel Hill isn't so bad in realistic and comparative terms, I pointed out in 1971, after reading a statistic that nationwide the average commuting time for driving to work was 16 minutes. By comparison, and through my good fortune to live in the old mid-town area of Chapel Hill, it took me only 18 minutes to WALK to work each day — which certainly was a touch of GLICH. That idea may have figured into the decision of the Village Bank some years later to innovate a "first" in GLICH, "a walk-up window at the pedestrian sidewalk, a place to serve vertical human beings unaccompanied by automobiles:"

... Tommy Mariakakis started it here in the 1930s when he sold hot dogs for a nickel to customers standing on the sidewalk outside his Marathon Sandwich Shop. ... As civilization "advanced," we traded all that for the drive-in and drive-through society. ... It's somewhat better to pass pleasantries with the clerk at the drive-in bank window. You can actually see somebody through the tinted glass of the bulletproof window. But that's not like walk-up personal service.

Woe be unto the pedestrian who dares enter the vale of autos for service at a fast food eatery, bank, or dry cleaning establishment. He's subject to being mowed down backside by entering motorists. Those facilities aren't built for

walk-up traffic anyhow.
(3/15/82)

Thus, the opening of Village Bank's "walk-up" window (in addition to its original installation of a detached drive-in banking shelter), at its Kroger Plaza office was, in effect, a revival of the earlier idea in Chapel Hill.

The aesthetics of GLICH have also been officially addressed by the Town of Chapel Hill, as you might expect, through its Appearance Commission. This citizens advisory body acted as consultants for the Town Manager back in 1970 and, after considerable research, recommended two-toning for our fire hydrants, a matter which surely makes Chapel Hill quite distinctive, if only in this modest category of pop art:

... As thoughtful arbiters of good taste, the appearance people have considered various fire hydrant color schemes over the past year. They pored over color samples, then had several plugs painted in both single and double colors — that is, all brown, all beige, or the bottom of one color and crown of another.

... Traditionally fire plugs have been red, in keeping with the color generally used by fire departments. In Chapel Hill they've been a dark green for many years to date. That seemed to be a reasonable color from the standpoint of inoffensiveness and blending with the natural surroundings But it was also, Town spokesmen point out, hard for firemen to find in a fast-growing town when a few seconds were crucial in hooking up to a hydrant. That task is often made more difficult by the possessiveness of some Chapel Hill householders who like to plant shrubbery and rock gardens around these utilities, too. The Fire Dept. wanted the stanchions repainted to a bright yellow — and understandably for them. People concerned with the spirit of Gracious Living in Chapel Hill balked.
(6/21/70)

The selection of rust and buff colors for two-tone fireplugs was thus a compromise, intended to offer both aesthetic appeal and visibility, picking up hues of both brick and the landscape. I wrote that it seemed to me that the colors chosen were at least better than the day-glo fluorescent plug paints used in some places, "or the sickly robin's egg blue that Pittsboro has picked up lately — or even the dull gray that the University is converting the campus plugs to display." But, I concluded back in those days of the perennial summer water shortage, "we'd as well be concerned with whether there's enough water in the hydrants."

The fireplug color issue is moot now, anyhow. Several years ago the Fire Department decided on its own hook to paint white silhouettes on the asphalt pavement of the street at each fireplug location.

Our official municipal colors apparently are something nominally decided by fiat of the Town Manager. Some years ago official public works vehicles were painted green and yellow—again with greater visibility as a safety factor in mind, by order of Manager Bob Peck. Now they've evolved to an over-all buff, or cafe au lait color.

The Orange Water and Sewer Authority had a big decision to make in this realm when it began operations in 1977. Inheriting its public utility vehicles from Chapel Hill, Carrboro, and the University, OWASA had them in a variety of colors. Executive Director Everett Billingsley admitted that a color decision had to be made. He chose a no-nonsense approach in designing their emblem—the acronym "OWASA" being printed on an orange panel inside the seal. He assuaged any concern about the fire hydrants too:

... And, Mr. Billingsley further assured, he wouldn't dare change the colors on our fire hydrants without first holding a public hearing on the issue, creating a citizens task force to study the matter, giving them the benefit of a consultant's detailed survey, and then staging a general referendum on it. Sure enough, if OWASA does this, it will be the instantaneous Chapel Hilliest of all.

(2/23/77)

OWASA, as the new kid on the block in terms of local public utilities, was even more assuring to its customers right away. Telephone calls to that office were answered simply, "The Authority."

... it simply confirmed to me that I was calling the right kind of place, and one, in fact, which was THE authority. Again, in the spirit of GLICH, I asked Br'er Billingsley how they arrived at that particular terminology for greeting telephone callers. Not one to dodge a tough question, he explained that "Orange Water and Sewer Authority" was simply too big a mouthful to unload on a telephone caller. "And if we answered 'OWASA' they might retort, 'Well, OWASA on you, too!' So we felt that 'The Authority' was right to the point."

I like it. In a community that is dedicated to higher education as the pursuit of truth, "The Authority" is right in spirit.

(2/23/77)

Quite naturally, with the passage of time, OWASA became as well known as AMTRAK or TV, and after a few years the OWASAns quietly substituted that acronym for "The Authority."

Concern for the colors available in natural beauty has received rightful recognition from the Town of Chapel Hill at various times in recent history. In 1971 I cited as a contribution to GLICH a tiny patch of marigolds planted in the sterile confines of the tiny median strip on W. Franklin St. at the Carrboro town line:

… Though this is one of the more topsy-like and congested corners in the community, the swatch of flowers amid the asphalt reminds the passerby that with just the least bit of effort, natural beauty can be utilized to enhance almost any spot. Credit is due the Town of Chapel Hill Street Department for this thoughtful concession to aesthetics. … I note that an appropriation for a Town Gardener has been included in the municipal budget for the first time this near fiscal year, and trust that this modest project is one of the first fruits of his worthy labors.

(8/1/71)

Other contributions to this spirit that I cited were the flowers so faithfully planted on the E. Franklin St. sidewalk in front of her home by Shirley Marshall. (She continues that practice to this day.) Another long-time volunteer steward of GLICH in this realm is Maurice Julian who has used the space around sidewalk trees in front of his mid-town store for well-nurtured and colorful bedding plants. A number of downtown stores have planter boxes in front of their buildings, but none presently use them for this simple pursuit of GLICH. The flower ladies who offer their wares for sale in the NCNB bank corridor (through the grace of the bank) obviously contribute to the ambience of downtown. They're no doubt much more comfortable there, too, but something of the informal and colorful aura of downtown was lost when town authorities in their wisdom chose to ban all sidewalk vending, and the flower ladies had to move onto private property.

A municipal contribution to GLICH was initiated by the Town of Chapel Hill some years ago when it announced a program to promote the planting of crepe myrtle all around the community, and set out quite a string of the long-flowering summer trees on some public sidewalks. Unfortunately, the initial effort wasn't pursued:

… It's still a good idea, and the promotional effort should be revived. The

vivid pink and purple hues of crepe myrtle – more and more of it – would add a lot of seasonal lustre to the Southern Part of Heaven.
(3/14/75)

Some day, we should yet hope, an imaginative local politician or munici-pal official, is going to re-discover this idea and make popular capital of it with the citizenry.

The University, with a much wider constituency and longer standing than the Town, has traditionally contributed to GLICH through its concern for natural beauty – as in the carefully-planted and well-maintained monkey grass strips flanking Cameron Avenue on campus, and, in more recent years, several rock-walled planter boxes along campus walks. Some little things pay big dividends in GLICH, too:

"Good fences make good neighbors," wrote the great poet Robert Frost. And so they do, especially in the case of the attractive new treated pine fence lately erected by the University around the former Best property parking lot at the Pittsboro-McCauley St. corner.

The University might well have simply left this as the junky looking parking lot (almost all parking lots are innately junky looking) it has been for so many years. It is destined as a building site in the fairly near future, so any temporary improvements would be an unrecoverable expense.

Instead, as a good "neighbor," the University erected a very nice fence around the lot, fairly well hiding the awesome and awry mass of automotive metal inside. The University also graced the fence with a natural border of photopinia shrubbery – a bright, hardy plant that sprouts red tips of new growth year-round. In this unsolicited stewardship, the University has significantly added to Gracious Living in Chapel Hill.
(2/11/80)

That same blessing will be realized in the concealment of the main midtown off-street parking lot of the Rosemary Square business develop-ment, since it is to be built above an underground parking garage.

It is inevitable that population growth has a relationship to GLICH, though from the various illustrations of it cited in this chapter it should be evident that this quality can also accommodate growth. Naturally we associate "Gracious Living" with the legendary "village" atmosphere of Chapel Hill. And that "village" has been a fleeting thing since the early days of Davie Poplar. Or, to consider this idea in a more modern idiom:

Chapel Hill as a village in name, or as a small city in fact, is a thing of growing conflict. The recent annexation of an area (Glen Lennox) enlarging the municipality by about 60 percent has made it all the more so.

From the chamber of commerce viewpoint it's easy to see the advantages of "the attractive little University village" or the "fast growing community of Chapel Hill – a small city of over 20,000."

... And, we predict, it won't be long before the Glen Lennox end of town will be wearing the informal tag of "East Chapel Hill," like it or not.

It might refer as much to the temperament as to the pocketbook, but there's one measuring rod, which to our thinking, keeps Chapel Hill still in the small town (or "village," if you must) class. Count up the number of Cadillacs owned by Chapel Hill residents. There's only 10, of vintage 1946 or later, by our tally. And a 10-Cadillac community just doesn't fit the tag "city"in our book.

(7/9/56)

That finding, published three decades ago in The Chapel Hill News Leader, would make Chapel Hill several times a city today, for its many multiples now of being a "10-Cadillac community."

Another comparison, to illustrate how that "village" of 1956 has "vanished," is to note the publication in which that Cadillac count was published in my Newsman's Notepad ("Incidental Jottings Culled From The Beat"). It was the Chapel Hill News Leader, which four of us – Phillips Russell, Ed Hamlin, L.M. Pollander, and myself, plus The News Inc. –- started in 1954 as a semi-weekly newspaper when The Chapel Hill Newspaper, then an every-Friday newspaper known from its 1922 beginning as The Chapel Hill Weekly, was sold to its present owners by its original editor/ owner Louis Graves. (I was at that time The Weekly's only reporter, sole advertising solicitor, and circulation manager.)

We started the News Leader as a semi-weekly (Monday and Thursday) home delivery newspaper with the slogan, "Leading with the news of Chapel Hill, Carrboro, and Glen Lennox." It was a noble and under-financed endeavor, and altogether a pretty good community newspaper, which lasted but five years. The slogan fitted Chapel Hill at the time as a lingering village, but wouldn't cover it now. (After the News Leader's demise, I continued seven years as Editor of the long-standing News of Orange County until it was sold to The Chapel Hill Weekly in 1966.)

Another indication of how the "village" image has perennially been fleeting is this:

Down at the Bank they're always trying to be helpful. Competitive banking has made the customer a king... So we were brought up short the other day in the NCNB lobby to be herded through a rat's maze of theater roping, then stopped to be ushered up one at a time to the teller's slots as a space became available.

... They wanted the customer's reaction. Wary of change, the hometown boy said he didn't like it: —More of the impersonal computer approach, "herding us around," we said. "Let us just pick our own line and take our chances."

... Well, the organized lobby line may indeed be the best plan. But it signals another Vanishing Vestige of the Village. Alas, it probably is a good thing. But this, like so many other fine improvements in our civilized life here in the blessed Southern Part of Heaven, just isn't Chapel Hilly.

(11/10/74)

Nowadays we all routinely accept the single-line herding process at the banks and in other business establishments with the realization that this is a practical and time-saving procedure. But we could scarcely say that it contributes to GLICH. There are other processes, too, that may be good ideas from the point of view of practical thrift, but they suffer this same falling from grace.

The Town of Chapel Hill has warily shown its concern for GLICH in the face of financial sacrifice, albeit a willing sacrifice of taxpayers' dollars in return for a particular kind of service. The issue is "roll-your-own" garbage, a thriftier way of municipal refuse collection.

No doubt we've not heard the last of roll-your-own, since it has excellent hucksters around the country, and the practice is growing in cities and towns all around us—for example, Carrboro, where it was adopted in 1980. Under this system, local government furnishes each householder with a big plastic two-wheel cart, in which he must deposit his garbage at the curbside on collection days:

... It's an interesting commentary on the difference between the brother-sister towns. (Decide for yourselves which is the sister.) Chapel Hill folk zealously insist that back-door garbage collection is a distinction that makes for GLICH. Carrboro pragmatists argue cost-saving and claim the patron-pushed perambulators will save more than their cost in the first year.

Fundamentalists of the Southern Part of Heaven acknowledge the economy, but point out the potential of the precedent: If everybody would simply haul their own garbage the rest of the way to the landfill—or dispose of it themselves – there'd be a 100 percent saving to municipal government. ... Where will it all end? What have our local governmental fathers wrought for us? The Chamber of Commerce should list "roll-your-own" and back-yard pick-up as alternative community assets for people considering moving to Chapel Hill or Carrboro.

(8/8/80)

The "roll-your-own" trend on the part of the Town of Chapel Hill led to what we labeled "The Notorious Trash Packaging Act," again an economy move for the municipal public works department. Public reaction against it was so strong that the Town Board killed it:

Thank you, Town Fathers for responding and relenting. This week you amended the onerous Trash Packaging Act, whereby natural litter had to be mathematically cut to size and bundled like parcel post packages. Now, in a return to Gracious Living in Chapel Hill, you have loosened the trash-tying bonds. You will have the sanitation workers pick up un-bundled stuff at the curb (up to 75 pounds per chunk) as their time permits. You will still remove trash that's tied to the legal specifications on a more frequent regular schedule.

Dear Fathers, we realize that anything we can do to make it easier for you to carry out the services we pay for with **our** taxes will be appreciated by you. In a complementary spirit then, we appreciate your compromising and contributing to GLICH by helping us out in the execution of this, your most fundamental service of all – helping to beautify the Southern Part of Heaven.

(5/26/78)

Town government wasn't inevitably the villain, a creature always to be reviled in hindsight. It merited praise for its "color-coded sidewalks," which served the purposes of both beauty and utility:

A sense of millenium is realized in the recent construction by the Town of not just paved sidewalks, but color-coded ones. It comes to a veritable embarrassment of riches where we have been so traditionally poverty-stricken. The reddish-brown slabs are sanctuaries for bicyclists, the regular cement white ones, for pedestrians.

... The Historic District Commission recommended that paved sidewalks in the historic sectors be of the more eye-appealing reddish-brown – closer to the color of our historic gravel sidewalks. With the passage in 1976 of the $325,000 bond issue for bikeways, the decision was made to extend the significance of the tinting even farther, and to have the red signify a bikeway. ... The rationale of the "red-walk" is further revealed in that they're on the biker's right going uphill. – The cyclist has his own private lanes where he physically needs them most.

... We raise a sincere "huzzah" for this sophisticated addition to Gracious Living in Chapel Hill (GLICH) – while at the same time blanching at the cost. Figure it out for yourself: $325,000 for 3.6 miles of bikeways, almost all of this for the red-walks. That's approximately $90,000 a mile, or $17 a running foot, and over $1.40 per inch. Chapel Hilliness has a precious price.

(7/27/79)

We've failed so far in our campaign to invoke a unique touch of sidewalk GLICH here that's gained treasured institutional status in London:

How utterly Chapel Hilly it was. The renowned and traditional Speaker's Corner at Hyde Park in London was just up the block from the hotel where our Carolina alumni tour group was staying earlier this month.

If you've lived in the free spirit of Chapel Hill for any time at all, you realize that the phenomenon of all kinds of people doing their thing on a public speaking stump is no big deal. But the performance is delightfully institutionalized in London. Every Saturday and Sunday, by historical fiat of who-knows-whom, the speakers take over this particular corner of the park. ... Everybody enjoys it, and speech-hopping is the order of every day for the listeners.

... –What a model for Chapel Hill, all of it! All we have to do is formalize what we already have here. The Pit on the campus is randomly used in this manner already. Back in the days of the Speaker Ban Law the campus boundary wall across from the post office was a natural platform spot for left-wingers or anybody who chose to speak against that loathsome and un-Constitutional statute. The downtown post office and NCNB bank sidewalk areas serve the spirit of Hyde Park already as locales for petition-signing and literature distribution.

All that's lacking is a structure. Gracious Living in Chapel Hill cries out for the creation of a Hyde Park "Speaker's Corner" here.

(8/27/79)

Since the downtown post office has become a municipal building, replete with an open brickyard patio at its front, this is the natural and ideal location for a Chapel Hill speakers' corner. There's historic precedent for this. In the mid-60s a youthful group of protestors campaigning for enactment of a local public accommodations law camped out in sleeping bags for six weeks at the base of the post office flag pole. That is the most heart-felt of a variety of campaigns carried out in the pursuit of Constitutional freedom at this site. I have talked with some municipal officials about formalizing or at least encouraging this program. They have been sympathetic, but the idea is still languishing.

Chapel Hill does have one of London's other famous institutions—a town clock. It doesn't have a bell like "Big Ben," a tolling tradition that was long ago pre-empted by the Morehead-Patterson Bell Tower on campus. But the Home Savings and Loan Association time-temperature clock in mid-town is an important if not uncommon fixture for a community such as Chapel Hill. It was set up in 1959 when the Durham-based financial institution first opened its Chapel Hill branch in the Carl Smith Building at the southwest corner of Columbia and Rosemary Streets.

When in 1981 the clock appeared to have a new format, changed from the original layout of flashing lights, I checked up and found out that it was the first "solar matrix" sign to be installed in this state. The explanation of what that meant was complicated, but HS&L Manager Toby Grady said it involved something of the principle of "UNC students flipping colored pasteboards to do the card stunts at Kenan Stadium football games." Its annual pro-rated cost, at that time, was about 50 cents an hour, which, they figured, was was not a bad deal for the public relations value involved:

Actually, the new sign could be programmed to spell out other messages. Like "BEAT DOOK" or "GO HEELS," but Grady admitted that "the Town of Chapel Hill is a bit sensitive about things like that," so they just stick to the fundamentals.

The good folks at Home Savings feel the sign even upstages their own business building. When people telephone and want to do business ... they sometimes have difficulty placing the firm's actual location. But when they learn that "it's by the time and temperature clock," they almost always remember.

People in Chapel Hill appropriately appreciate their nice new solar matrix sign. It definitely adds a couple of cubits to GLICH.

(10/23/81)

A now well-established and popular Chapel Hill institution that almost got out of hand has been recaptured and has retained its spirit of GLICH. This is the annual Festifall—and also the spring-time Apple Chill Fair, started by the town recreation department in 1972. These annual street festivals grew so massively, both in numbers of vendors and visitors from all around the state, that in 1979 the spring Apple Chill Fair became too much of a mob scene, with more than 20,000 people jamming the mid-town block on a sweltering Sunday afternoon. The sponsors decided to limit the number of vendors to a certain number and require that all be local or Orange County residents. This accomplished the purpose of keeping it strictly a Chapel Hill affair, instead of an incipient Woodstock:

SCALED DOWN? STERILIZED? – No, Festifall in its new dimensions was simply comfortable community. Yesterday afternoon's revamped semi-annual Chapel Hill fair gave off positive vibes.

Many of us weren't disturbed by the massive, crushing multitudes that jammed mid-town last spring and previously. But we'd also agree that the refinement to make it more of a local celebration was a pleasant alternative, too. This was a casual, strolling, easy-going Sunday afternoon occasion, yet lost none of the free-wheeling showy tumult that has made it a nice traditional contribution to GLICH.

(10/8/79)

For many years Chapel Hillians could revel in the uniqueness of their telephone directory. Since the public utilities were owned by the University, that influence no doubt figured in the decision to give us a scenic, rather than an institutional cover for this most popular piece of printed literature:

Another one of those little things that make for Gracious Living in Chapel Hill is the localized cover on the new telephone directory. I am glad and proud to live in a town that doesn't have to display the stock drawing of a telephone lineman and an operator on its cover – but can instead show off an attractive hometown photo scene of dogwoods in bloom. This new design was the deliberate decision of the UNC utilities people, who appropriately sensed the pulse of their customers on what could have been an easily overlooked issue. They commissioned several dozen color photo slides of dogwood scenes around the community to be made by Jock Lauterer last spring. After a painstaking process of elimination they settled on one – a shot made on Westwood Drive which shows off Chapel Hill at its glorious best in the spring.

(12/4/68)

Of course that touch of GLICH is now history here. When Southern Bell took over the telephone system here on March 31, 1977, it retained the coffee table-quality cover for a few years, then put Chapel Hill in the same mold as every other local exchange in its system. Thankfully, the University retains this touch of GLICH for its annual Student Directory, a book that rivals the local phone book in both quality and size.

It was an open question whether or not GLICH was advanced by some other public utility tools, despite the fact that they were truly unique. I wondered if we were going "logo loco" in Chapel Hill:

THE EYES HAVE IT— What you see is all important to what you think — and pre-think. You may not realize it, but it's true, or so the subliminal scientists tell us. Therefore every truly hep organization nowadays has its own unique symbol or logo...

... If the creators of the hometown hieroglyphics below are successful in

their objectives, these designs will become mind-joggers to instantly indicate their particular parent organizations.

At the left... is the eight-segment stylized Geneva cross, which is actually the International Red Cross. This is destined to identify everything it graces as being related to NC Memorial Hospital. ... The bold script-like marking of the logo(above right) was also sprung on us quietly this past week within a display advertisement for Chapel Hill Transit Lines. It is a "T" for "transit."

... What does it all mean to Gracious Living in Chapel Hill? GLICH is not necessarily advanced by symbols that replace words in this education-oriented community. But neither are they an all-bad idea. Chapel Hill, a unique island in this world-wide swirling sea of shorthand symbolism, must yet maintain a link to normal human frailty. Let our logos grow!

(9/29/80)

Two other local logos might have been included, as shown above, but they have wider significance, though they're based in Chapel Hill. The 16 three-dimensional squares in one is a logo that was used in an information book published by the general administration of the 16-campus University of North Carolina. The other logo is a symbol adopted by the Center for Public Television when it changed its name to that from University Public Television.

Another writer for the Chapel Hill Newspaper, expatriate Thelma Hinson, now in Florida, once cited the qualities that she felt were the various Life Support Systems that she appreciated:

This brought to mind the Life Support Systems unique to the Southern Part of Heaven that all of us here enjoy—little niceties that contribute to Gracious Living in Chapel Hill. Among these I number random things such as:

(1) Trees—Our local love affair with trees gives Chapel Hill a rare dominance over the otherwise inevitable onslaught of asphalt.

(2) Back yard garbage collection—This vanishing benefit is yet availed every Chapel Hill householder in an era when the "roll-your-onus" plan is a creeping curse.

(3) The University—By its fortunate location in the center of the community, it significantly abets the beauty and spirit of the place.

(4) Blue—Its coincidental identity as the Carolina color softly enhances the hues of the Hill.

(5) A sense of history—The people here generally realize there's nothing really "new" under the sun, or that even if there is it isn't necessarily better. —A reverence for our heritage.

(6) Tolerance—There is an attitude of live and let live; that differences of opinion are to be appreciated and even viewed as avenues to growth.

(7) Friendly atmosphere—This is a quality some may subjectively feel is absent or diminishing, but in the judgment of others, is still one of the every-day glories of the Southern Part.

(8/10/81)

Those being some of the more general touches of GLICH in terms of local "life support systems," I suggest that the following things, cited at various times through the years, also have abetted Gracious Living:

• (On the newly-passed municipal leash law) ... One of the facets of Gracious Living in Chapel Hill is the tolerance and appreciation accorded dogdom. There are now and inevitably there will be in the future some vicious dogs that ought to be kept on a leash at all times. But the terms of the Town's new regulations which permit well-behaved dogs to roam their own

domains as they please are well considered. So long as Chapel Hill is able to have freedom for dogs, it will continue as a friendly place.
(11/3/71)

• There should be a special place in the Eternal Kingdom for those humble but determined saints who second motions and move to end discussion. They are the souls who truly contribute to Gracious Living in Chapel Hill—the ones who are the most considerate of the time of other people and who want to get on with the job. ... Every minute of time wasted by a windbag speaker can be multiplied by the number of people in the room and the product will be the total amount of time lost in distortion of purpose.

The fellow who moves in at this point and gently makes the proper motion, seconds it, or calls for the previous question is the true man of the hour. He may be a quiet, self-effacing soul who never contributes anything else to the body of public knowledge. But he renders a valuable service.
(9/29/72)

• (Under the heading, "Banquet Bouquet")—This is the season of the testimonial banquet. We are invited to heap all glory, laud and honor on various worthies at dinner bashes staged for them. Sometimes the programs are long. The necessary niceties are inevitably tedious. ... Therefore, this is to call praiseworthy attention to a thoughtful and effective practice—a veritable boon to better banquetry—that was instituted last Friday by master of ceremonies H.G. Jones at the local program honoring Paul Green. Mr. Jones simply introduced all the distinguished people at the head table, and made a number of housekeeping announcements just as everybody sat down and BEFORE the meal was served.

... Banquet planners take note, heed, and copy. You have nothing to lose but the boredom of your listeners. Master of Ceremonies H.G. Jones has set a fine example for you—and has improved Gracious Living in Chapel Hill.
(3/24/78)

• GLICH is abetted by two little niceties recently: (1) The "YEILD" sign on the S. Columbia St. corner of Manning Drive has finally been taken down and corrected to "YIELD," thus removing a nagging annoyance to literate drivers; and (2) the United Fund campaign progress billboard at the main corner downtown has finally been removed, too. It was beginning to list badly and would have fallen over ere long.
(2/13/76)

• It was one of those pleasant, long, cool summer evenings last night.

Scattered around the front lawn at the Horace Williams House were about 70-80 persons—couples and families of all ages. Picnic baskets were abetted by lemonade and iced watermelons, the latter served from Horace Williams' massive old porcelain iron bathtub. ... The inevitable Chapel Hill dogs were on hand—occasionally racing pell-mell through the crowd. A young man read his poetry and sang contemporary country songs to his own guitar accompaniment.

It was good—and very Chapel Hilly. This is the kind of program the Horace Williams House is ideally suited to carry on. It contributes significantly to GLICH.

(6/25/76)

• (Under the title "A Good Y-ear")—They're too busy to do much formal celebrating of the occasion, but the Chapel Hill Carrboro YMCA will next week observe the first anniversary of its formal opening.

There have been growing pains, and a few un-timely faults found. But never can we recall any institution that has so quickly and completely become a part of Gracious Living in Chapel Hill. With 2,300 members and a jam-packed dawn to post-dusk schedule of activities, the "Y" has greatly advanced GLICH in The Southern Part...

(9/10/79)

• A final requirement for becoming an Eagle Scout, the highest rank in Scouting, is the completion of a service project. This must be a well-planned deed of significant benefit to the community, a school, or church. ... One of the best and most creative Eagle service projects was recently completed by David Herion of Troop 39, a Chapel Hill High School senior who will receive his Eagle rank at a court of honor this month. David had street numbers painted on the curbing in front of every house in the Estes Hills neighborhood—120 homes in all. His larger purpose was to do this as a pilot project and contact other groups to do the same in other areas of town—which he has now done.

Gracious Living in Chapel Hill has been abetted by this imaginative and useful work...

(5/23/80)

• (Under the heading "Surfeit of Experts")—One of the glories of The Southern Part is that there's at least one Expert-in-Residence here for every subject under the canopy of this Heaven. (We were shy an authority on persimmons until the late great Pete Ivey staked out and proved his claim in that exotic field. With that temporary exception, Chapel Hill has had a surfeit of knowledgeables for whatever the matter of the moment.)

It makes literary life dangerous for a columnist. We're fair game for every Tom, Dick, and PhD. ... Our real experts are welcome protectors against all manner of charlatans in this village.

All in all... there is no question that the wealth of legitimate experts we have definitely adds to GLICH.

(9/1/80)

Chapter 2

Chapel Hill 'Characters'

"You pick up and move down to Chapel Hill," the friend counseled. "There're so many strange people there you won't even be noticed."

A community whose reason for existence is to improve the mind is bound to attract and nurture a number of truly great people, as well as a body of rugged individualists. Many of the latter are true "characters," persons who are significantly and positively different from their fellow mortals, and who by their force of personality contribute to the spirit of Chapel Hill. The "characters" are truly as important to Chapel Hill as the "great" people, for without one we'd not have the other.

It is difficult to separate people in the two classifications, but it is also a necessary, if subjective decision. Some of the "great" people have been true "characters," and some of them have been "great" in non-conventional, or even minute ways. Some of the "characters" have been humble, scarcely-known citizens, others almost notorious. But there is an indefinable something that stamps them as Chapel Hill "characters."

Chapel Hill loves the "character" and eagerly clasps him to her bosom, if sometimes grudgingly or even only in retrospect:

... Case in point is that of the late Carl Boettcher, University craftsman whose years here are memorialized in his wood hand-carved circus parade at the Monogram Club soda shop [Note: Now in the Carolina Inn Cafeteria].

As the well-known story goes, Mr. Boettcher, a German immigrant living in Hickory, also became concerned for his safety in the late '30s. In light of the rising tide of Hitler's totalitarian regime, he imagined that people in Hickory were whispering about him, even suggesting he was a Nazi spy.

Mr. Boettcher asked a friend what he should do. "You pick up and move down to Chapel Hill," the friend counseled. "There're so many strange people there you won't ever be noticed." The Boettchers did move to Chapel Hill, and enjoyed many fruitful years here ...
(8/24/66)

The friend who suggested that Carl Boettcher move to Chapel Hill is himself a local expatriate, who still maintains his legal residence here. He is William M. (Bill) Cochrane, long-time administrative assistant to US Senators from this state and currently the Democratic Staff Director of the U.S. Senate Rules Committee. I wrote about Mr. Boettcher's move in light of the concern at that time of Harry Golden of Charlotte, long-time liberal Editor of The Carolina Israelite. I suggested that Harry, who was feeling himself out of step with the tenor of the times in 1966, ought to move to Chapel Hill, where he, too, might feel right at home.

This book draws its name from the words of one of Chapel Hill's finer characters, another ex-patriate and contemporary of mine, Jimmy Pickard, who presently lives in Forsyth County. Shortly after he left Chapel Hill some years ago, I wrote of him:

... One of the classic Chapel Hill anecdotes is credited to Jimmy Pickard. Whether true or not, it is certainly in character for him. Story was that when they began the massive excavations for NC Memorial Hospital 20 years ago, Jimmy went and looked at the hole and asked a friend what they were digging it for. "That's to bury all the damn fools in Chapel Hill in," quipped the witling. "—Well, who's gonna cover 'em up?" one-upped Jimmy, echoing his inimitable laugh.

The son of a meat cutter, Jimmy Pickard came from a large family and has a number of sisters, all living elsewhere now. His mother was widowed many years ago and lived quietly with him in their mid-town home. While hampered by epilepsy, Jimmy was always faithful, energetic, and very incisive to human nature. Through the years he worked at various downtown stores, and bantered with one and all of his legion friends as he swept the sidewalk or strode here and there across the town on business errands.

... He could and did, to a fare-thee-well, offer advice to one and all on how to solve public problems of the moment. Usually it was a common-sense suggestion.

If all of this sounds like a funeral oration, I am glad that it is not, for Jimmy Pickard is physically alive and in good shape. He is no saint, and has

MANNING A.SIMONS
Income Tax Consultant
Phone 942- 1200

NO *New Clients*
Accepted

Manning A. Simons – 'a unique Chapel Hill institution' – 1956; and his office on W. Franklin St. – 1962

human frailties and shortcomings common to all of us. But I know that he must miss Chapel Hill, as we miss him. ... For he is, and he should continue to be a part of the spirit of this community.
(5/21/69)

There are many great Jimmy Pickard stories – but the title of this book should stand alone as a singular tribute to him.

It's hard, even unfair to designate a favorite "character," but when I use that term the first picture that comes to mind is that of the late, great Manning A. Simons (pronounced "Simmons"). A rare individual who'd figuratively put his money where his mouth was, Manning was one of the most sincere – and literal – souls ever to live here. I should write a book purely on him. To condense the essence of Manning Simons is to serve him insufficiently.

An ancestor of the French St. Simons family which immigrated to South Carolina low country after the Edict of Nantes, Manning was in his 40-odd (a word used advisedly) years in Chapel Hill a real estate agent, graduate student, student teacher, and produce farmer/seller. He had a downtown office as a tax consultant, but a "closed" sign was nailed permanently on the front door.

Manning said he was "the only child of a physician who married late in

*life." "— That might account for some of my peculiarities, don't you think?" he
once said. He claimed to have been "an escaped lunatic" who came to
Chapel Hill from a Richmond asylum in 1936. His personal trademarks were
wearing earmuffs almost year-round, walking wherever he wanted to go —
because he enjoyed walking, and asking questions, questions, questions
constantly. He'd remember every syllable of your answers. Manning was
best-known for promoting conservative causes, and being privately generous
to a fault. Because he was much in the news in Chapel Hill, I wrote about
him frequently:*

... Needless to point out, he is a man of strong convictions, and a fighter
for various causes of the moment. In recent months he's worked with equal
vigor to oppose fluoridation of the public water supply or to bring about
adherence to the letter of the law in the township constable elections.

Tell him anything in the world one time and he'll remember it permanently. He'll also recall it to you some time when you least expect it. Ask
him a question and you'll most likely get a question in reply. And more than
likely the question will be "Why do you ask that?"

He's a serious and sincere person, totally frank, and not at all intimidated
by majority opinion. ... Most simply, Manning Simons is a unique Chapel
Hill institution.

(1/5/61)

*I grew to appreciate Manning Simons as a true friend for his sincerity,
generosity — he often gave me money to pass on anonymously to persons with
emergency needs — and for his extraordinary consistency. Once when I went
to Durham to consult a state tax agent, the agent asked me, on learning I
was from Chapel Hill, if I knew Manning Simons. I answered that I knew
him well. "— Most extraordinary man I've ever met," said the agent. "He was
in here yesterday and asked me a tax question, then interrupted me twice
while I was answering him to correct my grammar."*

*Before he died here in 1976, Manning bought a local restaurant, with the
avowed purpose of starting a newspaper in vacant space in the building. He
also was a partner in a Chapel Hill florist business. Nothing seemed to faze
him.*

*A kindred spirit in love for Chapel Hill and force of will was "Doc"
Blodgett, a fellow Chapel Hillian and reporter with me on the Durham
Morning Herald in the early '50s. A hulking, almost grandfatherly fellow
who'd returned from World War II service to earn a journalism degree at*

Carolina, "Doc" treasured the simple pleasures of life more than anybody I knew. Another friend told me of going with him to a popular Durham roadhouse for beer and steaks one payday evening:

The atmosphere, conversation, and beer were all just at the right pitch as the waitress served steaks.

Then a juke box suddenly blared out behind them. Doc seemed stunned for a moment, his long-anticipated evening of delight shattered. He asked the manager how much the juke box was worth. It was something like $60 or $70.

Without another word, Doc pulled out his week's bankroll and put it on the counter. Then he reached over and picked up a fire ax that was on the wall for emergency use. With one hefty swing he demolished the noise-making machine. That taken care of, he sat down to enjoy his supper, stone broke, but with a strangely satisfied smile on his face.

(12/18/58)

"Characters" have one common characteristic. That is supreme confidence so long as they're within their own arena of operations. I think of the late Brack Creel, major domo of a post-World War II beer joint aptly named "The Shack." In its post-Creel years it became known for bizarre trappings such as a fur-lined urinal and a well-advertised address — "just three doors west of the Police Station." Brack himself was a diminutive, contagiously friendly fellow who lived his last 20 years on borrowed time, content to preside over The Shack, which quickly came to adopt his own personality as:

... the watering spot for a mixed bag of students, faculty, and scholars. ... He was a man of strong convictions, yet one with due humility. In some ways, though, this Newsman felt Brack's career on earth reached a peak about 10 years ago when Gov. Bill Umstead handed him the appointment as Expert for The North Carolina Railroad Co. There was an honorary salary attached to the job, and he actually did make an inspection trip (in the company of a regular railroad official) of the Goldsboro to Greensboro trackage leased by Southern Railroad.

... His personality encompassed a sly, twinkling smile, a ready wit, and a unique yet knife-like drawl in his manner of speaking. The cult that Brack built is as much a part of the inherent charm of this town as the Old Well, trees, and dogs at commencement.

(1/31/85)

John and Sallie Umstead – on their
50th wedding anniversary, 1/21/64

*Brack Creel was also responsible for my early baptism in learning the
difference between discretion and a good story. As a reporter for the Chapel
Hill Weekly, I was an habitue of The Shack and was present when Brack was
telling about being appointed an "Expert:"*

... "What are you an 'Expert' at?" the young reporter asked him. "Well, I
reckon I'm an expert at getting $300 a year for this job," replied Brack with
a twinkle. The brash cub went back to his office and faithfully chronicled
these words in a squib for The Chapel Hill Weekly. Brack sent word that he
wanted to see me. When I finally dared go back in the place a month later he
still hadn't forgotten. "Now don't I look like an ungrateful SOB!" Brack
stormed at me. "What's the Governor going to think when he sees what you
wrote about me?" I wanted to tell him that I thought the Governor would
indeed agree that he was an Expert at getting $300 a year for the job. But I
didn't.

(11/5/67)

*The Shack was the center of operations for Chapel Hill politics for many
years, and at its center was the foremost local politician of that era, Orange
County Rep. John W. Umstead Jr. (the man, incidentally, who arranged for
his younger brother, Gov. William Umstead, to appoint Brack Creel "Expert" for the State Railroad). John Umstead was many men in one, as I wrote
in describing him at his death:*

... his gruffness and quick boiling point, but also his instant and oft-
unspoken generosity for legion worthy causes; his impatience – a keystone
of his energetic zeal, and also his contagious good humor – a unique chuckle

and that all-pervading, sly, one-sided smile; his penchant for wearing a hat at his desk, yet courtly manners and quiet thoughtfulness as the occasion indicated; the demanding way in which he pushed his chosen causes in public service—education, roads, prison reform, the University of North Carolina, and mental health ... and finally, his absolute ramrod personal loyalty to friends and allies of high and low station.

(8/25/68)

John Umstead was a 1909 UNC classmate of Frank Graham, the first President of the multi-campus University of North Carolina. Umstead was Orange County campaign manager for "Dr. Frank" when Graham ran for the U.S. Senate in 1950. That is significant because John Umstead, whom some of us admiringly called "The Bull of the Woods," was an absolute opposite to to the quiet, diminutive "Dr. Frank" in every facet of their personalities.

Strong-willed women are inevitably among the great characters of any community. That realization mandates mention of Mary Barnett Gilson. A retired federal labor arbitrator, Miss Gilson lived the 25 years of her retirement in Chapel Hill, where she died at the age of 91. That was a full decade after she announced to the world that she had incurable cancer and was going to lick it (as she did).

Mary Gilson couldn't abide drawing breath each day without speaking her piece. She cultivated many enemies, whom I'm sure she secretly cherished for the privilege of disliking them just as much as she loved her friends. Many an afternoon I'd stop by her home for a nip of Scotch whiskey with her and the pleasure of hearing her revel in her admitted "trouble-making." At her death in the activist days of 1969 a townsman remarked in sincere humor: "Too bad Mary had to die while all the student riots and unrest are boiling about us. She'd have enjoyed it so!" As a newspaper reporter, I followed her closely in the public forum:

... As a letter to the editor writer she was in her prime unmatched. Tact was not a factor in this field of confrontation for her. The Ku Klux Klan, conservative politicians, squirrels, and big dogs were frequent targets ...

In a public meeting, she was a rare and beautifully terrifying creature to behold. She could turn the most harmonious love-feast into an uproar at the mere drop of such a few words of invective ...

How delightfully she despised people, too. Of one particular unfortunate human being in this category, she said scornfully, "He's the best reason I've ever seen for retroactive birth control."

(3/16/69)

Johnsie Burnham and Paul Green – 1972

Of the same era in Chapel Hill was Otelia Connor, who moved to Chapel Hill as a widow and won both fame and notoriety as the campus "good manners lady." Otelia wrote a column for The Chapel Hill News Leader for a period and was an inveterate letter to the editor writer on issues of etiquette and courtesy. In her methods of promoting good manners she was more direct. She'd whack an unwary violator with her umbrella, then bless him out:

Otelia Connor proved that the age of gently rugged individualism need not die in burgeoning Chapel Hill. ... Otelia often waded in like a fiercely righteous angel where some of us journalistic fools feared to tread. Carolina's good manners lady struck fear of her ire into the hearts of many students and businessmen alike. She was a good gadfly for the University, both as a personality, and as a forceful influence for better etiquette.
(8/10/69)

Among other remarkable women of the Gilson-Connor period whom I occasionally wrote about was my next door neighbor, Johnsie Burnham (truly a "grand dame" in the best sense of that word) who died in 1980 at the age of 98. The moving spirit of the North Carolina Symphony from its earliest days and an accomplished concert violinist herself, Johnsie Burnham was widowed soon after coming to Chapel Hill in 1930. She was always a high-spirited soul. I dared not write about her by name, but did as follows, referring to her only as a "sprightly dowager:"

Jesse Robert
Stroud — self-proclaimed
trouble-maker and citizen of the
world — 1965

In casual conversation a friend inquired after her health. "To tell you the truth, I feel like hell," the octogenarian replied with vigorous conviction. "But if I stayed home thinking about it, I'd only feel worse." She is one of Chapel Hill's more lovable radicals and a woman who has in the past and still today contributes richly to our civic and cultural life.
(9/13/67)

Recalling letter-to-the-editor writers with abrasive personalities naturally brings to mind Jesse Robert Stroud, a member of one of the community's most prominent black families. In his declining years he was, self-proclaimed, "an embittered ex-alcoholic trouble-maker." He was more than that in positive ways, though. Jesse Stroud attended N.C. Central three years on a football scholarship and worked many years as a bellhop for the Carolina Inn. A compulsive talker, he had quite a way with words:

... "I used to think I was 'poor.' Then they told me I wasn't 'poor,' I was 'needy.' Then they told me it was self-defeating to think of myself as 'needy,' that I was 'culturally deprived.' Then they told me 'deprived' had a bad image, that I was 'underprivileged.' Then they told me 'underprivileged' was over over-used, that I was 'dis-advantaged.' I still don't have a dime, but you must admit, I have an atomic vocabulary."

He may have intended this humor as humor — but again he may not have. Another time he declared in a letter to the editor: "This is a difficult system, symptomatic of a sick culture, where all human values are obliterated by a thing called white supremacy. I am a cosmopolitan man — a citizen of the world." — That statement, I am certain, he meant in all seriousness.

Mr. Stroud (as I occasionally called him when he was on the warpath against me) was a familiar figure on the downtown streets. He claimed a foot disability prevented him from doing such jobs as would require standing much or moving around. "I know I'm no intellectual giant, but I'm willing to do any kind of work I can," he once told me. "Here I've been a great crusader for others all my life, and now it's me that aint got no job."To his friends of both races, Jesse Stroud was an abrasive, contentious, and simultaneously quite likeable person. He loved Chapel Hill and the "old days" at the same time as he spoke out for the elimination of racism on any and every occasion ...

(8/29/77)

Jesse Stroud claimed a mystical kinship with a prominent contemporary white Chapel Hill family, that of the town's first automobile dealer, Bruce Strowd. Strowd Motor Co. was opened in 1914 as a Ford agency and the building that housed it many years still stands at the northwest corner of Franklin and Columbia Streets. Regardless of any possibility of the mis-cegnation alluded to by Jesse Stroud ("They paid us to spell our name with a 'u'—'Stroud,' not 'Strowd,' " he once told me.), he was certainly a soul-mate with Bruce Strowd as a town character.

Bruce Strowd—Chapel Hill's first auto dealer—4/1/53

The Strowd home (also still standing) was in the center of Davie Circle. The meadowlands of the area around Eastgate and University Mall used to be known as "Strowd's Lowgrounds." The Chapel Hill Board of Aldermen, once angered by the auto experimentation of young Bruce Strowd, in 1908 passed a local ordinance specifically prohibiting him from driving his contrivance on the municipal streets.

The "Bruce Strowd" stories are classics. Collier Cobb Jr. liked to tell the one about how he came to be best man for Bruce at his wedding. Collier was having a haircut one day when the barber told him he'd heard that Collier was going to "stand up" for Bruce at his wedding the next day. Collier said he replied in surprise that Bruce hadn't said anything to him about it. But he decided to show up at the wedding the next day and did indeed act as Bruce's best man. Afterwards he asked Bruce why he hadn't said anything about it to him beforehand. "I didn't need to," Bruce supposedly replied. "I knew if I told it at the barber shop the word would get around and you'd be there."

That fact of village life of an earlier era brings to mind the true character of the barber shop itself as a bygone institution, as I wrote about it here some years ago:

Y.Z. Cannon in 'the last barber shop on Franklin St.' (customer: Peter Ness) – 1950

Collier Cobb Jr. (1962) – 'stood up' for Bruce Strowd

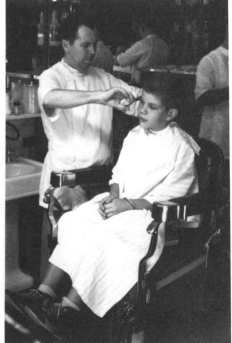

Last Barber Shop on Franklin St. Those words have a tragic ring — like "Last Train out of Atlanta," or even "Last man on earth."

Now there is another Vanishing Vestige of the Village insofar as its historic vantage point for more than half a century is concerned: Red Marley's grand old Carolina Barber Shop. Come Saturday the Carolina will lock its Franklin St. doors and with that the barber shop will be a bygone institution on main street in midtown.

... What mini-skirts along the sidewalks gave to the denizens of Red Marley's Carolina Barber Shop, the hirsute styles of contemporary American manhood took away. That is — just when the Carolina Barber Shop was about to reach its greatest potential as an all-American legitimate grandstand for the sidewalk girl-watching show, the clientele vanished. Slaves to style, people stopped getting haircuts.

... There was the day when the barber shop — and especially the old Carolina Barber Shop — was the center of the local Establishment. Ribald jokes, financial and political gossip, and tall sports stories were all freely exchanged across the floor sweepings. It was a meeting place — a verbal watering hole where you went to find out what was going on.

Now most of that is gone, a victim of television-oriented civilization. It's not all gone, admittedly. Not the ribald jokes anyhow. Nor the vantage point for a fish bowl oversight of main street bigger than life. But when Chapel Hill's last barber shop on main street closes for all times this Saturday noon, that great pastime will also be lost forever. Say a requiem for a fine bit of Chapel Hilliana.

(2/15/73)

Of course Red Marley still holds court in his Tar Heel Barber Shop on Rosemary St., but the glory of the locale where Bruce Strowd felt he could so casually leave a message of his impending nuptials is surely fading.

Collier Cobb liked to illustrate the unsinkable puckishness of Bruce Strowd by recalling an incident many years later:

... Methodist Minister Excell Rozzelle had been called back to town to participate in the ceremony (a Masonic dedication program). Bruce Strowd called him off to the side and gravely informed him "It's just awful about Collier. You know, he's just throwin' himself away." Taken aback, the Rev. Rozzelle solemnly inquired, "Tell me his problem. Is it drinking?" "Hell no," Bruce replied with a blue-eyed twinkle, "Collier's gone to working."

(3/7/73)

In his later years Bruce Strowd moved south of town and raised beef cattle on his farm, naturally named "HereFord." On the morning after it was announced in The Chapel Hill Weekly that the newspaper was being sold to a group including Durham banker Watts Hill, Bruce walked in the office, looked around with a twinkle in his blue eyes, and chirped, "Well it aint 'Chapel Hill' any more — it's 'Watt Hill!'"

He wasn't a brash joker like Bruce Strowd, but native son J. Wesley Thompson was also an audacious hometown business pioneer. Though a white, he was for many years the owner-operator of the community's only movie theater for blacks. Later he built and operated Chapel Hill's only drive-in movie theaters, the Valley and the Parkview. When television and racial integration took their natural toll of these enterprises he opened and successfully operated the first rug cleaning business here:

... But this was just moonlighting. Through all of this time, over 30 years, he was a full-time projectionist for the Carolina Theater in Durham. He'd also flown airplanes and built radios — just sidelines, too.

... Lanky, easy-going, pipe-smoking Wes Thompson was really Chapel Hill's resident philosopher without portfolio for many years. But unlike the typical philosopher, he was one of the hardest-working and most usefully-inventive fellows you ever knew.

... More important was Wes' quiet but plain-spoken manner — his unique ability to laugh at himself and the foibles of an uptight society. It was the way he was a doer and not just a talker, and the grace with which he accepted the changing and conflicting customs of society — always a laborer in the vineyard, never building up treasures for himself. If Wes read this, he'd just smile, pooh-pooh, and tell some anecdote puncturing a pompous personality.

(1/10/75)

He had a way with homespun metaphors that calls to mind another businessman character. Reciting a story about earlier days in Chapel Hill, Wes once said, "... The snow that day was as high as E. A. Brown's butt ..." That was a statement of superlative. Mr. Brown, as everybody knew, was about six-feet-six in an era when that would have been a record for a basketball player. A rock-ribbed Republican, he opened his first furniture store downtown in 1908, and continued in business for over 60 years:

... Not everybody took a liking to E.A. Brown, and no doubt the feeling was mutual, for he was, and no doubt still is, a rugged individualist. But to the needy and to the deserving he was often a friend in need — and more than

E.A. Brown in his furniture store – 1956; and Jim Phipps – sworn in as district court judge – 1964

that, a voluntary and a willing helper. Many a customer in his store received a price concession or a write-off at the grace of Mr. Brown.

He also appreciated and remembered what he considered to be favors. ... I was shopping for a particular piece of furniture and asked the price. He told me the price, then quoted a lower figure, stating that I had "always been good to the Party." What he meant was that as a newspaperman I had, in his estimation, given the Republican Party fair treatment in news stories. I told him that if that was true, it was no more than what should be required of any reporter. But I appreciated his sentiment, and the evidence of it, too. **(2/9/69)**

No mention of E.A. Brown can be made without also citing his partisan opposite, attorney L.J. (Jim) Phipps, long-time local court judge. In addition to being a devoted family man, Jim Phipps had three true loves in his life – the Baptist Church, the American Legion, and the Democratic Party. He served all in high office with quiet grace and good humor. Conservative native son that he was, Jim Phipps could maintain his Democratic allegiance through any political firestorm, as so often occurred in a community of fiercely held beliefs such as Chapel Hill. I recall him presiding at a public meeting on county zoning at which he was subjected to a volley of hostile questions from E.A. Brown:

... "F'r'instance now, Mr. Phipps, I'd like to ask you what the Supreme Court would think of a law like this?" The chairman replied that in light of recent Supreme Court trends he couldn't predict what the high tribunal

'Old Man Nevilles' – 1955

might rule on it, but he further suggested that the best way to prevent further erosion of states' rights by the federal government was for local government to impose effective self-control and make it work. The critic pondered a moment, then arose again to comment – "F'r'instance now, Mr. Phipps, I'd say that if a Republican had made that statement I'd call it a durn good statement."
(1/19/67)

Jim Phipps was never boastful, but he did appear pleased with his generally accorded title as Carolina's Number One football fan. He was in his 50th season of attending every single Carolina home football game at his death. He also took singular pride in claiming he'd predicted (and local witnesses so confirmed) Carolina's extraordinary 50 to nothing nationally-televised victory over Duke in 1959.

Attorneys are naturals for "charactership." I cite the late court prosecutor and long-time Town Attorney John Quince (Jack) LeGrand, who thought he was retiring when he moved to Chapel Hill. Courtly, conservative, peppery of temperament, and quick-witted, he brooked no foolishness as a public protector. Because of his chosen profession, I took to calling him "Jackleg Jack." He accepted the nickname for a while, then quietly suggested I drop it, which I was glad to do.

Another practically un-paralleled Democrat was E. W. Neville:

As long as I can remember, he always called himself "Old Man Nevilles" – a label he gave out with both pride and good humor. Certainly in all of Chapel Hill there was nobody prouder of the University community and his long heritage and relation to it than Everett Walters Neville, who died Thursday at the age of 93. That he could trace his ancestry back to the original donors of the land for the University here was a matter of particular pride for him; also the fact that he was, in his own words "a thoroughbred Democrat." (His blue eyes glinted when he said that.) Everett W. Neville was first known to some of us as a kindly custodian at the old Chapel Hill School for many years, and also a merchant in his "little store" at the end of W. Cameron Ave. by the University Laundry. "Characters" are wonderful persons for any town to have. They give it body, and healthy tradition. "Old Man Neville" was one of these in the finest sense of the word.

(5/26/68)

There are characters who know they are such and make the most of it. Chapel Hill as a haven for the creative spirit naturally nurtures these. Then, there are those who are un-intended characters. Before moving on to the dominant variety, I want to close with an anecdote that speaks more for the outlander than it does for our cherished hometown character. It is about Wallace Williams, who has operated an upholstering business in his own name here for many years. Several of us couples went on a Caribbean cruise a few years ago (and Wallace happened coincidentally to draw a cabin next to the ship upholsterer's shop):

… You meet people from all over the country on these trips. There were about 1,000 on this ship – including the inevitable ones from Brooklyn. Wallace, well-known as a fellow who kids a good deal, struck up a conversation with this New York woman. "You don't believe everything he says, do you?" we asked her. "Believe him?" the woman rejoined. "I can't even understand him!"

(1/23/76)

Then there were people like Leroy and Agnes Merritt, also "naturals:"

Things that are taken for granted, that are accepted as parts of the local scene like the Bell Tower and the Old Well, can't be so simply dismissed and forgotten. The only notice of their retirement and leaving was a modest script ad in Tuesday's Newspaper that "Agnes and Leroy Merritt will be retiring from The Pines as of midnight tonight."

Hold on, now. A restaurant is not just a place for good food. It is the people who make you welcome, who make its operation their total life, who are the cement that holds a community together. – What is The Pines without Leroy muttering about, moving table-to-table in a constant chatter, dithering from kitchen to cash register? – Can The Pines be The Pines without Agnes greeting you as a long-lost sweetheart when you enter, calling you by name, and fussing over your comfort?

These are people who care about Chapel Hill, the kind of people that make it go ...
(2/3/78)

A person who truly made Chapel Hill "go" in earlier years was veterinarian Dr. S. A. Nathan, whom I knew best as a neighbor:

One of the stalwarts of an earlier era in the village, "Doc" Nathan was a living legend—a massive (425 pounds) and masterly man of the times whom we children imagined could to anything. And he did—variously as local health officer, county commissioner, coroner, and most important to us—as everybody's "dog doctor."

The Nathan homestead on Pittsboro St. was one of those all important and essential places in every town: The eternal gathering spot for all the neighborhood kids, where we always checked in first to see what was going on. A quiet and kindly soul, Doc Nathan forebore us in all our youthful foibles—and no doubt, loved us in spite of ourselves ...
(10/23/78)

The best vignette of Dr. Nathan is given by one of his three children, my contemporary, Marx, who wrote to me on the first anniversary of his father's death:

... I remember my Dad; and the memories of the lion-head chair in which he sat; the two double-wide seats on the second row from the back in the Carolina Theater where dating couples hoped he wouldn't be when they went to the show; of the Saturday morning trip to the Railway Express office for his weekly weigh-in; of the calls to sick animals in the middle of the night; of the very expensive dog left in his safekeeping showing up at Kenan Stadium during a game; of my mother fussing at his eating too much and his picking up one biscuit in his fingers and palming three others; of his ever-present attendance at athletic events; of the farmers bringing eggs, hams and vegetables when they couldn't pay cash; of the way he carved a turkey or left an eaten fish with not a bone out of place; of the looks of disbelief when he was first met by a stranger; of the dry cleaners delivering size 62 pants; but mostly of the people whom he loved and who loved him just coming by for a chat. Yes, I remember. I do remember.
(10/22/79)

Another legend in his own time is Kemp Battle Nye, known by his own designation as "the Franklin St. Frenchman" during the lively years when he ran his music and record shop in a ramshackle downtown store building:

NOTE
PLEASE LEAVE
ALL BOOKS·BAGS
AND PAPERS
AT COUNTER
SO WE CAN WATCH
THEM FOR YOU !
- KEMP-

Kemp Battle Nye—'the
Franklin St. Frenchman' in
1955

One of Chapel Hill's great personal business institutions for the past
quarter century will close tomorrow, leaving a void in the swashbuckling
swath of free enterprise he has so colorfully plied.

... It all comes at the season of business revival that Kemp made famous
in downtown Chapel Hill. From his rickety record shop—now the parking
lot by the Presbyterian Church—he'd herald the beginning of the new school
year. Sometimes he did it literally with a trumpet, other times with a
billboard emblazoned: "Welcome Back Money! Keep Kemp's Green!"
Through the era of beatniks, McCarthyism, and the jaded 60s, Kemp
perennially stayed amid or ahead of whatever was "in."

It began here in the depression-ridden 30s when Kemp walked away from
the mountains of Grassy Creek up in Ashe County and finally caught a
Model-T ride to Chapel Hill. After a self-help fling at college, working in
Milton Abernethy's original Intimate Bookshop and in local boarding
houses, he joined the marines as a 17-year-old bugler ...

... For a third time he returned to Chapel Hill—again to work for the
"Chief," as he called "Ab," at the Intimate. The "Kemp" epoch of entrepre-
neurship began when he succeeded Ab in 1952.

Competitors, municipal officials, and University administrators were
alternately critical, cheered, or wrung their hands. Some also secretly
admired the unconventional "Franklin St. Frenchman" who always had a
twinkle in his eye and lived his life in stereo, both literally and figuratively.

(8/27/76)

A Chapel Hill minister also coped successfully with students during the activist years of the '70s. Langill Watson of University Methodist Church was the exception to prove the rule in attracting students to his church— without trying to be one of them—during this period. He did it with a fatherly interest in students and their activities, and perhaps also through his publicly-expressed passion for Carolina athletics. On returning from a three-month Merrill Fellowship at Harvard, he reported to a local civic club on life in that Ivy League institution:

... Langill evoked chuckling sympathy on recalling his handicaps in "identifying" with today's students on the Cambridge campus. "I asked directions to Harvard when I drove into Cambridge. They told me to turn left—and everything went left for me from then on. My wife sent me off with a change of clothing for every day of the week," he said. "It turned out to be an embarrassment instead of an enhancement."

Though he found the contemporary collegiate speaks in a saltier language than that normally used by a pastor, Langill said he had to admit—after the first few blushes—that it had "a kind of honesty about it—clearing away the verbiage." Not that he'd been able to personally adapt his own tongue to such blue hues, he emphasized.

... he admitted that living in a college residence hall with students generally half his age provided quite a challenge—albeit a truly rewarding experience.

(1/17/73)

Former Mayor of Chapel Hill Jimmy Wallace, in his nearly 50 years here since first arriving as a freshman from an eastern North Carolina hamlet, has also successfully bridged the gap betweeen the radicals and conservatives. From being the unintentional godfather of the local anti-establishment liberals, Jimmy evolved to the center of the establishment. After serving on the Town Council, he was Mayor 1975-79, and could surely have been reelected or gone to higher office, had he chosen. At his departure I wrote under the heading of "Wallace's Wake:"

Is it the mournful feast traditionally staged at the death of a member of the family? Is it the swath he has cut in charting the previously uncharted municipal waters? Or is it the way he verbally awakes one and all to enliven what might otherwise be a stultifying meeting or issue?

Gentleman Jimmy, our retiring Mayor, may well qualify on all three of these definitions as applied to his four-year stewardship in the Municipal Building ...

... Jimmy would've been unhappy himself if he hadn't made many people happy by his necessary but un-Coolidge-like decision. His Controversial Honor has respectfully and realistically anticipated enemies as well as friends. Jimmy is a practical politician, but variously a delightful iconoclast and muckraker. — Anybody who'd ever try to agree with him all the time would end up a nervous wreck. — So, no doubt, there has been quite a coterie of diners at the great Wake for Wallace.

What about the second kind of wake — the widening ripple effect his municipal stewardship has left? Nobody but nobody will deny that Wallace has left his mark. It's generally been more of a wallop — but no less final — than a surgical incision. ... If you take nothing more than the creation of OWASA with majority control by the Town of Chapel Hill, you have a significant monument in that alone to the determination of Jimmy Wallace ...

As for the a-wakening effect ("wake") of Mayor Wallace, it's been the most noticeable of all. While Jimmy is at his best with wits and words, he's also developed quite a versatile facial vocabulary from his very visible vantage in the Mayor's chair. By nuance of an eyebrow, a deliberately pained visage, or a quick, puckish smile, he has spoken reams ...

No, you won't find any deep, pithy memorials in this little write-up about our (literally) outgoing Mayor. It's quite enough, and quite appropriate, to simply say "Thanks, Jimmy," for caring and for serving ...

(12/3/79)

It's appropriate to conclude this limited recollection of characters with a note about the most deliberate and perennial of all of them, Professor of Law Emeritus Albert Coates. I think of an occasion when the North Caroliniana Society was engaging in what was during that program referred to as "North Carolina's favorite indoor sport — honoring Albert Coates:"

... Gladys (his wife), the main speaker, was introduced as the one who Albert said "cut my prose to pieces and added insult to injury by proving she'd improved it ..."

In tribute to her spouse's creative mind she recalled that "his invincible love of the picturesque has drawn him demonstrably aside from the dull line of veracity" — a quote from an editor's note in a Macaulay essay.

In his own response to his wife's tribute, Albert recalled how she'd read him a question and answer from Ann Landers' column one morning. A writer asked whether in the daily frustrations of life she'd ever considered divorce, to which Ann Landers replied "Murder, yes. Divorce, never."

"And so it is today," admitted Albert, then quoting from a love poem, "I have always loved her like a Christian loves sin, and still do."
(4/23/79)

An illustration of Albert Coates' force of will is a vignette from a personal scolding he once gave me. I'd displeased him by the manner I wrote something about him in the University's alumni publication. He sent word that he was going to have his say at me. It was a full six weeks before I saw him, and the occasion was my going to his home to remove some boxes of books from his basement. He planted himself in the middle of the basement to have at me. As I'd walk out the door, he'd stop in mid-sentence, then pick up again and continue when I came back into range of hearing. And so it continued for about 15 minutes. The power and glory of his fully-retained anger was so complete I admired it more than I feared it. — So it continues to this date. Whether in criticism or in praise, and he has plenty of both, Albert Coates is going to have his say. His favorite expression, "Aye, God," comes to the ear as "I, God," and the similar sound is appropriate.

Every true Chapel Hill character properly calls to mind another one, but this chapter is limited to those I happened to write about in The Newsman's Notepad. We naturally venerate those of an earlier era and are more likely to assign "characterhood" to somebody in historical, rather than contemporary terms.

Perhaps University Chancellor Emeritus Robert B. (Bob) House understood this, too. He and a friend were reminiscing one morning in front of the old Chapel Hill Post Office when the friend asked him "What's happened to all the town characters we used to have in Chapel Hill?"

— To which Chancellor House replied quite aptly and succinctly:
"We are they."
Of such is the coterie of Chapel Hill characters.

Chapter 3

Anecdotes

"Why not just let Chapel Hill form a state of its own!"

Classic stories that illustrate the unique nature of Chapel Hill are legion. Typical of these is the unfounded legend attributed to US Sen. Jesse Helms some years back to the effect that North Carolina didn't need a state zoo. All that was necessary was to put a fence around Chapel Hill.

I personally overheard a statement in this realm while covering a public hearing in Raleigh on the so-called Pearsall Plan. This was a proposal, subsequently adopted and later discarded, whereby under certain circumstances (meaning racial integration) North Carolina localities were empowered to abandon their public school systems:

Our cloakroom reporter at the Legislature's recent hearings on the Pearsall Bill in Raleigh picked up an off-hand suggestion by one of the august Assemblymen that could well have gained a lot of attention as an alternate acceptable proposal in the current situation in Tar Heelia.

Seems he was seated near the door to Memorial Auditorium along about the end of a hot, sticky afternoon. From time to time various legislators would step to the doorway for a smoke and a breath of fresh air. It was just after one of the Chapel Hill opponents of the Pearsall Plan had spoken that our agent heard one man, in passing by his seat, say to the other: "Why not just let Chapel Hill form a state of its own!"

(8/6/56)

While it may be difficult now to imagine the tenor of those times, Chapel Hill harbored considerable sentiment different from the rest of the state on

41

the race issue then. At that same legislative hearing I recall that one of several witnesses from Chapel Hill was a University professor who testified vigorously against the optional school-closing plan, and flatly spoke out on the virtues of racial integration.

At the end of his statement a legislator arose and asked him if he were a native North Carolinian. The speaker hesitated, then admitted he wasn't. "Well, where did you come from?" asked the legislator. The professor hesitated again, then answered quietly: "South Carolina."

It's important to remember, too, that Chapel Hill didn't escape its own trials on racial issues. For months during 1963 there were frequent downtown parades, then called "demonstrations," in behalf of the enactment of a local public accommodations ordinance. It was a tense period:

Old words take on sudden new meanings nowadays. The scene was a momentary period of quiet in the newspaper office a couple of weeks ago. The community was fairly seething with uneasiness during the period of picketing, integrationists' parades, and in anticipation of the civil disobedience tests.

A salesman came into the office hawking a new machine. When his prospect showed some interest the huckster, with more enthusiasm, declared, "Let me give you a demonstration." – The Newsman, uneasy anyhow, almost jumped out of his seat.

(8/1/63)

In that era, as so often today, the spirit of Chapel Hill marched to a different drummer. Witness this recent experience from fall 1985 as related by a friend – and which should be labeled "Only in Chapel Hill."

A local businessman was stopped for speeding in midtown early one morning. The policeman naturally asked him for some identification. Consider, if you will, what a policeman would normally have in mind when he asks a driver for some identification – and also consider that Chapel Hill, literate, erudite Chapel Hill, is the higher educational capital of the region.

The driver of the car, in this instance, asked the policeman what kind of identification he wanted him to produce. The policeman responded: "Do you have a library card?"

– And that, I submit, is the ideal illustration of something that would happen "Only in Chapel Hill."

The following occurred some years earlier, as I happened to write in the column, also under the headline "Only in Chapel Hill:"

It was late of a social evening and several couples were sitting around a pitcher of Michelob. The talk was of many casual issues – religion, televi-

Billy Arthur—in his hobby store—1962

sion, and politics. There was a momentary lull in the conversation. Then a helpful young hausfrau asked brightly: "What do you think about Liz and Eddie?" "Liz and Eddie? I don't believe I know 'em," replied another contributor. "Who are they?"

At the telling of this to a friend recently, he declared simply—"Only in Chapel Hill—and aren't we glad!"

(5/31/62)

That friend, by the way, was a devoted Chapel Hillian who probably knew both Elizabeth Taylor and Eddie Fisher personally from his previous days in Hollywood: The recently deceased Kay Kyser.

Such blessed anonymity can at times be a drawback, as in another social vignette locally:

There has been an interesting and not un-natural reaction locally to the announcement by Chapel Hill's own Edwin W. Tenney Jr. that he expected to become a candidate for the US Senate on the Republican ticket. Almost invariably the reader or listener asks "Who's Ed Tenney?" It recalls a vignette that Edwin tells on himself—and which Billy Arthur first revealed in his Chapel Hill Weekly column six years ago. Billy and Edwin were attending a reception ... when Billy noticed an attractive petite woman pouring punch. He turned to the guy standing beside him (who happened to be Edwin) and asked "Who's that woman at the punch bowl?" "That's Ed

Tenney's wife," replied Edwin. "Who's Ed Tenney?" rejoined Billy.
(1/24/68)

Ed Tenney, who'd led the ticket in running for the local School Board, didn't get far in that race for the US Senate, and Sam Ervin was subsequently re-elected for his triumphant final term. But Tenney profited from the above-noted social episode and distributed a bumper sticker that became a collector's item at the time: "Ed Who??"

Of all the Chapel Hill anecdotes I ever wrote up, I know of none that I thought more delightful for choice of words on the part of the original teller, long-time gas station owner Eben Merritt, than this:

A couple of guys came in and stuck a pistol in Mr. Merritt's face as he stood at the cash register in his place. "I took my hand and pointed the barrel west," said Mr. Merritt later, "and told him not to point that thing at me. Then one of the men said, 'Mister, this is a real hold-up.' " The robbers then took a considerable sum of money from Mr. Merritt and fled.
(1/20/66)

That's gospel as Eben Merritt told it to me. The reason I especially appreciated it was for Eben's preciseness. As he stood at his cash register facing the robber and pushed the pistol barrel away from him, it was indeed pointing "west."

The quick-witted retort is also deserving of the spirit of rugged individualism so well-known in Chapel Hill:

… Local citizen who had a disabled driver permit recently pulled up to a campus space reserved for the handicapped. Another motorist had already parked there and was just leaving. "Do you have a handicapped permit?" he asked the departing driver. "No, do you?" "Yes." "What is your disability?"

"I am totally blind."

—Now where else but in Chapel Hill would you hear a snappy reply like that?
(8/14/81)

Every column item about "Only in Chapel Hill" happenings seemed to spawn other recollections on the part of readers. These were called in after the item above was published:

First off there was the one about the late Miss Madge Kennette, an independent soul if ever there was one. She drove downtown from her East Franklin St. home one morning to purchase a loaf of bread at the Hill

Bakery. Finding no parking place at the curb, she simply left her car in the middle of the street, while she went into the store and made her purchase.

Returning to her car, she found a policeman writing a ticket for this offense. "I had to have a loaf of bread," she told the policeman, then got in her automobile and drove off. And that, you should believe, was the end of that.

The other story was on the lovely Mrs. Ruth Sloan. One day she stopped at a downtown traffic light. A young man opened the door of her car, got in, looked her over and said, "Oh, I didn't know you were an old woman," and promptly got out and walked away.

Ruth told her husband, the late Bill Sloan (whose father was chief of police) about the incident later. "Did you call the police?" Bill asked. "No," Ruth replied. "I called the beauty parlor." ...

(8/2/82)

Barber shops are the stuff that hometown anecdotes everywhere are made of. I don't recall ever writing this one up, but it was a personal experience out at the two-chair Carrboro Barber Shop that Jess Hackney and John Williford once operated. I patronized it because I liked them, but also because haircuts there were only 75 cents—half the prevailing price in Chapel Hill.

It was one Saturday morning, a popular time for haircuts of course, when several of us were waiting our turn, and the usual buzz of conversation was going around the shop. Then I heard Mr. Williford say to his customer, "Oh, I may be old, but I aint sick. —But there's one thing I can't do any longer."

All other conversation in the place stopped instantly. I sat on the edge of my seat waiting expectantly, as Mr. Williford then said, quite casually:

"I can't stay up late."

Such a scene about what appeared to be a delicate matter was once judged to be too delicate. Witness this item turned in for my column in 1980, under the heading "It Really Happened," but which was never printed because of the misconceptions it encouraged:

Scene: The busy lunch hour in mid-town NC National Bank. Among the multitudes waiting in the line for teller service in the bank lobby are a mother and an unhappy four-year-old lad. The tot's restlessness finally gets to the mother. She picks up her child, takes him to a nearby sofa and plops him down. "Now you've done it, momma," charges the lad. "What have I done?" rejoins mom. Everybody in the place is looking on in hushed anticipation. "You've crushed my balls!" cried the boy.

With that he pulled two ping pong balls out of his back pocket. The bank lobby erupted in a gale of laughter. A man walked over to the "crushed" kid and handed him a five-dollar bill. "You've made my day, son," he declared.

And it really happened. — Only in Chapel Hill.

Personal experiences should be pardonable if they're good true stories. The following one I did write up, concerning the old oak stump that stood on the sidewalk in front of Mrs. John Lasley's home on East Rosemary St. Mrs. Lasley often said how she enjoyed the flowers that I planted in the stump, but she'd also add that she'd called the Town of Chapel Hill to have it removed. At least 10 years after she moved away, and long after her death, I reported the following:

One day last month the present owner of the home, Bill Chandler, was working in his front yard when he noticed a Town maintenance truck pull up on the sidewalk. He asked the workman if he could help him. The friendly fellow explained that Mrs. Lasley had asked him to remove the stump and he was now ready to do so. Bill explained that Mrs. Lasley had been gone many years — and that if it was all the same, he'd appreciate the town's leaving this fine, natural flower bed to reap its own eventual reward.

The town's faithful servant agreed, hopped in his truck, and called back to Bill as he drove off, "Just let us know if you ever want the stump removed." **(7/23/82)**

And surely every parent has had a personal experience in this realm, as happened one summer evening when his mother and I called our six-year-old bike racing son over for a brief word:

… "Do you know which side of the street you should ride on?" we asked the boy. "Sure — the wight side," the young epitome of brilliance quickly replied. "And which is the wight side?" his mother inquired. A pleased smile of knowledge crossed the youngster's face. He immediately threw up his hand — his left hand.

Mom gave pop a slant-eyed look and spoke like a Solomon: "Perhaps we'd better call off the races in the street for tonight," she gently declared. **(8/10/61)**

Politics are natural grist for the anecdotal mill:

… A well-known public spirited local citizen was appointed to fill a vacancy on the Chapel Hill Board of Aldermen and served quite ably. However, when the time approached for expiration of his interim term he chose not to stand for re-election. Instead he filed for election to the Chapel Hill School Board. In the large field of candidates running for the school posts he didn't win election. But his comment of explanation to friends was appropriately revealing: "I just can't get as interested in sewer lines and streets as I am in the schools."

(5/28/67)

I believe the late UNC Prof. of Business Administration Dick Calhoon would not at all mind my revealing him as the person who said that. Local elections inevitably provide a laughable look at local life, too:

... It was scarcely a score of years ago that we stopped voting on township offices. Until then there was a ballot for two offices in each township — constable and justice of the peace. The constable was a rural (township), part-time, but fully sworn policeman.

The late Republican stalwart Louis Sparrow was one of the last to serve that office locally. I recall one time during a League of Women Voters candidates meeting when a woman in the audience asked him, in his bid for re-election, how many people he arrested in a typical day. "Well, some days I don't arrest as many as I want to," Mr. Sparrow inveighed, "and other days I have to arrest more than I want to."

That reply, I've always thought, was one of the greatest pearls of wisdom unleashed since UNC Baseball Coach Bunn Hearn first gave out his annual pre-season prediction that "We'll win some; we'll lose some; and some of 'em'll get rained out."

(8/6/82)

It was also at one of the early League of Women Voters candidates meetings that I heard Hubert S. Robinson Sr. show the combined folk humor and common sense that helped him become the first black person to serve in local elective office. He was one of a number of candidates running for the Board of Aldermen. As the meeting was about to be closed the woman presiding asked if any of the candidates had anything else to say.

Mr. Robinson arose and calmly declared: "Now you've heard all these other people tell you all the good things they'd do for you if they're elected. I just want to say that if they're elected and I'm not and they don't do what they've said, I'm gonna go down to city hall and h'ant 'em." His seizing the moment to come up with such a statement demonstrated to me Hubert Robinson's ability to see the real humor in every-day life — a quality that I felt carried him through many difficult moments during his long service on the Town Board.

This one came out under the heading, "Yes, We Have Only Bananas," and occurs to me as another example of the humor that abounds in our life experiences every day.

It really happened at NC Memorial Hospital here recently. Doctors received a call from an eastern North Carolina physician concerning a man there who was suffering serious convulsions. It was agreed the patient would be sent to Memorial Hospital for treatment, and he was scheduled to arrive that afternoon. By nightfall he'd failed to show up there. ...Next day about noon a man walked in and handed the Emergency Room staff an envelope containing detailed information on the case. The doctors started to discuss his condition with him.

"Wait a minute," the new arrival said, "I'm not the patient." "Well, where is he?" asked the puzzled doctors. "I don't rightly know," said the man. "We stopped at a store on the highway yesterday and he went in to buy some bananas and that's the last time I saw him." "Do you know what town that was in?" pursued the doctors. "Well, no sir, I don't believe I do. You see, I aint never come this way before ... But the doctor back there, he told me to be absolutely sure I give you this envelope, so here I am ..."

– Now, if you see a rather disturbed fellow standing on the roadside down east with a sack of bananas –

(7/14/66)

Under the heading of Great Stories About Good Old Days, I place this one, told by Chapel Hill High School classmate George Pickard at his 25th class reunion here:

... There was that time back in the summer of '42, he recalled, when his dad made him take math as a summer school make-up course after he'd flunked it. In addition he had to take a job scraping dishes at the University's Lenoir Dining Hall, arising at 4:30 each morning. On the pre-dawn morning of his final summer school exam, his dad came in to wake him and shouted that he'd better get up, that the school house was burning down. George uttered a customary oath and rolled over, then opened one eye and could see by the glow in the sky out his bedroom window that the school, a block away, was indeed on fire.

"I jumped into my clothes and started out the door," he recalled. "Then I saw that math book on the dresser and stuck it in my belt, hopped on my bike and rode over to the school. It was in full blaze. Standing at the back corner of the building I pitched that book into the fire – just as my dad came around the side of the building." His father made him go to the principal,

William H. Peacock, to pay for the book, George recalled. But the principal pointed out that the books were insured, and he wouldn't take the money ...
(6/26/68)

The Southern Part of Heaven ought to be a place to draw out the creative best in its citizenry. A touch of romance always helps:

The spirit of romance can thrive, even in the doldrums of these summer-time Dog Days. Lcdr. Harry Buzhardt of the Naval ROTC faculty at the University has proven it. Lately he decided to propose to his sweetheart, Amanda Gainey. An appropriate method and setting was needed. The inventive suitor came up with it. He obtained a fortune cookie, steamed it open and put his written request inside, then had it served to Amanda when he took her to dinner at their favorite Chinese restaurant—yes, she accepted.
(7/14/78)

If you think that's high "camp," what about this from the Orange County Bicentennial celebration of 1952. The late Judge Jim Phipps was general chairman of the program, which included a historical pageant and several sidelight attractions to spice it up:

One such attraction—quite in the mood of that less-jaded era—was a bicentennial beauty pageant. As a piece de resistance to climax the selection of the bicentennial queen, US Senator Alton Asa Lennon of Wilmington agreed to come to crown the winner. Before the assembled multitudes looking on in Hillsborough, the senator placed the crown on the head of beaming young Miss Patsy Ann Poythress of Chapel Hill.

Then he paused, looked around, and with a sincere smile of his own asserted almost credibly: "This is the greatest honor that has come to me since I have been a United States Senator."

And why shouldn't it be?
(9/27/82)

You have to appreciate a guy who does his thing with style, don't you! Some crooks have that flair, also:

Prof. and Mrs. Claude George left their home on Coker Drive for an hour last Saturday morning to go to the grocery. On their return they discovered that a thief had broken in and taken a great many of their belongings—including a color TV set. An incidental loss, too, was a packet of personalized stationery which Dr. George had received as a Christmas present. Two days later he received a letter from the robber, postmarked from Raleigh, and written on this very same monogrammed note paper. Addressing him quite properly as "Dr. George," the culprit expresed his regret for stealing the stuff, but helpfully enclosed pawn tickets for the goods from a hock shop in Rocky Mount.

(1/7/68)

Claude George as a man who enjoys his own foibles was kind enough to tell me that one on himself. No doubt he really enjoyed this one more, as I happened to witness it myself:

Business Administration School Associate Dean Claude George was presiding in his customary easy-going gracious manner last week at induction ceremonies for new initiates into Phi Beta Kappa. As each student was called forward, Claude would state where he or she was from and what they were studying. This was a beneficial way to fill the moments as the scholars walked to the stage, and it helped the atmosphere of the appropriately dignified proceedings.

All was going well until Dean George called forth Jonathan Gregory McKenzie and found himself announcing that "Jonathan is studying Charlotte and he comes from a business major." After the laughter subsided the proceedings moved along even better.

(4/23/79)

There are myriad anecdotes that have naturally grown up with the passing of years at the First State University. Among such a number of them, this is perhaps the oldest as a tradition:

In earlier years of the University the hazing of freshmen was a recognized practice. ... The fashion was to leave a telephone message for the first-year man to "Call Frank Porter" at such and such a number. The boy answering the message would find he was talking to Consolidated University President Frank P. Graham—always a gracious and sympathetic soul in dealing with the duped youngsters.

Now the fashion is to leave a note on the greenie's desk to "Call Bill" at a given number. Upon "returning" the call the poor soul eagerly asks "Is that you, 'Bill?' " University President Bill Friday, who discerningly recognizes this type of call in the greeting or inquiry of the caller, then carefully and kindly lets the boy down as gently as possible, cautioning that he doesn't mind his calling him, but that this is the President of the University, and somebody has played a trick on him.

(1/8/67)

Another fad that comes and goes through the years is the telephoning of bomb threats:

… It was early in the morning during an exam period when the telephone rang in the Naval ROTC Armory building. A veteran chief petty officer, accustomed to crises of many serious kinds through the years, was the only person on duty. Picking up the phone, he was told there was a bomb in the building, set to go off in a short while.

Quick as a flash, the chief calmly replied, "Sorry, wrong number," and hung up, no doubt totally confounding the caller.

(6/4/72)

Actually in that case the building was quietly checked out anyhow, but exams went on there as scheduled that day.

The fact that college education doesn't insure preparation to deal with the common sense realities of life was illustrated by this one, which occurred at the end of the academic year:

Maybe he was deep in meditation within that mythical ivory tower all the time he was here. At least that is the only explanation that immediately comes to mind. According to the staff at the UNC Photo Lab this fellow came in early last week and asked where he could pick up his diploma. They explained to him that he was in the Photo Lab, and his diploma was probably over at the Central Records Office. "Where is the Central Records Office?" the newly-graduated senior asked. "It's in Hanes Hall," they answered, citing the well-known central campus structure in the nearby business administration court. "Where's Hanes Hall?" then asked this pillar of knowledge who was so imminently preparing to pick up his certificate of learning and go out to face the brave new world.

(6/9/68)

That recalls the classic involving the long-time Director of the UNC Photo Lab, Ross Scroggs, who also taught a very popular physics class in photo theory. His wife, Mary Scroggs, was the long-time administrative manager of the physics department. She recollected the creative intrigue by which one student attempted to gain admission to Ross' closed-out course one semester:

… "I'm a special friend of Mr. Scroggs," he told her unknowingly and to no avail. "Mr. Scroggs will be upset if you don't register me. I guess you don't know Mr. Scroggs." Mary Scroggs pondered that for a moment, then responded, "Well, I've slept with him for 30 years." It was, she admitted, "one of my finest moments."

(2/4/80)

Absent-minded professors are inevitably the target of academic anecdotes, and sometimes with justification. Ferebee Taylor, when he was University Chancellor, once stopped at a gas station while traveling down east with his wife. Not realizing she'd gotten out of the car during the stop, he drove off and didn't miss her till he was some distance down the road, and thought he was speaking to her in the back seat. Mrs. Taylor was waiting patiently, if a bit bewildered, when her husband returned for her.

An earlier Taylor on the faculty, the late great English Prof. George Coffin Taylor, was an archetypical absent-minded scholar:

Prof. and Mrs. Taylor, according to a story that Editor Louis Graves delighted in publishing in the old Chapel Hill Weekly, went back to his home in Columbia, SC, one weekend. On conclusion of the visit he drove all the way back to Chapel Hill before he realized he'd come off an left his wife back in South Carolina. He had to drive back there to fetch her.

They tell another one on Prof. Taylor—how before he left for a trip one time, his wife admonished him to remember to write her while he was away. The good professor failed to do that, but he apparently made a good try. Some time later when his wife was cleaning out one of his suit coats to send it to the cleaners, she felt something bulky in a pocket. Reaching inside, she pulled out a stack of postcards, each addressed to her, and each bearing the identical hand-written message, "Having a wonderful time ..."

(2/1/80)

Naturally so many of the great Carolina stories involve sports. — This one is from Football Coach Dick Crum's first year in Chapel Hill:

A special showing of the new Carolina alumni slide show, "Hark the Sound," was given recently for Carolina Football Coach Dick Crum and his assistants, almost all of whom came here this year from the University of Miami in Ohio.

As various scenes appeared on the screen in the Kenan Fieldhouse projection room, one of the coaches recognized a slide from gridiron action during last fall's Carolina-Miami football game in Chapel Hill. "Hey—that's us." he exclaimed. "No," came the authoritative voice of one of his fellow coaches in the darkened room. "That's them!"

(6/9/78)

Needless to say, the ardor of some Carolina sports fans is legendary, and almost painfully real, too:

That was a real gem tucked in Gene Upchurch's sports column the other day—the one about the guy who called the UNC Sports Information Office to ask whether a certain Saturday basketball game this coming season would be in the afternoon or night. Told it was a night game, he responded, "Good, I'm getting married in the afternoon, so I'll be able to make the game."

It recalls that classic nugget about the Tar Heel rooter in the season ticket 50-yard line section at a jam-packed Carolina-Duke football game one year. Noting a vacant seat beside him he asked the fellow next to it whose seat it was. "That's my wife's," was the reply. The dialogue continued "Couldn't she come?" "No, she died." "Oh, I'm sorry. Well couldn't you find a friend to use her ticket?" "No, they're all attending her funeral."—And that's really Chapel Hilly!

(9/14/79)

Outlanders simply can't understand the little niceties of Carolina sports, sometimes. This one happened many years ago while the Tar Heels were in the national basketball playoffs. The young daughter of a friend from South Carolina was in Duke Hospital for an eye operation:

... Brave little moppet that she was, she chattered away friendly-like with the doctors and attendants as preparations for surgery were completed. And she was quite a basketball fan, too, real dyed-in-the-wool for Carolina. That was the University up here, she figured. At least, that's obviously what she meant when she looked up at the medical team around her and said real chipper-like, "I guess y'all are real proud of your UNC basketball team." And she's still probably wondering what all the silence was about.

(3/19/69)

A recollection of University anecdotes may also rightfully include at least one seldom-told tale about alma mater, for reasons which will become obvious:

The story can never be verified genetically, but there is significant evidence in historical lore that President Abe Lincoln was the son of a member of the first graduating class at Carolina. But for the circumstances surrounding his paternal parentage, Abe might well have followed his natural father to Chapel Hill instead of acquiring his book-learning by candlelight in a Kentucky cabin. ... Dad is said to have been Adam Alexander Springs, an early landowner in the Gaston County town of McAdenville. Adam was a classmate of the first student at UNC, Hinton James, and received his diploma in 1798. In fact, his is the earliest diploma now in the University archives.

Young Nancy Hanks and her sister were sent from Virginia to live with a brother in the Gaston County community of South Point. Nancy was said to be working for Adam Springs when she became pregnant by him. Springs had her sent away so that his indiscretion would not become known. And so the 16th president was born in Hodgenville, KY, and grew up in the family of Nancy and Tom Lincoln. McAdenville descendants cite as proof some old pictures of two other sons of Adam Springs. Their features bear a striking resemblance to Lincoln's distinctive dark-eyed angular countenance.

The muse is now whether the early curriculum — and extra-curriculum — of Carolina actually played a role in the birth of Abraham Lincoln.

(2/26/82)

University anecdotes should certainly include some of the favorite stories of contemporary Carolina "greats," such as this one which Albert Coates included in his book, "The Story of the Institute of Government:"

The professor writes that ... it reminded him of a nominating speech for the President of the Phi Society that was made by a fellow student at Carolina many years ago: "Mr. President, I have in mind a man ..." At that point a critic rose to a point of personal privilege and rejoined: "Mr. President, I would like to observe that that man is in a mighty cramped position ..."

(5/7/82)

— And the classic of Chancellor Emeritus Robert B. House:

When invited to speak at the various college class reunions each year, Chancellor Bob invariably would start off his talk by announcing with sober authority that "This is the greatest class that ever attended the University of North Carolina." When the applause died down he'd continue, "I know that to be a fact, because I have announced it at every class reunion for years and nobody has ever disputed it."

(7/19/82)

Chapter 4

Chapel Hill Traditions
and Customs

What, to us in the Heavenly Southern Part, is Chapel Hilly, and what really isn't — or isn't any longer?

So many mundane activities elsewhere are given exalted status in Chapel Hill. What would be a routine public hearing in Anywhere, USA, is a sophisticated ritual in Chapel Hill. The public hearing here is a unique species, suffice it to say. Other activities take on trappings that are unique to this community, and are worthy of observation, study, and comment.

But the public hearing in this academic community would be worthy of a doctoral dissertation:

... In political science it might be entitled: "The Hearing — Servant or Subverter of Political Action?" In English it could be "Circumlocutions as Expressed in the Public Hearing." The zoology paper might be on "The Rare Genus Chapel Hilliana as Observed in Public Hearings." Or in psychology the candidate could prepare a treatise on "Group Mental Paralysis: Case Studies from Public Hearings."

Having sat in on several hundred of these exercises during the past 15 years, I consider myself a fair-grade appraiser of public hearings. The need for them, if only as a defense mechanism for action in a representative form of government, is unquestionable. Unfortunately, they are all too often exercises in futility. The persons often most concerned with the business at hand aren't heard from, generally through their own indifference. On the other hand, too, the intimidating effect of a public hearing on an inexperienced participant is fearsome. We have many "pros" on this circuit, and

The Flower Ladies – still on the downtown sidewalk in 1955

they can fairly demolish an unwary first-timer.
(1/14/70)

Public hearing speakers include the "so long as I'm here" types who came to the meeting for some other purpose, but decide to grab a piece of the action; the real experts, who diligently study the issues and speak out at almost all hearings; and finally, the self-designated experts, such as the one who reasons logically that his PhD in comparative literature makes him a natural savant on the vagaries of the exotic language of zoning-speak. In light of this, I concluded "... public hearings are as much a part of Chapel Hill as Davie Poplar, dogs, and the flower ladies. Long may we rave."
(1/14/70)

The flower ladies as one of Chapel Hill's noblest institutions have been shoved from grace by what I call from my prejudicial point of view "municipal arrogance." They continue a 50-year tradition of individual enterprise in downtown Chapel Hill and are no doubt more comfortable than ever in the protected climate of the NCNB Plaza corridor. But the gain there has been the loss to the sidewalk scene. This came about through the futility of a supposed egalitarian spirit, another quality that occasionally confounds our community.

The flower ladies simply sold their home-grown wares on the sidewalks for years, in mutually-recognized violation of a local ordinance against such. Everything was fine. The practice was recognized as a unique activity,

which, as the Dickens saying in "Oliver Twist" went, made the law "an ass."
Then in the activist era of the 60s the beatniks moved in with all kinds of
craft gimcrackery, including paper flowers. The Town Council, in a belief
that it had to find a legal answer to all problems, felt it had to act — naturally,
after staging a public hearing on the issue:

... Will the genius of a new municipal administration — eight aldermen
and a mayor who can resolve the mighty problems of municipal government — be able to finally set this situation aright as it should be? Will they be
able to draw up and pass a local ordinance to put the flower ladies back on
the main sidewalk where they reigned so long amid their radiant natural
creations until the fateful "progress" of legal red tape did them in?
(12/22/75)

The Town, prodded to and determined to handle the issue, did so by
banning all sidewalk sales, and the flower ladies as a sidewalk institution
died.
Another unique institution locally which I fear is dying, a victim of both
technology and overkill, is the League of Women Voters candidates' forums
before elections. That I may avert the righteous wrath of the League, let it be
understood that I highly respect this project and hope it will continue. But its
role in community politics is diminishing from the status it held for three
decades prior to this appraisal:

Candidates were made and broken by their appearance before this formi-
dable forum. Woe betide the hopeful who failed to appear or faltered in his
presence at this occasion. The good women of the League, well-informed
and sternly impartial, were not to be trifled with. The single candidates'

League of Women Voters-sponsored candidates meeting in West Franklin
St. Elementary School Auditorium — 5/13/54

meeting they sponsored invariably drew a full house to the high school auditorium, and its proceedings were comprehensively chronicled in the press. The old pols learned they could not jolly the ladies of the League. The smoke of their political backrooms gave way to the mercy of a two-minute alarm clock on their pleas to the public. Some quailed and failed before the incisive questions posed to them by the League. What, then, has happened?

(5/2/80)

What has happened, of course, is that a good idea has spawned multiple offspring to the extent that the many of these forums have become primarily media events where the press sometimes outnumbers the "live" public:

... Think what it'll be like when cable TV envelops us. We'll be up to our ears and eyeballs in public service candidate forums right in our own living rooms – but with escape from such significant knowledge only the twist of a dial away. Yea, for all its fine purpose and heritage, we fairly mourn the imminent passing of the candidates' forum of yore. Technology, and our own good intentions, have done us in.

Now one of these days in the great sweet by and by, some smart candidate is going to re-discover those greatest of all political weapons from back in the dark ages – doorbell ringing and the personal handshake.

(5/2/80)

Speaking of the handshake, there used to be a species of that which was uniquely Chapel Hilly. It was the tri-partitite shake that was singular to the late President of the University, Dr. Frank Porter Graham:

... Though so diminutive that he was invariably outreached, President Graham was a handshaker without a peer as a part of his natural, warm, social grace. You knew you'd been shook, and in the finest fashion, when he finished with you.

Remember, too, that "Dr. Frank" was a fine physical specimen – a man of moderation with a justified reputation as a feisty competitor. In the friendliest manner, he'd always get the grip on the "shakee" first. What followed could have been in any of three stages – or all in progression.

Most often he'd grip your hand in both of his own – a gracious supplement to the standard form of greeting – as he inquired of your and your family's health and happiness. Often, he'd advance to firmly grasp your elbow with his free hand. Not infrequently the handshake was a simple entry to a hefty hand around your shoulder. Nobody greeted a friend or stranger in a finer

Frank & Marian
Graham voting in
Chapel Hill's
South Precinct,
11/7/50

and fonder fashion than did Frank Graham.
(9/13/82)

The community tradition that's come to draw the widest mass participation is the Apple Chill Fair, the annual spring festival, and its autumn equivalent, Festifall. This Sunday afternoon mid-town happening sponsored by the Town Recreation Department was an instant success and has grown steadily in stature:

For the first time in its eight-year history, Apple Chill became a full community-wide celebration yesterday. By spilling over onto the historic McCorkle Place on the University's main campus, this annual rite of spring came to epitomize both figuratively and literally the coming together of town and gown.

The revelry of the occasion did no irreverence to the memories of the Confederate Soldier, the Caldwell monument or even Davie Poplar. In their era the village WAS the University. In Apple Chill yesterday it all evolved together into community.

Many years ago at this season the University sponsored a delightful arts and crafts fair called the Dogwood Festival. After several decades aborning, that spirit and program has now found new life in Apple Chill.
(4/17/78)

The spring and fall street fairs continued to grow to the extent they became regional mob scene attractions until restrictions on exhibitors were imposed to restore them to community status. I always enjoyed recording them in vignette form:

APPLE CHILLINESS – (As witnessed from the Rec. Dept. Desk on the Post Office Porch): A lissome lass in bikini blue jeans – revealing and hiding, enticingly. ... Looking like a lost soul in a strange land, she wanders by, toting the Sunday NY Times – and sits a few moments to try to sort out the strange, teeming scene. ... "Do we have any safety pins?" Sorry, that's one overlooked item of foresight. ... What an incongruous pair – that girl in skin-tight denim slacks, balancing on four-inch high heels, and holding hands as she browses along with the barefoot guy. ... Tiny tot, rear cheeks akimbo, casually wetting right there on the pavement. ... Nattily-dressed dandy in immaculate two-tone green sport coat and slacks, carrying a color-coordinated matching tray of newly-purchased tomato seedlings. ... Inevitable bombed-out beatnik in a tank shirt, murmuring "Don't mess with me, man, I'm cool." ... A mature moppet of eight coming up to calmly report her loss of her mother. ... Closely followed by a tear-streaked darling wailing over loss of her helium balloon.

– Yes, Apple Chill Fair is all of this, but much more. How can you capture it in a paragraph – the colors, odors, the noise – the garish gaudiness and the beautiful harmony? But on this hot Sunday afternoon there's something purely rewarding to the soul, just looking on as Chapel Hill in this playful rite of spring again becomes Apple Chill.

(4/23/79)

Even commercial hype can gradually develop into local tradition. One of these that was a natural was the annual Christmas season men's night champagne showing of lingerie by the Night Gallery store. As self-appointed saloon editor, I chose to "review" this well-staged happening. So popular was it that admission to it was by written invitation only. I never received one, but took advantage of the invitation mailed to my Number Three Son:

... Yule-timed sales promotions like these are not intended as entertainment, but they're involuntary captives of that end. Success is insured. The menfolk have the benefit of transference vision in considering purchase of all the lacy stuff shown off by the lovely leggy models. And they can't help enjoying the scene, with its inevitable mildly raucous fellowship, abetted by the complimentary bubbly beverage.

George and Marion Spransy – with '39th birthday' loot – Feb. 9, 1965; George Spransy and Wallace Williams

… Don't expect me to evaluate the quality of the models or merchandise. At my age, both looked like sheer dynamite. Suffice it to say there was attractive Christmas potential in just about every offering – from the $4.50 nylon side-tie bikini to the top-price merino wool kimono ($224).
(12/5/80)

That was my only "review" of this comparatively new, but steadily growing hometown tradition. One barometer of its success is that fact that staging it required as many off-duty cops for security as there were lingerie models.

Another Chapel Hill entrepreneur did pretty well for himself, too, by creating an annual occasion that was self-proclaimed for his own benefit. The late George Spransy did it with style:

The printed invitations are out again, calling attention to George Spransy's annual "39th birthday" this Thursday (Feb. 9). New note in the anniversary proclamation this year is the too subtle recommendation for "quality rather than quantity." Hand-painted neckties only, George pleads.
(2/8/67)

*George, who also made "bald is beautiful" a popular hometown cult, was a natural showman in addition to being a devoted family man and an energetic civic service contributor. He was a perfect model for Benjamin Franklin and dressed like him annually for the downtown (E. **Franklin** St.) Ben Franklin Day sales promotion. His size and hearty laugh also made George a natural for Santa Claus, whom he portrayed for many years in the Merchants Association-sponsored Christmas parade. George could make a*

'Persimmon Pete' Ivey – inspecting the crop by Caldwell Hall on
UNC campus – fall 1959

good thing out of almost anything, and enjoyed life to its limits. I remember
on a special train to the Gator Bowl in Jacksonville, FL, one time that
George wanted to liven things up a bit. He picked up a pie plate and started
walking down the cars shaking the plate and calmly imploring "Give!" It was
such an outrageous idea that his fellow travelers fairly deluged him with
coins – which George soon lost again in an all-night penny ante poker
game.

  Chapel Hillians for at least 14 years observed Button Gwinnett Day and
hoped it would catch on nationally. This was the the idea of some staff
members at the University Press, and it had both sentimental and practical
potential:

… Mrs. Frank ("Gwinnett Gwen") Duffey explained its origin. Several of
them noticed this unusual name listed as a signer of the Declaration of
Independence and looked him up in the Dictionary of American Biography.
They found Gwinnett to have indeed been a tragic figure – a man who died
penniless in a duel and left no descendants. With hearts full of remorseful
charity, they decided to designate July 2 annually as Button Gwinnett Day.
They had the practical notion that if it caught on nationally there'd likely be
a three-day holiday for the Fourth of July.

  It hasn't caught on nationally yet, but in the Charlie Brown spirit of those
who observe Beethoven's birthday in December, the local chapter continues
to lionize Gwinnett during a coffee break each July 2 (with) … the reading

of odes to the honored one — acrostics on his name — and a bit of good fellowship to continuing the fine old tradition.
(7/2/67)

I was primarily responsible for the rise to prominence of another very personal local tradition, but, as happened with Gwinnett Day, I couldn't perpetuate it. University News Bureau Director Pete Ivey was a natural-born humorist and a competent promotor. But, as Pete considered his personal status in the scheme of learned things, he found out early on that in a town full of PhD's, he as an un-lettered generalist wasn't very significant. So he decided to seize upon a specialty of his own and become the ranking authority on it.

Through logic that I never divined he settled upon the persimmon, and soon became the "patron saint of persimmonry" — with the willing conniv-ance of others of us in the press who aided and abetted. Many feature stories were written about "Persimmon Pete," including one I wrote in 1959:

… At that time I quoted him as feeling "We persimmon lovers are a dying race. It's a good fruit, but there's too much misunderstanding and too many false tales about 'em. I'm afraid there's no great future for persimmons." Of course Pete lived to see better than he forecast in that statement 16 years ago. Through his diligent research and promotion (and a modest bit of supplemental press agentry), he's seen the world become much more tolerant, even appreciative of persimmons.
(12/29/75)

On writing that shortly after Pete's death, I offered immodestly to carry on the good fight in behalf of persimmons, and even announced a campaign to have it officially declared the state fruit. Apparently I didn't have Pete's panache for that bill never made it to the Legislature.

Friends even planted a persimmon tree in the University's Coker Arbore-tum in Pete's honor, but perhaps it was because of the absence of his personal oversight that the tree died. I wrote about persimmons from time to time, but couldn't successfully continue his heritage.

Not unique to Chapel Hill, but certainly lingering local traditions, are dogs and trees. Because of the big tract of public open space strategically located in the center of town, dogs for many years had a much freer run in Chapel Hill than in other comparable communities. Campus dogs, both strays and local ones that were self-adopted, often gained exalted status. Some are yet legendary, like Prof. Lee Wiley's "Dan, the Dog" who was a celebrity for students of the late 40s. There was no dog control law in town until 1971:

Mrs. A.M. Jordan, Chapel Hill Humane Society matriarch with Newfoundland puppy given by friends, 1955

The town's new dog control program will preserve Chapel Hill as a canine haven, we hope. One of the facets of Gracious Living in Chapel Hill is the tolerance and appreciation accorded dogdom. There are now and inevitably there will be in the future some vicious dogs that ought to be kept on leash at all times. But the terms of the Town's new regulations which permit well-behaved dogs to roam their own domains as they please are well considered. So long as Chapel Hill is able to have freedom for dogs it will continue to be a friendly place.

(11/3/71)

Two years later more dog laws were passed:

… as another Fleeting Vestige of the Vanishing Village we learn that we'll have to have a leash law for dogs. Cats will have to be licensed and vaccinated, too. Those of us unlucky with, or unwary for our pets, may be fined $25 for this oversight, and the danger to the public therefrom.

No, we'll not flat-out say it was better in the Old Days. Citified civilization must and will prevail. But we certainly mourn the passing of the era when dogdom was at liberty locally. It all seemed natural and good.

(10/4/73)

Trees, like dogs, continue to have exalted status in Chapel Hill. Many's the time when the possible cutting of a tree has been front-page high drama in the local newspaper. I recall an occasion about 1952 when the Town

proposed to cut a sapling near a busy corner to improve motorists' vision. An
editorial campaign was mounted against it. One night the Town removed the
tree — and it was several days before its absence was noted.

— Not so, other trees. Although Davie Poplar on the campus contains
much more concrete than wood, the mere mention of tampering with it, as
necessary from time to time, evokes indignant controversy. Gavels made
from branches pruned from Davie are highly-treasured souvenirs.

An out-of-town owner of a local food franchise operation this year
unwarily, or perhaps accidentally, had or permitted trees to be cut on the
public right-of-way by his property. In the resulting public furore he agreed
to a costly replanting. The firm's patronage suffered significantly and the
place closed down.

Chapel Hill's "Old Fashioned Fourth of July" celebration in Kenan
Stadium (and in more recent years, Carrboro's own family-oriented observ-
ance) has gained status as a worthy hometown tradition. I well recall the
original one, started as a benefit for the local chapter of the American Field
Service, as I wrote about it some years later:

... The first year it was staged back in 1960 it brought in about $600
profit — a real windfall then to co-chairmen Bob Boyce and Roy Martin. ...
The idea of a community-wide celebration on old Emerson Field caught on
quickly. In addition to the fireworks there was a picnic dinner, band concert,
pet show, pony rides, and contests. One year the Fire Department brought
out a hydrant hose and sprayed all the kiddies who dared run through the
stream. (— That was one of the least expensive and most popular "entertain-
ments" of all times.)

The age of television and spectator spectaculars, no doubt, is doing us in.
— You wouldn't want to go back to the "good old days" again. But the profits
for American Field Service — over $3,000 on some of the "Fourths," made
them worth more than simply the fun and tradition of the moment.
(7/8/77)

One of the community's most valid historic traditions in observance of
Independence Day is a newer celebration. It is the noon-time July Fourth
ringing of the Tom Collins' bell. Originally used to signal shift changes for
American Tobacco Co. workers in Durham, it was obtained by the tradition-
minded and patriotic newspaper columnist Tom Collins in 1965 and was
mounted in his yard. The Collins' made a neighborhood festival of the bell-
ringing at noon-time each July Fourth. After the death of their parents, the
three Collins sons gave the bell to the Chapel Hill Preservation Society,

which in 1985 renewed the annual tradition. The bell was moved to the yard of the Society's Horace Williams House.
  — What's especially Chapel Hilly about Christmas, the occasion with the greatest of all traditions? This from earlier years:

... How well I remember the community Christmas tree lighting party that was an annual affair, signaling the beginning of that exciting season for the village. As I recall, the Christmas tree was set up on the sidewalk in front of the mid-town Methodist Church. On a designated evening, as announced in the Chapel Hill Weekly, the lights were turned on, everybody gathered 'round for carol singing, and Santa Claus was there to talk to the children and pass out candy. How simple, but how grand ...
(12/20/70)

... Incidentally, back in an earlier and far more innocent era when this was more of a "company" town, the University used to decorate all of the main block downtown. There were lighted strings across the street between each lamp post and lighted laurel roping all along the sides. ... We proudly claimed the display to be the best outdoor Christmas decorations in the state. Whether that's an exaggeration or not, it is a certainty that these decorations have never been equaled downtown since then.
(12/17/78)

The University attempted vainly to restore some of this grace a few years ago:

... The campus Physical Plant Office is responsible for installation and decoration of the very attractive lighted tree across from the post office.
  I wondered at the time it was erected two weeks ago how long it would last, since many University students and other Chapel Hillians have an unfortunate penchant for swiping everything that isn't welded down. Inquiry reveals that to date — with Christmas still a fortnight away — the tree has had to be refurbished three times. More lights have had to be put on twice to replace those stolen. On another time wiring had to be put up, since a vandal yanked some of the lighting array off. Even the star on top was knocked off, and many of the ornaments taken.
  Sad, isn't it. We all seek the outward trappings of Christmas, but some of us can't understand that the real Yuletide spirit is giving — not taking.
(12/17/78

That item appeared under the headline "Grinch Steals Christmas." The University did not continue its community Christmas tree after that season.

Christmas decorations in downtown Chapel Hill – 1962

But the Preservation Society had created a fine new Chapel Hill tradition that has continued and prospered:

The extraordinary success of the past weekend's Christmas Candlelight Tour in the Historic District should inaugurate a new community tradition. While it exceeded the expectations of the sponsoring Chapel Hill Preservation Society as a profit-making project, the benefits were far greater. It was a worthy exercise in pardonable community pride – the many "favorite thing" traditional trappings of local families on display for everybody's appreciation and admiration. Further – and most important in the cheery Christmas spirit, it gave Chapel Hill an opportunity that was amply accepted: To become re-acquainted with itself and its interesting and significant historic heritage. Thank you, Preservation People, for starting this fine new tradition – won't you please?

(12/19/77)

The Christmas Candlelight Tour has become a growing annual tradition, and in 1984 featured a "Dickens Christmas" subscription banquet in the Gimghoul Castle, the first time the meeting hall of that secret University order had ever been opened to the public.

An unlikely Christmas tradition I suggested in the column on several occasions was this:

If I were the Almighty himself, I believe I'd proclaim Christmas to be on

Sunday every year. I'd do this not just as a matter of convenience the way we've so neatly set up Washington's birthday, Memorial Day, and Veterans Day on quarterly Mondays. Christmas is just more Christmas on a Sunday than in all the years when it falls on other days.

After all, Christmas is an annual celebration of the weekly **Sabbath**. There is all this talk about putting Christ back into the Yuletide, retreating from the commercialization, and remembering that which Christmas truly commemorates. No, I am not proposing to take the fun out of it and wouldn't Scrooge up any of our Christmas pastimes.

... Sentimental fools like me are the ones who dote on the notion of a Christ-mass every December 25. We're thankful it works out naturally every few years because Christmas really and truly is a Sunday day.
(12/26/77)

More than any tradition could ever do, our children help us to truly appreciate Christmas, as I came to realize in this simple incident:

"Watch out, daddy, you'll lose your Christmas spirit!"

Those were the gentle but firmly reproving words that brought The Newsman up short this Yuletide to the revelation that there's something basically changed in our Christmas nowadays.

It was seven-year-old Bill, bless his sincere and ever enthusiastic heart, who opened this new world of fact and shattered former fancy.

Occasion of the new dawn of realization was my reprimand, for the I-don't-know-how-many'th time, of the children who were fairly running rampant around the household in their natural pre-Christmas exuberance.

The stern warning shot back with a melting smile — "Watch out, daddy, you'll lose your Christmas spirit!"

There it was all of a sudden, clear as a White Christmas. Today it's the parents — not the children — who'd "better watch out, better not cry, pout, etc."

Time was, we recall, when the kids were by tradition and discipline of Santa's generosity to nice children, just naturally better boys and girls around Christmas time.

... How did it come about then, the Newsman not-too-seriously asked himself, that nowadays I'd better "watch out" or I'd "lose my Christmas spirit!" (And, I'll add — the boy's switcheroo on my reprimand worked 100 per cent — for him!)

... A fellow doesn't complain about this reversal of roles, and wouldn't if he could. Christmas is for the children, unquestionably. And it does us all a lot of good.

It's just that — well, I'm gonna have to watch out mighty carefully from now on to not lose the Christmas spirit!
(12/31/59)

Restoration of traditions is often to be cheered. While I agree we should all be rightfully concerned for the dropping of racist images of the past, this effort sometimes amounts to straining at a gnat. During the mid-century period of honorable activism for extension of civil rights, the singing of that grand old song "Dixie," was gratuitously labeled racist, and was generally dropped from the public repertoire. That, too, it seems, has passed:

"Dixie," yet, as a college fight song! We thought that went out, forcibly, when the misguided civil rights thrust effectively silenced some of Stephen Foster's finest songs and other great compositions to which contemporary bigotry was inappropriately attributed.

But there it was the other day, right on Saturday afternoon regional television. The Citadel, a deep South institution admittedly, but a military college, too, was playing Davidson in basketball. The Citadel wanted to rally its partisans, so the band played the school fight song: Dixie. And nobody rioted or protested it as a slur on members of the minority race. Is true tolerance returning, or are stiff-backed vigilantes asleep?
(2/21/74)

The tides of public attitudes inevitably ebb and flow, but it does seem more recently that we're doing a better job of protecting both minority and majority rights.

The bumper sticker craze brings a new homily to Chapel Hill every few weeks. But in the case of at least one of these, we've exported ours to another place. For several decades a popular saying in behalf of UNC-Chapel Hill has been "If God is not a Tar Heel, why is the sky Carolina blue?" A few years ago I spotted what appeared to be a copy-cat of this in the University

If God is not a Tarheel Why's the sky Carolina Blue!

If God isn't a Longhorn Why's the sunset Burnt Orange?

of Texas' alumni magazine: "If God isn't a Longhorn, why's the sunset burnt orange?" Sure enough, as it turned out, that newly-coined phrase was the enterprise of a U. of Texas fan who was the son of a Carolina alumnus. The boy from Houston adapted the new saying for his bumper sticker after seeing Carolina's while in Chapel Hill at Coach Dean Smith's basketball camp.

One tradition I decry is that of "crowdsmanship" at entertainment events, particularly concerts, and which I call "the herd instinct of spectators to applaud insincerely, or far more than necessary"—a "cheapie" ploy, I called it:

... The spectators, at least some of 'em, hope to wangle an encore out of the entertainer, and figure the way to do it is to go wild, show signs of historic ecstasy, and thus win an extra on the program at no additional charge. This compliments the spectator's own prowess in the sense of crowdsmanship. He is often shouting his "bravo" to make his attendance a better bargain, or at least to reassure himself it was worth the price.

But just as often the crassness of crowdsmanship occurs because of the timidity of the majority of spectators. There are always a few people who sincerely feel the particular number of the performance they're applauding was truly out-of-this-world. That is fine—let 'em clap. But the rest of us ought to be free to sit on our hands courteously if we don't hold the same judgment.

... Of course there are some smart performers who skillfully draw these curtain calls and encores. But that's to their credit. We in the audience are perfectly fair game, but we paid for our seats, and aren't obliged to more than proper courtesy ...

(3/14/74)

Hallmarks of contemporary life in Chapel Hill may be noted by our changing judgments as to what's "in" and "out." After reading a chronicle of what activities and addresses were chic in a trendy national magazine, it occurred to me these notions could be applied locally:

... what, to us in this Heavenly Southern Part, is Chapel Hilly, and what really isn't—or isn't any longer? In an effort to be helpful, we have compiled a list of "ins" and "out"s for the Compleat Chapel Hillian ...

... the following activities are "in" in Chapel Hill: Weight-watching, flying Old Glory, Ted Kennedy jokes (not exclusive to CH, by any means), racquetball (pronounced "rack-a-ball," please), Mike Cross, Bo Derek ... and old-time religion, particularly the Chapel Hill Bible Church ...

Out—are Jimmy Carter jokes, marijuana, steam baths and saunas for weight-watchers (—trendy, but just won't do the trick), and ERA—a noble cause, but one that's due a few days benign neglect for its own sake.

"In" places include mid-town addresses, any seat in Carmichael Auditorium, and Dip's Restaurant; and the" outs" are such as New York, Durham, Charlotte, and Iran; the main post office in Chapel Hill; by-the-drink rip-off price places; and the The Four Corners (Nobody goes there any more—the place is too crowded.)

And so, wishing you a happy, well-adjusted new year "in" all Chapel Hillity ...

(12/31/79)

A blessedly helpful organization that modestly contributes to gracious living here—and everywhere its tenets flourish—is SEWERS, an acronym for the Society for Encouraging the Wearing of Emblems on the Right-Hand Side. Started by UNC alumnus Pat Gaskins '35, who lived here in recent years, SEWERS has as its motto "Some of our best people are found in sewers." It more usefully promotes the wearing of name tags on the right-hand side for easier recognition. There is simply more visibility to the name tag worn on the right side, the side where the eyes naturally focus in hand-shaking. Pat Gaskins bequeathed the mantle of promoting this movement to me, and I do so through membership cards awarded to those who practice its preachments.

A similarly useful organization, which I've yearned to see as a national movement is SITDOWN—my own creation as a banquet-inspired acronym:

... The letters could stand for "Stop Insulting The Diners Over Worthless Nonsense." ...

SITDOWN will function purely through the voluntary common spirit of its membership, which can take action in keeping with any given occasion. In time, it is likely that banquet speakers, so un-waveringly hypnotized by the sound of their own .voices, will catch the spirit and join the ranks, too. At that point the nation's economy is expected to gain a real boost through the millions of dollars worth of time saved. ...

Wasting the time of listeners in a captive audience is one of the greatest discourtesies—in fact, one of the most inappropriate affronts to human intellect—that can be perpetrated by persons who are otherwise most careful to exercise the normal amenities of obvious courtesy.

(11/21/63)

As an illustration of the need for SITDOWN, I later cited this:

... At an annual banquet meeting for which I was arrangements chairman, an outside speaker who was thrust upon us extended his designated five minutes to 13. The program was long and had to be carefully timed. Even if he meant well, he was vandalizing his listeners. Even worse, he started to conclude three times before finally doing so. I sent him a note telling him to end it all, but my wife mercifully (for him) intercepted it. After the meeting was over, I told his sponsor that the windbag had wasted six hours of our collective time, multiplying his nine minutes overtime by the 400 persons in the audience. And I meant it sincerely. This was an annual affair, important as a civic event. The boor who took advantage of us not only wasted time, but harmed our cause and scared off people from coming the next year.

(12/6/72)

This idea ought to be retroactively applied to some speakers for commencement exercises:

... Graduation exercises should be for those who are graduating – not for the benefit of some windbag axe-grinder or a celebrity conned (or paid) to speak for the occasion. Our local high schoolers this year elected various ones of their own number to speak on a related theme of timely significance to themselves.

Likewise, some recent speakers at the UNC commencement exercises have used the occasion to foist off some esoteric scholarly finding in their own academic specialty on the hapless graduates and their bored parents. – No wonder so many seniors skip commencement exercises. Let's return the program to those for whom they're intended!

(6/19/78)

It was the acknowledgement that "time is money" – at least that we should be thrifty with it – that motivated this:

... I am going to start a new organization: The Society for the Banishing of Night-time Committee meetings. SBNC may not win any awards for alphabetical propriety. But its members will be sainted toilers in the vineyard to eliminate a scourge on Chapel Hill living. Committee meetings should be staged at hours when they won't interfere with the precious little time we have left for home life, anyhow. Like over the luncheon table, or while we're cleaning our fingernails, looking at television, or washing

dishes. Yes, committee meetings may be a necessary evil. But they ought to be meshed in with some such useful activity as this.
(9/10/67)

Finally, I urged just one more organization as a new and pragmatic tradition:

Breakfast should come into its own right as a legitimate act of dining. For as long as I have recognized the dreary sameness of the stereotyped bacon and eggs diet, I have advocated that people free themselves from this unnecessary and even un-nourishing way to start each day. (The price of it has generally eliminated bacon nowadays, but the cult lingers on.)

Now a nutritionist at the University of Nevada has publicly joined the cause. In a news story this week she's quoted as urging that nutrition be the main consideration. Pizza or a taco has much more to offer your body than cholesterol-loaded eggs, she notes. I'd add that an easy-to-fix meat and tomato sandwich—too often the prize in your lunch pail—would be just as tasty a treat to charge you up for the new day.

Or why not heat up some of the left-overs from the night before to make breakfast more exotic? Some dishes actually improve with a bit of age. As a soul (and sole) member of the League for Better Breakfasts, I say, "Down with the dreary bacon and eggs cult! Up with breakfast as a real meal!"
(9/7/73)

Chapter 5

Cameron Henderson

I found him gradually developing into quite an authoritarian person, yet a fellow to be respected, and a chap with beneficial insight into matters of the day. I slavishly admired him and accepted without questioning his high-handed manner ...

The spirit of Chapel Hill is epitomized in a fictional hometowner — an admitted autobiographical idol whom I named Cameron Henderson. In addition to that being a rather pleasant-sounding name, it utilized the initials of the name of our town. The name is based on two major streets that memorialize persons significant in our community's history. They are University benefactor Paul Cameron and Major Pleasant Henderson, the University's first steward and later a local merchant and justice of the peace.

Cameron, Cam, or C.H., as I variously called him, was theoretically a contemporary of my childhood days and a personal hero of that era. He left the hometown many years earlier, then mysteriously turned up again in an event recorded in my Newsman's Notepad column in The Chapel Hill Newspaper in the summer of 1978.

I was sitting on the wall downtown the other day, speculating on the whimsies of the new academic year, when a vaguely familiar face hove into view. "Cameron Henderson," I called out, recognizing the visage from years gone by in the old hometown. "You have come back to life, scarcely scarred from years out in the real world." Cam, the only person I ever knew with a name in Iambic Pentameter, took it all in stride. "Hello, friend," he responded quietly. "Yes, it is me, returning to live in the hometown homestead. May I add, though, that the ravages of Space Age civilization appear to have taken their toll on your mortal body." Cam always was one

for frank speaking — yet a well-meaning soul in his quaint ways that I knew so well from the days of our childhood in Chapel Hill ...
(8/27/78)

The location of our repatiration is significant to the spirit of Chapel Hill, also. I have always imagined that the ideal place for people-watching was the rock wall in front of the mid-town University United Methodist Church. I pointed out, also, that Cameron Henderson's pleasant-sounding name was in "Iambic Pentameter." A reader some time later informed me that was incorrect. Cameron Henderson's name rolls off the tongue in syllables of Dactylic Dimiter, this knowledgeable reader declared. I'll not dispute that, nor dwell further on this aspect of his name, but I like both the sound and the local significance of Cameron Henderson.

By his opening greeting to me, furthermore, my old friend revealed his personality: That he obviously felt a rather genial contempt for me, yet acknowledged our long-standing friendship from days of yore. In using the spirit of Cameron Henderson to chronicle the Chapel Hill scene, I found him gradually developing into quite an authoritarian person, yet a fellow to be respected, and a chap with beneficial insight into matters of the day. I slavishly admired him and accepted without questioning his high-handed manner of often addressing me a "dummy," "dolt," or "clod."

This was exemplified, for instance, in Cameron Henderson's expected reaction to the allegation by the local Appearance Commission that the traditional downtown Christmas decorations put up by the Merchants Association several years ago were "garish." Cam had no tolerance for this unwarranted attitude of superiority, as he saw it:

"They are killing Santa Claus," angrily charged Cameron Henderson. "What manner of monster have we manufactured in this erstwhile Southern Part of Heaven?"

"Calm down, Cam," I responded, knowing my old buddy still remembered the Chapel Hill of his childhood. "Scrooge lived in your younger days here, too. I am glad you still cherish Christmas, but pray, explain your vociferous riddle ..."

"You know what I'm talking about, dolt," he continued (as I knew he would) ...
(10/13/78)

I begged Cam's indulgence, urging him to consider the fact that the Merchants Association was in the process of reorganization then, and the Town Council has even suggested it might contritube some public money toward the Yuletide decorating project. Cam was somewhat mollified by that possibility, which he called, "not only heart-warming, but amazing." He continued, "Let us applaud together and give a round of ho-hos in appreciation."

This time it was I who sounded a Chapel Hilly caution. "Hold on, Cam," I hedged. "It's a nice idea all right, but if you know Chapel Hill—and I do—somebody is still liable to come along with a Constitutional injunction against public funds being used in support of a religious observance. Just don't rush the season-to-be-jolly right now."

That fictional observation proved prescient in an allied sense. Four Yules later, in response to a civil liberties-based complaint by a UNC faculty member, the University Chancellor directed that the traditional Christmas star be removed from the Morehead Planetarium dome. A state-wide furor ensued. It was resolved only in 1984 when a US Supreme Court decision on a Pawtucket, Rhode Island, lawsuit was decided on a split vote of the high court justices in favor of permitting a Christmas display on public property. Chapel Hill dotes on controversies like this. They arouse emotions, but also nurture the spirit to be appropriately concerned for serious issues.

Cameron Henderson was, of course, the natural enemy of the bureaucratic spirit. That same fall of 1978 he argued the law and common sense when the Town Council carped at Bell Telephone Company's plans to erect its mid-town exchange building. The historic old Methodist Church building at the corner of Henderson and Rosemary Streets, occupied by James Webb's architectural office, might be endangered by excavations for the new building, some argued. Bell officials' insistence that they were conscious of the situation, had investigated it to the best of their ability, and accepted responsibility for the old building's continued structural soundness, were insufficient for some Town Council members. Cameron Henderson was furious:

"I've been looking for you, wise guy." The sarcastic voice came from behind me. Cameron Henderson strolled up aggressively. I knew the sage of old Chapel Hill was on the warpath. "What has our fair community done to trespass on your heritage?" I asked, anticipating that C.H. had a lecture to deliver. He was not amused. "Don't try to make light of it, you clod. I read The Newspaper and that stuff you write about me in your column. It's time you got something right." I was trapped ...
(9/29/78)

Cameron went on to recall the controversy raised over the proposed Bell

Telephone exchange building project. Bell was obviously "hooked," he pointed out — legally obligated to preserve the adjoining property from any harm its construction might cause. Then he concluded characteristically:

"... So how come all the clucking by the noble aldermen? — Must we presume they have superior insight on every problem? Or does all this foofaraw happen every time somebody hollers 'preservation?' "

"Cam, I am but a mortal," I countered. "How can you expect me to refute such logic by you or our worthy town fathers?"

(9/29/78)

Cameron's contempt for vested authority misused was typified in his view of the Chapel Hill Town Council's 1978 reaction to the proposed construction of the I-40 highway across the Land of Orange:

"Explain it to me, old friend," begged Cameron Henderson. "Something has happened to Genus Chapel Hilliana in my years of absence that I just do not understand."

Cam was off again, I could tell. Naturally he didn't need my invitation to proceed: "Look here, old buddy. I know we're a bunch of crazies, if only from my dad's observations on all his own kids. But will you riddle me this: Our local elected Establishment, esteemed leaders of our public fate, seek out and have done right well in glomming off federal and state money for our streets and buses. — Then at the same time, they file a lawsuit to stop the money-givers from building a federal highway — that I-40 thing — across the county toward Raleigh. — What gives?"

I responded, groping for the elusive answer, "This is simply the up-to-date genus of we-the-people-of-Chapel Hill. This is what's happening. 'Bite the hand' is the 'in' thing. Never mind that for 20 years we've been vainly demanding a four-laning of NC Highway 54 toward Raleigh for our convenience. There's been a moat of new highways all around, but not into the Southern Part of Heaven. Still, the message that should convey falls on deaf ears."

"You read the papers, I guess," pursued Cameron. "The State Transportation Board voted to delay local public hand-outs for state roads in Chapel Hill because of that I-40 lawsuit, then they relented. — Lost their nerve."

"Ahhh, Cameron, Cameron. I guess you're right," I admitted. "The message is there as it has been all these years. But in this fine center of higher education, we don't seem to hear or heed. — They just can't comprehend our unique folkways in this fair village."

(9/15/78)

As it turned out, both the Chapel Hill Town Council and the Orange County commissioners ultimately dropped their bootless lawsuit against construction of I-40 and began concentrating on how to preserve the local environment in light of the dramatic effect its construction was bound to have.

The old curmudgeon also had a streak of environmentalist in him, too. On occasion he'd combine this with his natural attitude toward local authority. Again in the fall of 1978 he took the stump when a reader urged me to write something about the scourge of "green boxes" and dumpster trucks in the community. Cam Henderson was most sympathetic:

... "Yes, it is time you were writing about something really important in that crazy column," said Cam. My effusive friend of yore was clearly stirred by this matter. "The Dumpster is fast sneaking up on us as a Big Brother monster."

Instantly I realized that the notion had been subtly lurking in my thoughts for a long time. We cry out for preservation and natural beauty nowadays, then stick a big bin of garbage in front of it. We promote the sale of posh condos, then shatter the sleep of the owners with Dumpster truck alarms at ungodly hours.

Our consumer affairs people threaten violators of the noise pollution laws, but do nothing about the scourge at the back door of their office.

Cameron Henderson had struck the touchstone. — Why, in the first place, must we in this Enlightened Civilization be so accommodating to the Green Box Syndrome, instead of vice-versa? Why can't the same technology that sent space ships to the moon put sound-deadening rubber bumpers on the Green Box? ... And why can't Detroit invent quieter machinery for the garbage truck out of the same concern it revealed for muffling the sound of passenger automobile engines?

Cameron Henderson, the purveyor of these all-significant alternative questions, didn't have the answer himself. "No, I am not really the all-knowing genius that you think I am," he modestly admitted. "But I can tell you what everybody here ought to do."

"Write your alderman. Collar him and demand to know how he stands on the great Green Box issue. ... Organize a picket line around the Dumpster. Call for a public hearing. Demand that the Mayor appoint a task force. Write letters to the editor. Get with it, man. That's the Chapel Hilly way."
(11/3/78)

To show he was a well-rounded Chapel Hillian, Cameron was also

concerned about local issues with wider implications. During UNC Foot-
ball Coach Bill Dooley's 11th and final season in 1978, Cam took up the
cudgel of sportsmanship. On a post-game Sunday afternoon I spotted him
sitting on the downtown wall, all decked out in a Carolina blue blazer, Rams
Club necktie, and sporting a "Go Heels" button:

... "Cam, old jock, the game isn't till next Saturday. Handsome and loyal
fan that you are, I don't dig your get-up for this Sabbath afternoon." "I'm not
here for your benefit, Sonny," he retorted with curled lip. "It's those lynch
mob types that I want to confront — those what-have-you-done-for-me-lately
types who too early proclaimed the demise of the Tar Heel coach and
football team ..." "Cameron, I agree, you are Carolina blue to the marrow,
but won't you admit that our football fortunes have left everybody less than
satisfied so far this season?"

"I'll overlook your admission to falling from grace as typical ignorance,"
he continued. "To make it easy for you, I'll give an example: Let's say you
were smart enough to run a big business outfit. One morning you find that
every one of your key people are gone, and you have to instantly replace
them. — Do you figure that would affect your operations on a business as
usual basis? ... Too many Carolina fans are the least sympathetic in the
country. Since the days of Charlie Justice and Frank McGuire they've
become victims of their continually unsatisfied rising expectations. Always
they want more and more. Why do you think they call it 'Carolina Fever?'"

Cam, despite his customary self-anointed brilliance, had unraveled
another of life's local dilemmas.

(10/16/78)

Of all topics, Cameron Henderson was at his self-confident utmost on
politics, an area in which he seemed to admit blandly he was the oracle I so
devotedly believed him to be. As an erudite hometown patrician, he was a
natural for this role. He was experienced in politics and accepted it for both
its necessary processes and built-in hypocrisy. I also fancy he truly enjoyed
it, though he'd certainly not admit that publicly. His deliverances encom-
passed victims in both high and low locales. His oft-acid comments on
politics were exceeded only by his freely-expressed opinions on the press,
that natural hand-maiden of politics. During the mid-term election season
in the fall of 1978, Cam took on the press analysts, who were generally
touting the early political death of President Carter. The occasion was a
supposed wedding reception:

"Have some peanuts, pardner," urged Cameron. "These will be in high style for some years to come," he warned. ... With my mouth full of peanuts I was an easy mark. "I have been listening to the talk from the sheep around this room," he said for openers, while I wondered how his crusade of the moment would develop. "... You guys have written Jimmy Carter's obituary and now you have quite a few gullible souls believing those notices. You tasted blood with LBJ and Nixon and just got in the habit."

... "Here we have a President who for a change doesn't claim to walk on the water, who is refreshingly open and honest with the press and public, and whose biggest downfall so far may be his candor."

"For a change the country is at peace, so he can't demand drastic action – like Washington, Lincoln or Roosevelt. Crisis helped those guys. Meantime, in this instant mass hysteria, the effete snobs come down on Carter because they think he doesn't have class – because he's not 'one of the boys' like them. ... Listen old friend, the trouble is that the writers and commentators are themselves creating the ailing Mr. Carter. – Sure, he may stumble and not make it back to his feet one of these days, but he's the kind of guy I can relate to. You'd better stick with him and keep your head on straight. Better still, why don't you write something good about him in that little column of yours?"

(9/4/78)

As it turned out, Cam Henderson was both right and wrong. President Carter survived his early political obituaries and made a close race for re-election two years later. His failing at that is generally attributed to a happenstance that neither he nor any other political savants anticipated in 1978 – the Iranian hostage crisis, which he was unable to resolve.

That same election season in 1978 Cameron Henderson was among the multitudes who were unable to decide who to vote for for US Senator from North Carolina – the mercurial State Insurance Commissioner John Ingram, who'd escaped with the Democratic party nomination, or the conservative Republican Jesse Helms, then running for his second term in office. North Carolinians in general, including C.H., were traditional Democrats, but the extent of Ingram's integrity and intelligence ·gave many of them pause – again including Cam Henderson:

... "You can tell your readers, sonny boy, that old Cam is turning 'em loose to their own peril this time." "Horras, Cameron," I replied. "You mean you have no edict from On High to tell us who the Good Guys are on all those ballots?" ... "You heard me right, kid," he replied sagely – betraying his concern. "There aint a clear decision on that one at all. You can build a damn fine case against either one of 'em. But it's tough to go much farther than that. And the ballot doesn't have a box that lets you vote against 'em."

"I might make one small suggestion to you, kid," he added. (Was there a twinkle in his eye?) "Over there in the blank box under Libertarian Party, you can write in the name of Cameron Henderson, if you don't like Ingram or Helms."

As always I was awestruck. Good old Cam had resolved my dilemma. Cameron Henderson, the people's choice – for US Senator.

(11/6/78)

That is as far as Cam's campaign for Senator ever went, and Jesse was handily re-elected. But Cameron's uneasiness with his natural Democratic inclination presaged the voters' verdict the next time Helms came up for election. In 1984 the Democrats' intra-party division and reactive negative campaigning again provided the margin of victory for the Republican senator.

The personal patriotism of C.H. came out again the following year, as the local election campaign was beginning. Mayor Jimmy Wallace hadn't declared for re-election and subsequently decided to retire. Many other names were being bruited about, but nobody had made the plunge yet:

"Hey, stupid!" – The voice was as un-mistakable as the gracious form of address. Before I turned to acknowledge, I knew that it was my good friend Cameron Henderson. Patron saint of all that is old Chapel Hillity, Cam had been absent so long I feared he might have fled his hometown. "Well, dummy, I see they are quoting you in The Newspaper about not running for Mayor," said Cameron. "At least that's one favor you've done the voters ..." I reminded him that I had, in fact, resigned as an alderman and offered for Mayor a short 10 years ago. "Don't remind me, you tool. I was here then, and long before. You almost got elected, but we were lucky. ... To be blunt, so you can understand it, there are too many 'patriots' offering for so-called public service this season ..."

... "Cameron, dear Cameron, why are you so cynical?" I asked. "Is there no health in the elective process of local government?"

... He seemed not at all lugubrious at the prospects. ... "Chapel Hill has taken some pretty hard knocks over the last century. Hell, with Teddy Kennedy showing how neatly it can be done, I might take a fling at it myself."

– At last, the dawn of the obvious answer: Cameron Henderson for Mayor.

(9/28/78)

Cameron's suggested groundswell in his own behalf was no greater than his offering for the US Senate a year earlier. Joe Nassif was elected in a mild contest over his close friend and political ally, likewise a former alderman, attorney Robert Epting. The potential spoiler in that race, incumbent Gerry Cohen, failed in his second try for mayor and retired from local elective office.

I had personally and publicly supported Nassif for Mayor in the 1979 election—a decision too complicated to explain here, and beside the point. But I was quickly critical of Nassif in my newspaper column early in his term for what I felt to be his failure to provide effective leadership. So I used the Newsman's Notepad column for a bit of rare introspection on this issue. It was the spring of 1980, and Cameron Henderson had naturally just returned from wintering in Florida:

... The friendly old curmudgeon greeted me graciously as always. "Hello, dummy. I see you're up to your endless tilting at windmills again." (My boyhood chum never wasted time on undue civilities, such as saying hello.) "Welcome home, Cam," I responded in spirit ...

He continued: "That stuff you've been writing about His Nibs—Nasser, or whatever. You're right, I'll have to admit. But what of it? Anybody who reads that stuff just says, 'Well, there's old Roland doing his thing again.' Tell me, boy, what have you accomplished by your grand crusade against the munificent mayor's power grab?"

"Well, for one thing, he wrote me a brief thank-you note," I replied ... "But he's gone right ahead at his empire building without lawful authority. The plain fact is, the people don't care enough. Joe comes off as a good ole boy, so the steady, subtle change he's bringing in our form of government doesn't concern people ..."

... "Trouble with you is that when you write that little column of yours, the local folk read it as a personal attack. That distracts from the real issue. ... Now don't go gettin' the big head just because you happen to be right for a change."

(3/28/80)

What brought on all this was my writing in the Newsman's Notepad column against the upgrading in title and salary of the Mayor's new "executive assistant." I'd long questioned the authority of the Mayor to employ an assistant who was not under the supervision of the Town Manager, because I felt the Town Charter significantly mandated that the Manager be the direct line superior to all municipal employees. With the further "executive" upgrading of the job and its salary, I renewed the issue. It failed to excite anybody else, but had some eventual effect in another way.

Chapel Hill's mayor drew what I'd called a "bloated" salary of $10,000 a year for his part-time job. That sum was exceeded in North Carolina at that time only by the $11,000 paid the Mayor of the state's biggest city, Charlotte (which, I also pointed out, was the only other NC municipality that gave its mayor more than secretarial help, and even that position was under supervision of the city manager). Several years later, amid some backstage antagonism, the Mayor's salary was reduced to $7,000 a year on the basis of that figure being closer to the statewide average for municipalities of comparable size.

My adulation for Cam Henderson and his brilliant intellect is no doubt exaggerated and at least partially the product of my natural sentimentality for old friends. His penchant for puncturing the balloons of pompous bureaucrats is scarcely heroic. They're easy targets. Also, I'd written scathingly about them for years from my vantage point as an ex-insider through 12 years service on the Chapel Hill Board of Alderman. So I was naturally impressed by Cameron Henderson's kindred spirit. One winter morning he lectured me on the latest folly of the elected town fathers:

"... You remember just a few years ago when the Town Charter Commission was doing its study. They said we needed more stability in local government; ought to have the Mayor's term for four years instead of two; give continuity to the Town Board, and give the Mayor time to see through his programs, and all that?" I nodded in agreement and recollection.

"They did it—changed the term to four years. Now they're about to change it back to two years, out of an abundance of opposite logic." "What's the reason for the change, Cam?" I asked, responding to his invitation by pause.

"They changed to four years to give continuity," he said with a flourish. "Now they're about to change it back to give a chance for change—so a majority of the Town Board with the Mayor will be elected every two years."

"It figures, Cam," I replied. "—Just like the weather in Chapel Hill. If you don't like it, don't worry. It's bound to change soon."
(2/12/79)

Through amending its charter again, the Council did in fact change the Mayor's term back to two years. Cameron Henderson and I wholeheartedly endorsed the change for the stated reasons that the action was taken—to give the voters the opportunity to elect both the Mayor and Council members at each biennial election. But I suggested in the Notepad that just like the original change to four years, the reversion "happens to suit expeditiously the political needs of the moment for prospective mayoral candidates." That is, it was favored by Nassif, who became the next Mayor, but who, curiously, was also Chairman of the 1975 Town Charter Commission which recommended the original change.

The heart of election politics in Chapel Hill is not in the mythical "city hall gang," nor in the blue smoke of back room offices. For many years it's been in the non-partisan local candidates' forum sponsored by the Chapel Hill Chapter of the League of Women Voters. Now that various special interest groups and the media are sponsoring a multitude of such forums, this original one doesn't have the clout it did a quarter century ago. But it's still a success story for the theoretical "little old ladies in tennis shoes." I tried to put this noble institution in perspective through the words of Cameron Henderson, in a column that was headlined, "Forum Or Agin 'Em?":

It was a slack night for TV and a fine, balmy, harvest moon evening. Those facts, as much as the attraction of civic concern, drew us to the League of Women Voters' candidates forum last Thursday night. The meeting was well under way when we slipped into a back row corner seat in the new downtown post office courtroom ...

The hopeful patriots in front were bashfully admitting their capabilities for service in the State Senate when I felt a sharp jab in the ribs. The citizen to the right of me spoke firmly but softly: "It's about time you arrived, stupid. Things are getting out of hand ... The good women of this group are about to do themselves in. They are scaring 'em off." While I'd not figured this meeting was his natural briar patch, there was Cameron Henderson, on the personal stump again.

Puzzled, I noted that the hall was middling full, replete with reporters busy scribbling every pearl uttered by the various speakers. Cameron didn't wait for a rejoinder, but rushed on: "Used to be this forum was a make-or-break thing for the candidates. They feared to come just as much as they feared not to. Now, you will notice, none of the Congressional candidates — the top race this fall — have come."

"Yes, I noticed. How do you figure that, Cameron?"

"For one thing, they can't get away with just blowing smoke any more. The ladies — and too many other local citizens — are asking the tough questions and finding their weak spots. At the same time, there's overkill on the political scene and too much competition for the voters' attention. We're becoming victims of our own sophistication. ... That doesn't mean that campaigning is unimportant. Personal contact is still the key. But there are so many opportunities for public exposure this has come to be just one more of 'em."

"I appreciate and believe your sage analysis, Cam," I replied, "but if all that's true, then how come you're here?"

"Well, old buddy," he replied with just a tinge of warmth, "there wasn't anything good on TV, and it was a nice evening, so ..."

(10/11/82)

The Oracle, wise as he claimed to be, did not look upon everything with jaundiced eye. Occasionally, to my surprise, he'd find silver lining around the clouds. Such an occasion was the day after the 1980 national elections:

Rare for the hometown curmudgeon, Cameron Henderson was in an expansive mood yesterday. ... "Ho, Cameron," I greeted him. "You look pleased with yourself."

"... We tossed 'em out," he responded. I bade him explain. He needed no urging. "Nothing personal against 'em," he confided in a fatherly manner. "No doubt they were convinced of their own benevolence. But that's the point: High office personality comes to feed on itself. The ring of your own voice sounds steadily sweeter—and purer. Every now and then you need to send a message as to who's really the boss. If you don't, you yourself may start believing their legends about their own virtue and infallibility."

"... You seem to feel that the republic will survive—that a new crop of saviours will arise and do some good before they have to be turned out themselves. Is that it, friend Cameron?"

"You got it, sonny. And don't forget it. The buck doesn't stop in the Oval Room. It's with you and me."

(11/7/80)

Interestingly, thus, Cameron Henderson found virtue in Reagan's land-slide victory over President Carter, just as he'd seen refreshing qualities in Carter when Carter's preliminary political obituary was being touted two years earlier. In that spirit, early in Reagan's term, he called for patience on the part of the public:

He was back in the canned goods section, pondering the prices of pork and beans when I spotted him. ... "Cam, we have missed you during your winter's hiberation," I opened. "What brings you back on the hometown scene?"

"Hope, sonny boy, pure hope," he responded. "I am laying in a stock of staples—in keeping with the President's plea for austerity. ... Yes, lad, it's not that difficult. In fact, even you may have noticed that the Democrats aren't quibbling over the basic issues. They merely argue that the President's tax cut proposals may be too much and too late. And the Republican leadership is already calling for even greater cutbacks in spending."

... "President Ronald may or may not be a good doctor when he tells us to bite the bullet. But it is too early to condemn his prescription before we give the bullet a good shot." There it was, crystal clear in sparkling metaphor: Cameron Henderson, leading the way to good times through hard times.
(2/23/81)

In that same constructive spirit, Cam waxed philosophical on the scene in Chapel Hill at one of the quieter times of the year. The occasion was a balmy afternoon during the Christmas holidays:

... "Ho, ho, Cam," I greeted him. "Ho, ho, and one more ho to you, too, my good Yuletidy friend," he returned. I asked Cam how it was that he appeared at such peace with the scene. —Were there no remaining hassles with the Establishment?

... "No, lad, none of that," replied Cameron. "Let's be content with today for its own sake." ... "Have you thought about it?" he asked. "What a singular time of the year this is in the Southern Part—how close this comes to reverting to the village we knew here as knee-britches lads? Sure, we miss the students. We clasp them to our community bosom as the reason for Chapel Hill's existence in the first place. And we'll be glad to see 'em back early next month."

"But aint it nice, too," he continued reflectively, "to have the old home-town all to ourselves in this leisurely and folksy fashion for just a few days."
(12/26/78)

His feeling, akin to the surprise many Chapel Hillians feel in the several annual University holiday seasons, was best expressed by the late great University Vice President Billy Carmichael Jr., who's supposed to have proclaimed that "Chapel Hill would be such a great place to live—if it just wasn't for all the students!" Like every hometowner, too, C.H. had a strong feeling about the sanctity of springtime in Chapel Hill:

Always showing up like a bad penny, there was Cameron Henderson, decked out in his Sunday finest on this Easter Monday morning. Sitting on his accustomed campus wall downtown, he waved some papers at me. ... It turned out to be third-class postal matter he'd lately received. He appeared outraged at the unsolicited appeals, so I tried to calm him. ... "Well, you understand that ploy, Cameron. People appreciate something more if they pay for it."

"Like Hell I do," exploded Cam. "I'd rather pay not to receive anything like this. Do you realize, man, here it's barely springtime, and we have over six months 'til the local elections. — Now here's mail from the candidates already. — The Hell with it!"

(4/16/79)

Cameron Henderson also helped me out of tight journalistic spots occasionally, exposing my misplaced viewing-with-alarm. He did so conveniently after I'd fired one of my perennial favorite editorial fusillades — the need for the State Legislature to legally limit the length of its sessions. The occasion was just after adjournment of its short off-year budget-revising session:

Cameron Henderson was waiting for me in the shade of the downtown post office as I arrived for the morning mailbox ritual. "Hey, kid, you'd as well say you're sorry for all those scornful words about the Legislature," he opened.

"Help me redress my wrongs, Cam," I bade him, knowing he needed no encouragement. He plunged on. "You were up to your customary finger-pointing when the Legislature convened this month — all righteous about 'nothing being safe while the Assembly's in session.' Well, they met for 15 days, did their necessaries, and adjourned the 'little session.'"

"Right you are, as always, old friend." I admitted. (Immediate acquiescence is the better part of valor in dialogue with Cameron Henderson.) "All these years I've been railing about the Honbles trying to make a full-time job out of their legislating. At least they kept their word this time — cut the budget melon, took up some special interest stuff, then adjourned for cooler parts ..."

(6/30/80)

Another popular traditional target in the Newsman's Notepad was the Chapel Hill Bus System. With Cam's help, I moderated that crusade through a new twist for the moment:

Chapel Hill's veritable city within a city will soon have its own bus system. An open-air tram will shortly begin hauling people between the front door of NC Memorial Hospital and the parking decks across Manning Drive – a grand distance of one-quarter mile.

Hospital authorities cite the need for the tractor caravan in that disabled motorists will thus have easier access to the hospital – though park-and-retrieve attendant service is already offered for handicapped persons from the front door. Benches also will be installed at the parking deck end of the new bus line to ease the wait for tram passengers.

It is well and good to proclaim and justify the need for this new service. It will no doubt be patronized even more heavily (and at a better price, since it'll be free) than the widely-acclaimed Chapel Hill Transit Lines. It's in the same spirit (but pretty small potatoes) as the air-cushion computer-dispatched automatic trolley service between nearby Duke Hpsoital and the newly-opened north section of that complex.

Hometown curmudgeon Cameron Henderson takes a dim view of this grand innovation in our village. Asked his opinion, Chapel Hill's self-appointed oracle responded: "People in general would be a darn sight healthier and need hospital services much less if they'd walk their quarter-miles to the front door of the hospital – and most other places they choose to go." The need for bus service, Cam observed, is in direct ratio to the well-proven slothfulness of Space Age human beings, and thus can be cited as an absolute necessity.

(7/14/80)

The Hospital has since then abandoned the tram transportation from the parking garage, but still offers free rides via a shuttle car.

Cameron Henderson wasn't automatically against all changes in the village, however. Surprisingly, he found one of its newest, and certainly more uncharacteristic institutions, to his liking:

... "Cameron, long-gone Cameron," I said in dismay, "something is obviously bothering you. Please unload on me."

"Certainly, sucker," he responded. That was better. The veritable soul of the old C.H. yet survived. " – You know where I've been? – Out at the new Hotel Europa. And you know what that means: The end of the village!" He said it as a warning, but with a tinge of admiration.

"You figure we have managed without the place for 200 years, boy, but Europa lives up to its press notices. – No place else, nowhere, can put down Chapel Hill now, in price or posh."

... "Why, they even have a liveried doorman—but nothin' for him to do on the door; one of those electric eye things opens it for you before you can touch it. And talk about marble halls! There's more of that fine-vein white rock on the floor and walls of the Europa than you've seen in the entire Chapel Hill Cemetery and every plush toilet stall partition in Orange County ..."

(11/16/81)

Applying the changing fashions of society to Chapel Hill was always one of Cam's favorite indulgences. He seized on this several years ago on learning that in New York City the latest thing was "an adult education course on how to move up in society—in short, instruction in jet-setting for those still traveling on square wheels."

Cameron Henderson suggested that Chapel Hill, as a trend-setting capital of higher education, stage a similar course on "Chic for Chapel Hill." He explained a few of the New York society conversational fillips then being taught in the new adult course, such as "Meet me at the club ..." or "I'd NEVER spend August in Florence ..." I began to catch on how this would work in Chapel Hill:

... "For instance, I could casually say, 'No, I don't sit on the 50-yard line. The action's ALWAYS down at the goal.' Or: 'Carmichael Auditorium's just getting so congested, I declare I'd almost rather watch the games on TV.' — And how about '... Yas, I HAVE been considering joining Republicans for Ike Andrews.'" Shock value, I divined, was as important as implied status in this verbal gamesmanship. I looked to Cam for approval.

"I'm surprised. For someone as naturally dumb as you, I believe you're catching on," he said. "Mind your transportation, too. Cars are passe in Chapel Hill. You may need one to get around, but keep a bicycle in the trunk or at the office. At the least, carry a white helmet around with you, or a cable lock slung over your shoulder."

"What about The Bus, Cam?" I asked him. "Nahhh, not the bus, sonny. They were 'in' until '78 or so, when gas was $1.50 and people were still buying cars on time. Nobody rides the buses anymore, anyhow. They're too crowded. You might even jog—if you can manage to look happy while you do it. Now that's what the really hip Chapel Hill types are doing nowadays."

"I suppose you want me to join the 'Y,' too, Cameron?"

"Well, it would be a promotion from your present lifestyle," he admitted. "But why not widen your horizons? Just talk about your 'personal Nautilus.'"

Don't worry about what it is. Weight-lifting has clout in Chapel Hill now ..."
(10/25/82)

° *Of such was Cameron Henderson, legendary spirit of Chapel Hill, and now again vanished. But his ideas surely live on, debatably square or chique. And Cam himself may again turn up on the hometown scene some day.*

Chapter 6

Memories

Or a little farther out, still, was the old Scout Cabin—about a 45-minute hike from Chapel Hill ... The nearest water was a house out in the country on the Raleigh Road, about 15 minutes walk from the cabin. Now it's [the cabin] covered by the Glen Lennox apartment development.

The passing of years increases the glamour and superlative qualities of things we recall. The old-timer likes to upstage anything with his own recollection of how much moreso it was "way back when." That is often valid to the extent that the days of yore were less complicated, and also because memory tends to gild the extremes and dim recollection of the norm.

Weather is a good example. As a 12-year-old delivering the Charlotte Observer all over the village, I recall checking the 5:30 AM temperature on the big thermometer at Pendergraft's Service Station at the main corner downtown. On various occasions it registered zero or below. —Is that a trick of memory, or an appropriately vivid historical fact?

... Three decades ago there was never a winter without at least a six-inch snow that provided a week's fun for the youngsters. Ice skating was a popular pastime on Hogan's Lake, and the surface would sometimes be frozen over for a week.

A century before that, according to local historians, sledding and ice skating were the town's most popular winter pastimes. As a regular practice then, the University declared Washington's birthday as a holiday from classes so that students and faculty alike could adjourn to local mill ponds and streams for ice skating.

(1/13/66)

There is, however, no question about the memory of one of the prime joys of winter in my boyhood days in what was then really a village:

... Time was when the sledding hill for the entire town was automatically "Odum's Hill" – the fine slope down Brierbridge Lane, which was little used anyhow. It provided an exciting toboggan ride down the curving lane and across the stone bridge at the bottom.

(1/15/67)

One correction: "Windy Hill," the main part of Hillsborough St., was then and still is (to the extent it's available for sledding) the longest and most exciting ride in town. I definitely recall "Odum's Hill," so named for the Howard Odum family who lived at its top. Sledding down it one day, I crashed head first into the stone bridge at the bottom – an accident that left me bruised and bed-ridden for a week.

Surely the worst weather any living locals can remember here was a freak storm I recalled following a similar scare many years later:

... That pseudo-tornado on Monday brought to mind "the real thing" last time it hit Chapel Hill. It wasn't a tornado, but there was no question as to its identity when Hurricane Hazel struck at 1:08 PM on Friday afternoon, Oct. 15, 1954. Pokey Alexander was announcing on WCHL that the storm was expected to hit between 2 and 3 PM when it knocked the station off the air. In the next hour an estimated four inches of rain fell, the wind was clocked at 68 miles an hour, and the mercury dropped from 75 to 51. Just as it did this past week, the main fury of the storm swept through the eastside – the University Mall area. Wes Thompson's newly-opened Valley Drive-In Theater was flattened – that being about the biggest business operation out in the lowground [Note:Eastgate] area.

(3/28/75)

The water shortages of recent years offer natural opportunities for earlier-day superlatives:

... One savant recollects that back in 1921 the start of University classes had to be delayed a week until October 4 because of the water shortage. There'd been almost no rain since mid-May, gardens and crops withered away, evergreens in the Arboretum withered, and even pines and oaks were dying. New Hope Creek was dusty dry for six weeks, and Little Creek east of town, a mere trickle ...

(9/18/68)

... To meet the situation the University administration did just as this year: Authorized the laying of a special water line. This was a six-inch pipe to Morgan's Creek. To make up for the missed class time, the scheduled Thanksgiving holidays were canceled.

(8/30/76)

The simpler times a half-century ago made one of the big holidays in Chapel Hill quite a different occasion. Thanksgiving today is likely to be a very quiet time hereabouts — a time for mass weekend vacations. Back then:

... A band was parading down East Franklin St. preparatory to the afternoon's 40th annual playing of the Carolina-Virginia football classic in Kenan Stadium. Though classes at the University were recessed for the holidays, the streets were jammed, and a capacity crowd of 20,000 was expected for the season's closing game at Kenan Stadium. ... On that earlier Thanksgiving Day the Carolina football team rebounded from its bitter 25-0 upset defeat by Duke the previous Saturday and demolished Virginia 61-0. ... That same week Coach Carl Snavely publicly complained that there were no good places to eat in town and his football players were all losing weight — where they usually gained 20 pounds a season ...

(11/16/76)

Celebrations of great moments in Carolina's sports history have become spontaneous festivals. Vic Huggins, then Carolina's head cheerleader, well recalls and recounts with gusto how he led a parade of jubilant students all the way to Durham on the night back in 1924 that the Tar Heels won the national basketball championship in Atlanta.

More vivid in the minds of so many of us is the post-midnight excitement in downtown Chapel Hill on March 23, 1957, when Carolina defeated Kansas in a triple-overtime contest for the NCAA basketball title:

... With no designated plan, but just as the natural thing to do, thousands of students and townspeople suddenly jammed the main business block. A bonfire was set in the middle of the street from toilet paper, slats, haberdashery, a roll of hose, and anything inflammable that wasn't welded down. There was a parade, too, as everybody marched up the street to Chancellor House's residence and swapped small talk with the University's first family. Certainly anybody still in Chapel Hill today will recall that post-game victory celebration just as much as the details and facts of the game itself ...

(1/17/77)

... At the height of the celebration, fearing things were about to get out of hand, I edged over to Police Chief Bill Blake on the fringe of the crowd and

Celebrating Carolina's national basketball championship on Franklin St., downtown, March 27, 1957

asked him fearfully, "How are things going, Bill?" Without a moment's hesitation, he grinned from ear to ear and replied "Just fine!"

(3/27/74)

Carolina football was just as big a deal locally then, but there was one occasional difference to the festival of it:

... The regular UNC football train specials of a quarter-century ago and previously when the railroad tracks ran right up to the middle of the Carolina campus. The 10 to 15-car coach and Pullman combination trains would pull up onto the Pittsboro St. siding and take on hundreds of students, faculty, townspeople, the band, team, and cheerleaders.

For many of the intersectional games huge trainloads would come to Chapel Hill from elsewhere, grinding to a halt at that same humble siding on Pittsboro St., almost in shouting distance of Kenan Stadium. Perhaps the biggest such invasion occurred for Carolina's gala homecoming game with Fordham back in 1937. More than 1,000 rooters for the Bronx team piled off an 18-car train that stretched most of the way back to the University Laundry plant. They got their money's worth, too. That was the year Fordham whipped the Tar Heels on the famous Statue of Liberty play, with the aid of a fabulous all-Polish first string of linemen ...

(1/9/64)

It was also the occasion of the first great riot in the then fairly new Kenan Stadium. The Yankee visitors, jubilant at their victory, rushed onto the field for what was to them a routine ritual—to tear down the goalposts. However, the concrete-planted Kenan Stadium uprights resisted their efforts and Carolina fans, unfamiliar with that custom, defended the goal posts with a fervor that fairly matched the opening guns of the Civil War.

In the Chapel Hill of today with seven different commercial banks it's hard to imagine how it all began, but it wasn't really all that long ago:

Chapel Hill's unofficial but most knowledgeable local historian, Carl Durham, was reminiscing at the grand opening for Wachovia Bank the other night. Looking across the Bolin Creek flood plain at the doorstep of the new building, he recalled how the old Strowd's Lowgrounds, as we used to call this section, was one of his favorite duck hunting spots. Chapel Hill's first bank, he continued, was started by Charlie Lindsay before the 1900s in a kind of lean-to beside a downtown store building. Mr. Lindsay simply opened shop for persons who wanted to leave money with him, and took the funds home at night for safe-keeping.

(8/11/71)

Chapel Hill's first bank robbery—actually the Bank of Chapel Hill branch in Carrboro—was not until July 28, 1954. But Chapel Hill as a popular crossroads has historically had a fair share of sensational crime. One that old-timers often talk about was the 1934 robery and assault of a hot dog stand owner:

Chapel Hill Police Chief William D. Blake investigating robbery of Bank of Chapel Hill branch, 7/28/54 (foreground, Manager Hubert Neville)

... Town Policeman Ernest Rackley had only a motorcycle, so he commandeered the help of Ashby Penn, a wealthy young student from Reidsville. Riding in Penn's flashy Auburn, they drove out NC Hwy. 54 west till they came upon a car with a flat tire. There they stopped, and the policeman handed Penn his pistol as they got out. The men in the car ahead warned Penn not to come any closer, then shot him in the stomach. The student was rushed to the University Infirmary back in town, where he lingered in very serious condition before recovering. Some time later the culprits were captured in New York, returned and convicted.
(1/19/69)

Recollection of the downtown scene of that era also came to mind when a new ice cream parlor, the first one in many years, opened here a few years ago:

... Will it become as popular as the local hangout – THE place to meet – as the predecessor Sloan's Drugstore corner was? ... Or as the old Durham Dairy Products ice cream parlor of 40 years ago – in the quarters now occupied by Julian's College Shop?

The idea is certainly as popular. But price tells the sad story of inflation: One carefully-weighed three-ounce scoop for 28 cents (plus tax) today, versus one long brimming trowel-full for a nickel back then. – That was one of the few things about the "good old days" that really were verifiably "good."
(12/20/74)

In that same column, taking note of downtown business establishments, I wrote:

What a weird place this is. Think about it. You can go to The Library, The Town Hall, and The Electric Company and still never set foot inside a public building. But you can sure order a beer at any of them. – Only in Chapel Hill.
(12/20/74)

Just how Carl Durham himself came to be Congressman is quite a true story, too. The hometown pharmacist, whom Editor Louis Graves dubbed "The Great Common Adviser" because of his unstinting civic service, liked to tell how he was at the counter of Eubanks Drugstore one morning when Orange County Rep. John Umstead walked across the street and abruptly asked him "– You want to go to Congress?" "What kind of liquor you been

Carl Durham
(right) presents
Merchant of Year
award to Clyde
'Boss' Eubanks in
his downtown
drugstore – 1964

*drinkin','' Durham responded. Umstead left, then proposed Durham's name
to Chapel Hill's "Skipper" Coffin, the County's Democratic Congressional
Committeeman. The four committee members, one each for the Sixth
District's four counties, Durham, Orange, Alamance, and Guilford, were
deadlocked in choosing a successor to the nominee who'd died since the
primary and before the general election. Durham accepted the nomination
and served 12 terms in Congress.*

*Albert Coates, in a talk before the Chapel Hill Historical Society, recalled
an especially colorful character of his era (1914-18) as a University
student:*

... about the late great Colonel (his actual name) Swain Pendergraft,
swashbuckling local bus operator and merchant of a half-century ago. A
passenger arriving at the Durham train station had made a reservation to
ride to Chapel Hill on Mr. Pendergraft's jitney bus. When a competitor
solicited him, the passenger noted his reservation, and the rival bus driver
said "Well, I'm Colonel Pendergraft" and drove him to Chapel Hill for the
50-cent fare. Learning of this later, the outspoken Mr. Pendergraft is said to
have remarked, "He can call himself Colonel Pendergraft for 50 cents if he
wants to, but I'm damned if I'd call myself him for that much."

(11/11/74)

The best illustration of Colonel Pendergraft's pragmatic approach to life is his explanation to an acquaintance why he had, at a mature stage in his life, chosen to join a local church: "They say it's a good thing, and that it'll help your business, too."

The changes in Chapel Hill in the short years since World War Two eclipse the almost 200-year evolution of the University community. Its growth has been mainly in the south campus area, the wellsprings of which are easy to recall:

Even Kenan Stadium ranks as a newcomer to south-side Chapel Hill. Shortly after arriving in Chapel Hill about 35 years ago, our family lived in one of the University-owned rental houses that stood on the site of the giant public health building [Note: Rosenau Hall] now under construction. ... My parents recalled the clattering of rocks and rubble on the composition slate-shingled roof of this house while construction dynamiting was going on at Kenan Stadium.

... Despite the solid attractiveness of the pharmacy building [Note: Beard Hall] now, many hometowners driving by on the Pittsboro Road still do a double take there. The mind's eye yet sees the two-story wood-columned brick building that housed the high school on this same site from 1937 till it burned in the late summer of 1942.

"Stadium Woods" where the mammoth complex of Memorial Hospital now stands held a special place in the hearts of neighborhood small fry. With toy cars and imaginative minds, they spent endless hours—even days—building cities in the light wilderness across the highway from their homes. ... About all that's left of the old Stadium Woods today is a one-acre glade around what was known for several summers as "Utley's Dam." This is the patch of woods between the Hospital entrance drive and Wilson Hall.

There must have been at least two dozen stout young hearts involved in hard labor over most of a summer, building a dam under direction of Freddie Utley on a tiny trickle of a branch that dribbled down the draw into the Stadium bottom. The resulting four-foot-high dam and swimming hole was a thing of beauty and a joy for several summers to the youthful constructors. The new geology building [Note: Mitchell Hall] that will soon rise on this site will recall to a few local citizens yet left of this hardy band of young engineers the man-made geological wonder that previously occupied the site.

(9/6/61)

One wilderness of sorts remains on the old campus today. In this commu-

*nity where the words "open space" are a civic call to arms, I'd wager not one
citizen in a hundred has explored it:*

... Battle Park, a beautiful sylvan glen of 65 acres, courses along the
branch that bears the name of the University President, Kemp Plummer
Battle, who loved it and cut the original paths through it a century ago. ...
There was no public recreation building in Chapel Hill when The Newsman
was a lad here. But Battle Park filled a great deal of this need. A fine picnic
pavilion with both indoor and outdoor fireplaces sat on a bluff high above the
stream, just a few yards from East Franklin St. Weather permitting, this was
traditionally the site of most birthday parties and family outings ... ... best
of all, there were beautiful, open woods for running games, a creek to dam
up, and fine trees to climb. ... They're still there—as the few students and
townspeople who now frequent Battle Park know. The "open spaces" are as
attractive as ever—places that President Battle gave sentimental names such
as Fairy Vale, Lion Rock, Flirtation Knoll, and Dogwood Dingle ...
(2/24/66)

*There've been occasional calls to revive and restore the natural splendor
of Battle Park, but the onslaught of contemporary society has brought with
it so much vandalism that the fruitlessness of such an effort is generally
acknowledged. There was one other bygone wilderness adjacent to the old
village, and located today in the heart of Chapel Hill's largest subdivision:*

... Or a little farther out, still, was the old Scout Cabin—about a 45-
minute hike from Chapel Hill, located on the former R.J.M. Hobbs
property east of town. The nearest water was at a house out in the country on
the Raleigh Road about 15 minutes walk from the cabin. The lads would
camp out there on weekends during the school year and by the week in the
summer. Now it's covered by the Glen Lennox apartment development ...
(6/20/63)

*The development of fine public recreation facilities in Chapel Hill only in
recent years climaxed a long public campaign for these amenities. Still, for
countless decades we didn't seem to miss what we didn't have:*

... in retrospect there was certainly no shortage of good swimming
places. And this doesn't include the old swimmin' holes, which this town
had in plenty. King's Mill on Morgan's Creek was the favorite natural
swimming spot of 30 years ago. While there's still good potential swimming
there for any enterprising lad with a bit of imagination, the area is now
surrounded by a sedate and fashionable residential neighborhood ...

The acme of all summertime fun was Sparrow's Pool on the south side of Carrboro. Built by Mr. and Mrs. Joe Sparrow as a commercial venture in 1921, Sparrow's Pool flourished through the swimming seasons, year after year, until the private pools of recent years gradually made it less profitable. Mrs. Sparrow closed it four years ago; says she still misses it a great deal.

Favorite place in The Newsman's recollection was the old University Lake swimming area. When the big Lake was built along about 1930 or '31, the University also scooped out the Morgan Creek channel right below the spillways and lined the south-side of the bank with a high rock and mortar wall. This made it much like a regular swimming pool. There was a large picnic area in the shade alongside and on a warm summer afternoon there'd be well over a hundred swimmers of all ages splashing in the shallow and deep sections ...

(7/25/63)

Make-your-own-recreation offered so many other exciting possibilities:

... in what was more truthfully then called "the village," the boys and their parents thought nothing at all of bicycling over to Durham to see a movie — or just for the fun of it. ... That 12-mile trip, taking about an hour, was likely no more dangerous by bike then than the eight-mile whiz via the boulevard is in a car today. But any parents who'd let a boy ride his bike to Durham on the public highways nowadays would be nuts.

(3/1/67)

The coming of that grand new boulevard in 1951 was an exciting prospect, as I wrote in a Durham Morning Herald feature story, citing by comparison the existing road:

... State highway officials were calling the tortuous 12-mile 52-curve Durham-Chapel Hill Road (an 18-foot two-laner) "the most dangerous highway in the state." And the $1.5 million project was due to be completed within a year ... The much maligned "football highway" as Gov. Kerr Scott has termed it, planned and panned for 15 years, will be open by the 1952 gridiron schedule. It would cost, we figured in an armchair calculation, the fat sum of roughly $10,000 for every goal-to-goal 100-yard stretch of it.

Hopes were high ... There was a movement to make it a "parkway instead of a Broadway" and even mention of a plan to have it zoned like the Blue Ridge Parkway against commercial construction. ... Planners are determined to keep honky-tonks and auto junkyards off its borders ...

And so, for all the fond and fine fleeting hopes of a quarter-century ago,

Old Durham
Road – near Bolin
Creek – before
opening of new
Chapel
Hill-Durham
Boulevard – June
1951

we have today's product, headlined in the more recent Newspaper feature story, "The Boulevard: A Necessity or a Headache?"
(10/2/78)

The man who guided the corporate destiny of Chapel Hill in that era was Mayor Edwin S. Lanier. At the completion of the new roadway a big barbecue was staged at the county line and the Mayors of Durham and Chapel Hill made speeches about what a fine thing the boulevard would be. Ed Lanier was a remarkable person – self-described as an "humble and a poor man," and then the University's Director of Student Self-Help Services. The Laniers lived in a University-owned bungalow at 620 Park Place, the lone remaining dwelling today of quite a colony of 12 houses at the time. When the Chapel Hill Preservation Society decided to lease that house from the University to preserve it, I wrote, recalling Ed Lanier:

In public stewardship he served on the Chapel Hill Board of Aldermen, then successfully ran for Mayor in 1949 in what may yet be the Town's most heated election and with the highest voter turnout. Lanier topped three-term incumbent Bob Madry 811 to 589 with 84 percent of the registered voters casting ballots. … The photo shows Mayor Ed with his pride and joy – typical of his spirit of humility – his 1932 A-Model Ford coupe, parked by his Park Place homestead …

Earlier tenants of the same house included then Dean of Students Francis F. Bradshaw and his family. Some of us youngsters always envied them –

and the Ed Laniers, too—because their home was so convenient to the town's best playground and community picnic shelter a short distance down the trail in Battle Park ...
(3/31/80)

As the center of higher education in North Carolina, Chapel Hill ought to have the best public schools in the state. The NC Superintendent of Public Instruction said that in a Chapel Hill High School commencement address some years ago. It was no surprise. Traditionally, we always thought Chapel Hill's school **was** *the state's best. Under the administrative structure of that period almost all the teachers were senior professors in the University School of Education and used the school as their practice teaching laboratory:*

... Old CHHS was a good school even with its functional but box-like design, dark hallways, and "tin can" for a gymnasium. The new school completed in 1937 on Pittsboro Road was a palace by comparison—replete with a home economics room, fine science laboratories, a large library, and typing room ... That the new building was a comparative tinder box didn't occur to the pupils until after it burned on a summer night in 1942.

In the old village it was normal to walk or bike home for lunch—and still have 15 minutes for play period before afternoon classes took in. The Newsman lived in a University house next door to the Pittsboro Rd. school. Quite often he'd wait until he heard the 8:30AM school bell ring to casually pick up his books and saunter across the street for the day's class session. No Chapel Hill school in the future will ever be able to match that convenience.
(11/9/66)

As the trappings of contemporary civilization whittled away at the vestiges of the village I knew, the call of the vanishing wild still beckoned, and offered a nostalgic refuge:

Sunday afternoon and there was plenty of reading and indoor work to do. But the time of winter after Groundhog Day is numbered and the mood of the mind shifts to spring. On this balmy eve exactly a month before the vernal equinox, the outdoors beckoned us from hibernation. It was time to renew acquaintances with the countryside along Bolin Creek.

Down the wooded hillsides you venture, looking for familiar signs. There is reassurance in the constancy of nature, albeit ever evolving. The old landmarks are comforting, even as they grow and change. With all the frightful talk of pollution you pause to survey the Creek. It still runs clear,

Chapel Hill Mayor Ed Lanier with his trusty A-Model Ford, May 6, 1951

fast, and cold with no tell-tale traces of man-induced bubbles or heavy-colored streaks around the rocks and algae. Rains of the past few days have raised the level slightly. Bolin always looks healthier, the nearer it is to bankful.

On down towards Tenney's Meadow, the oaks rise to regal heights, still lords of this lost pocket of wilderness in leap-frogging Chapel Hill suburbia. In the field the afternoon sun feels good and takes the trace of a chill off the body as you lie in the broom straw. Along the rough sandy beach you see where a new generation of youngsters have discovered the glory of the vines that drape the banks. Two new ready-made trapezes have been cut loose at strategic spots to span the stream in an easy swing.

Walking back up the hill through the pine-carpeted woods you hear a startling muffled drum-roll off to the left. A single quail has just departed. Here and there are new sprouts poking up through the leaves. As surely as it is only mid-February there will still be some dying gasps of winter. But its grip has been broken. Soon it will be Chapel Hill in the spring
(2/25/70)

Struck by that same muse on a New Year's Day afternoon a few year's later, I discovered in that same area:

There was the old spring, shaded by the towering sweet gum trees in a dell of watercress. Up the pathway was Billy Hill—once a picturesque knob overlooking a vista of broad hillside meadows, now a young forest. We recalled seeing a graceful young fox glide through the broomsedge there years before. The slope turned into a glade of shortleafs carpeted by a thick covering of pine needles. Down in the valley was the perch hole—a favorite fishing spot of yore. And the well-worn path along the creek showed that countless others enjoyed (and, for the absence of litter, even respected) Chapel Hill's last frontier.

To the west, just a few yards, was a shopping center; to the north, two apartments developments and a fashionable subdivision; to the east and south were more apartments and an old neighborhood of town. Civilization has leapfrogged this vestige of Chapel Hill's vanishing open spaces. And all of this, for the nonce, is just over a half-mile from the downtown post office. **(1/2/76)**

Elements of these and other memories of earlier landscapes in Chapel Hill yet remain, but they're all fleeting—yet important to recall.

University Presbyterian Church fire, Feb. 20, 1958

Chapter 7

How, Now, Chapel Hill?

... being a Chapel Hillian is actually a state of mind — a matter of loyalty and sense of community ... The Compleat Chapel Hillian isn't an instant creation, the self-appointed philosopher charged. Some "feel" for the uniqueness of this sylvan vale is necessary.

What quality, what event, or what attitude best illustrates the true nature of Chapel Hill? The answer eludes proof. But out of the thousands of items published in The Newsman's Notepad over three decades I simply remember this short, short love story, and nominate it for a starry crown of Chapel Hilliness:

They'd only lived here about three years, but everyone in the family had come to love the town and their particular neighborhood. That dad received an offer he really couldn't refuse to move back up north didn't placate the children a bit. The "For Sale" sign was put up in the front yard. The day of departure drew closer. Then last Saturday the parents finally decided "to heck with it."

When the nine-year-old daughter came in they shared the joyous news with her. "You can go take down the 'For Sale' sign in the front yard," they told her. Pleased as she could be, the child cried out, "I want to put up a bigger sign saying 'We're Not Moving!' " And that's real Chapel Hilly!
(4/7/75)

The founding of The First State University at the New Hope Chapel Hill crossroads, and the University's actual opening two years later, are popularly and properly associated with the actual founding of Chapel Hill. Actually the Town of Chapel Hill dates from 1819, 25 years after the University itself opened. It was in 1819 that the General Assembly formally

authorized the appointment of five Chapel Hill town commissioners, empow-
ered to establish its boundaries and pass laws for it.

Because there are various other "Chapel Hills" in the country, ours may
not be the original one. But at least one other namesake is an offspring of
ours, and a variety of other articles, objects, and ideas, have been born
from our particular "Hill."

Best known, perhaps, is Chapel Hill, Tennessee, a hamlet about 40 miles
south of Nashville. A native of that town, William Garbard, was a graduate
student at UNC-Chapel Hill some years ago and told me his town was
founded in 1828 by one of his ancestors, John Laws of Chapel Hill, NC, who
on graduation from the University here followed other settlers there from
Orange County.

Laws opened a school there which was attended by the illustrious Civil
War Confederate General, Nathan Bedford Forrest. The names Forrest and
Laws are to this day well-identified with Orange County families, so the link
to the Chapel Hill in Tennessee looks likely from that standpoint:

... Thus the public educational spirit of Chapel Hill was continued in its
namesake – and perhaps even spurred that great Confederate general to his
renown strategy to "git thar fustest with the mostest."

I have always had a warm spot for Chapel Hill, Tennessee – an association which some other local postal patrons may have shared back in the dark
ages before ZIP codes. Tom and Nell Fulton had Post Office Box 44 in
Chapel Hill, Tenn. I have "44" here. I regularly received their doctor bills
and sundry other window envelopes ... We became pen pals and exchanged
Christmas cards for some years ...

(5/30/80)

On checking with the skilled reference researchers at the University's
Wilson Library, I learned that North Carolina and Tennessee have the only
two corporate municipalities in the country by that name, but that there are
a variety of them of varying status:

... The US Atlas has three Chapel Hills (mailing address listed in
parentheses): Chapel Hill, KY (Adolphus), pop. 125; Chapel Hill, DE,
(Newark), pop. 1,100; and Chapel Hill Estates, MA (Pembroke), pop. 100.

Rand McNally listings contain quite a spate of rural Chapel Hills –
neighborhoods with no identifiable boundaries – in Arkansas, Georgia,
Pennsylvania (within Huntington Valley), Virginia (within Alexandria),
and confusingly nearby in Maryland, but also in greater Washington, DC.

Logo for Chapel Hill – 'Virginia's
most exciting new
community' – Annandale, VA – 1966

They are also in Mississippi (out of Utica), and Missouri, out of Bates City.
There's even a Chapel Hill Shopping Center in Akron, Ohio, and a
Chapelhill, Indiana, as a part of Indianapolis. Texas, true to its wide open
"bigger and better" tradition, has two varieties of them: Chappell Hill, a
rural community of 400 in Washington County, and New Chapel Hill, a
hamlet of 595 persons in Smith County, addressed via Tyler.

Surely all of this tends to support the saying we have perpetuated about
the far-flung alumni of the First State University – that you can find little bits
of Chapel Hill all over the country.

(5/30/80)

*A Texas firm was marketing an item for the University's General Alumni
Association several years ago, erroneously spelled Chapel Hill with the
double-P Texas spelling. Rather than go to the expense and delay of
reprinting, the Alumni Office made a cost-conscious decision to go ahead
with the mailing of over 100,000 of these misprinted flyers. Dozens of
literate alumni spotted the typo and wrote their Alumni Office in understandably irate language about the error.*

*The Chapel Hill subdivision opened in Annandale, VA in 1966 as
"Virginia's Most Exciting New Community" was even promoted with an Old
Well logo. Perhaps it was a good thing, because the Washington Post also
advertised in 1977 "The Chapel Hill Institute" for weight loss by the "Diet
Meditation Plan," which guaranteed that through its program you would*

"lose weight with the power of your mind." I telephoned the listed number in Washington, an answering service, but was never rewarded with any further information about the highly-touted Chapel Hill Institute.

The attractiveness of our name, plus nostalgia for alma mater, gave our name to a preppy-looking short-sleeved, broadcloth men's shirt. I ran across and purchased several Chapel Hill Shirts at a factory outlet store several years ago. The manufacturer in Wilmington, as you might expect, was a Tar Heel alumnus.

A natural play on words made it easy for another alumnus to name his private four-bedroom railroad car the "Chapel Hill." Owner of this 1922-vintage rolling stock, originally built for the E.F. Hutton family, is Ohio business executive Dewitt Chapple, member of the UNC class of '56.

Just to show how far you can carry a good thing in the realm of commercialization, a Greensboro entrepreneur in 1982 had middling success with his "I'd Rather Be In Chapel Hill" game, an adaptation of that all-time parlor favorite, Monopoly.

More historically legitimate was the "Chapel Hill Victory," a 7,600-ton transport vessel built during World War II. It served the Allied cause successfully as a war-time troop and supply ship, then plied the seven seas commercially for 30 years thereafter before being scrapped in 1974. Less fortunate was another Chapel Hill-related liberty ship, the "Cornelia P. Spencer." Christened in the Wilmington, NC, shipyards on April 26, 1943, she was sunk by a German submarine off the East African coast about two months later.

Just how far-flung is the name of the old hometown this historic happening illustrates:

Chapel Hill is well-established locally as the "Southern Part of Heaven." The name was given general fame by illustrator and Chapel Hill native William Meade Prince in his 1950 book and oft-repeated legend by that title.

Tacit recognition to the name has now been given by the US Postal Service. A letter recently addressed to the General Alumni Association …"Southern Part of Heaven, NC 27514," was promptly delivered to the UNC Alumni Office.

(5/2/75)

The well-known writer, Frances Gray Patton, gave a lyrical definition of Chapel Hill and Chapel Hillians in a bylined article she wrote for Holiday magazine:

Hometowners on pilgrimage to christening of the 'SS Chapel Hill Victory' – and the ship at launching – 1943

... "The worst thing you can call them is 'suburban.' They are Chapel Hillians. This is a place in which individual idiosyncrasies are indulged or ignored just so long as they don't happen to make life awkward for the whole."

"There is plenty of gossip in Chapel Hill, but it is directed, in general, at fair game – the vain, the fatuous, the mean – and even then is tinged with human sympathy." From this the writer notes parenthetically "The very beatniks appear middle class because their nonconformity is so stylized and because in Chapel Hill, they wash ..."

... "Its residents like the town because of its willingness to let the chips of truth fall where they may, so that no one need fear to air his views." In this regard, "Chapel Hill has an air of being entirely unperplexed about what it is, was, and intends to remain. It has an air, also, of expecting everybody to fall in love with it at first sight. And almost everybody does."

(7/24/66)

Another eloquent spokesperson for the spirit of Chapel Hill was the late Miss Cornelia Love, whose name appropriately expressed her sentiments toward her local heritage. Recalling the village at the time of her repatriation in 1917, she included in her paper-back book of local sketches a fine yarn about the local general storekeeper, "Doc" A.A. Kluttz:

... one day Doc was playing checkers in the back room of the store when he heard a customer enter. "Let's keep quiet, and maybe he'll go away," Doc advised ...

(9/26/70)

It's especially interesting for us in Chapel Hill to see ourselves as others see us, and even moreso as an expatriate does. Time Magazine's Atlanta Bureau writer, Pete Range, lived here as a boy—for a period in the historic Horace Williams homestead. That was the basis for an article he wrote about the old hometown for a Sunday edition of The New York Times:

... "Chapel Hill has produced a marvelous melding of the intellectual vigor of youth and the wisdom of longevity ... In Chapel Hill a favorite pastime is talk, be it metaphysics or gossip ... The town is too cosmopolitan for serious parochialism. ... Words are currency in academe." That's pretty heady wine for old vintage Chapel Hill.

... I come off with the feeling that the writer has discovered this little jewel of an island where the folk are right up to date, yet succeed in living a simple but rewarding life. Chapel Hill seems to be a place that is somewhere on the nether reaches of nowhere conveniently close by. And here we'd lulled ourselves into the notion that Chapel Hill had been forging ahead in bringing North Carolina and the region into the mainstream of contemporary society.

There's really nothing to quibble about on this score. Just sort of a strange feeling of being in the zoo, instead of roaming free with the other animals in the forest.

(12/22/72)

Another nugget of the local personality is this from the 1953 Orange County Bicentennial issue of The State Magazine, by its publisher, Bill Sharpe:

... "Many towns with less than Chapel Hill's 9,177 strive to be called cities. Chapel Hill blandly ignores the census and speaks of itself as a village. Because of its dispersion, leisureliness and perhaps a conscious effort to make its dreams come true, this city is closer to the warmth and humanity of a village than are many hamlets a tenth its size."

In the 13 years since these lines were written, The Newsman observes that only one slight change has been made. Chapel Hill, in reality, has evolved into a "town," as it is legally designated.

The village, as fine a place as the present town, was a mood embodied in The Chapel Hill Weekly published by the late Louis Graves. The "town" of today is not necessarily any better nor worse—just an inevitable evolution. —But may the Lord forever save us from becoming a city.

(11/2/66)

That plea rings true today. The village, yes. The town, yes. Either one fits

all right. But the "city" of Chapel Hill, never.
The evolution of Chapel Hill came to mind once when a woman who'd
been here 10 years asked me "When do you really become a Chapel
Hillian?" My response:

... I first recalled to her that when I was a lad here the saying was that no
one was a Chapel Hillian who wasn't here before World War I. Of course
this fiction is no longer even suggested, I continued, and the fact is that
some natives who've been here a half-century aren't really Chapel Hillians.
Purely as a personal point of view, The Newsman then proclaimed that
being a Chapel Hillian is actually a state of mind — a matter of loyalty and
sense of community; a feeling of pride and pain, and of doing as much as
saying; of determination to be a part of Chapel Hill, rather than purely talk
about it. Notwithstanding this, The Compleat Chapel Hillian isn't an instant
creation, the self-appointed philosopher charged. Some "feel" for the uniqueness of this sylvan vale is necessary ...
(10/15/67)

As a half-serious criteria for when you really become a Chapel Hillian, I
suggested "... when you can find eternal solace and even warmth in '50 to 0;'
when you are always glad to see the Blue Devils lose in basketball, football,
or baseball; in short — when you really 'don't give a damn for Duke
University.' " I was obliged to add that "The above is purely an aberration of
sports, however. Duke and Carolina contribute to and complement each
other more and more each day."
(10/15/67)

While it's not a general qualification for being a Chapel Hillian, there is,
a friend once told me, a quality of some strong-willed locals that gives the
hometown a distinctive community personality:

Just what makes the Chapel Hill animal function and dis-function is a
favorite and perennial topic. Discussing it the other night, this newcomer
suggested that every community needs a certain balance of leaders and
followers if it is to have a well-rounded community personality. Wherever
he's been, he declared sagely, there'd been this situation. For their own
unique needs, some places naturally develop more 'leaders' or 'followers'
than others. But not Chapel Hill. Trouble here is that there is a third
category of people — a strong-willed group that refuses to stay in either
category — the independents. And that, he suggests, is what keeps our
corporate vale of tears in such a turmoil and throws its potential for a well-

developed community personality out of kilter—too many independents. —
So much for Chapel Hill on the couch.

(1/7/68)

Another facet of community personality was also cited by a long-time civic servant and University staff member:

Every now and then, being one of the native species, I have referred to the "peculiar animal" that is the "Compleat Chapel Hillian." It is occasionally healthy to grovel in such inward looks, because the normal attitude in this educational center is one of superiority.

In this spirit I thought Ross Scroggs labeled the community pretty fairly when he spoke to this topic. Calling Chapel Hill a "jungle," he said that what we get for our "so-called enlightenment" is "polysyllabic bigotry" and "ignorance enshrined in deathless prose." (Newspaper columnists probably make their fair contribution to this product.)

Now I am going to defend Chapel Hill vigorously against any "outside agitators" who pour contumely upon us. But I reserve the right to do the same within the family. It can be factually established that Chapel Hill is superior in its academic book learning and family income to much of the rest of the world around us. Pity is that we deliberately alienate ourselves from that world, and from each other, by flaunting this so ungraciously. As a grab-bag of specialists, our vision is inevitably too narrow to accept people as just people.

(10/20/71)

An ideological soul-mate of Ross Scroggs in his above-expressed point of view was a colleague of his on the Town Council, that renown hometown renaissance man, former Mayor Jimmy Wallace. A master of the quick quip as well as of such verbose circumlocution as he might happen to choose, Wallace obviously recognized this penchant of Chapel Hill types. In exasperation, as presiding officer over the Town Council, he once admonished his fellow Council members to "cut out all the garbaginous verbiage." To this day that's still a code word for un-necessary discussion in Council chambers.

Back in 1971 when Wallace was a member of the Chapel Hill Board of Aldermen he added considerable spice to the late summer doldrums with a running battle in doggerel that he started perhaps unintentionally with Hillsborough Mayor Fred Cates. It began with an off-hand remark Wallace made in public about Hillsboro, which had just formally added its original "ugh" back to its town name. Cates, who grandly adopted the title of "Lord Mayor," retorted with a sonnet, and the poetic war was on. As an unrequested "second" for both parties, I offered my own literary volley:

... Chapel Hill, Hillsborough, and indeed, Orange County as a whole, has needed just such a controversy – something of better substance than the mundane agenda of zoning, taxes, and sewer lines.

The late great journalism Prof. O.J. (Skipper) Coffin put it aptly when he admonished us as aspiring writers to heed that greatest commandment, "Thou shalt not take thyself too damn seriously."

... With the conviction that the poetic epithet is mightier than the shouted sabre, I submit:

> The doggerel war of Cates and Wallace
> Is surely the height of literate folliece
> And if depicting political intellectuality
> Explains our governments' ineffectuality.

(8/8/71)

Somehow the battle languished after that. But in its aftermath Mayor Cates, as a confidant of Gov. Bob Scott, recommended Wallace for appointment to the state board of environmental control, and he serves on it to this day.

A reason for the confused community mind-set in Chapel Hill is our constant turnover in population. I was surprised by the new census figures for 1970:

... Chapel Hill has more than doubled in size – 103.1 per cent, actually – over the past 10 years. Of course, much of this increase in the municipal population is the result of annexations to the town. But a good deal of the annexed area was wilderness in 1960, so the notion that the community has doubled since then is pretty accurate.

... Chapel Hill's proportionate growth 1960-70 was the greatest of any city in the state except Fayetteville, which was a shade ahead. But I expect that an age survey would show Chapel Hill to be by far the youngest town in the State since all UNC students living inside the limits are counted in the census figures here.

(1/20/71)

While I've already commented on the time frame for "becoming a Chapel Hillian," there's a more recent development that's cropped up in this realm. It

is the Glory of the Newcomer, and the Demise of the Old-Timer. I can't recall
where I heard it, but I distinctly recall that in the late Sixties I heard a
definition of an Old-Timer in Chapel Hill as being anybody who'd lived here
more than two years. In the Notepad column I once wrote that anybody
who'd lived in Chapel Hill since the previous election, before the local bus
system, or whose recollection pre-dated University Mall was certainly an
old-timer. Our community's penchant for human innovation and irreverence
toward experience is evident in local politics. Local longevity is nominally a
liability likely to identify a person with being in the stodgy establishment,
while the newcomer is looked upon, not always without justification, as
somebody with fresh new ideas.

The Chapel Hill Newspaper once surveyed 400 local residents for an
interesting Sunday feature series on the nature and future of Chapel Hill.
Most of those quoted had a feeling of foreboding about the future here and
felt Chapel Hill needed a new image, while retaining its "old charm:"

The respondents to the survey so far quoted dislike "the inbred nature of
the place," "find it difficult for newcomers to get acquainted," and that "the
natives are the coldest." (– That last one really chilled me.) They also seem
to like the "village," but not its purported penchant for quaintness – and
generally don't want it to grow any bigger.

Well sir, since we "natives" haven't had our say yet, I'll put both the
questions and the answers: (1) "What do you, Mr. Old Timer, think about all
the changes in Chapel Hill?" Answer: "We weren't smart enough to know
how bad off we were in earlier days, but we'd rather try to accommodate
ourselves to the present and future than turn back the clock."

(2) "Is the Town too big – and if so, what about it?" Answer: "Grandpa
thought it was too big back in '96, and I understand Gen. Davie's son
complained about the congestion, too. There must be some truth to it. But as
I recall in my own young life here, just about everybody has felt Chapel Hill
was 'just the right size' back when they first came here."

(3) "You admit, then, there are a great many problems in this growing
community. Are you pessimistic about the future?" Answer: "Well sir, my
rose-colored glasses are becoming a mite tarnished. But well-meaning
friends and spiteful enemies have both been trying unsuccessfully to kill off
Chapel Hill for many years ..."

(6/20/77)

For all the travail of life in The Southern Part of Heaven, I concluded, "...

nobody is forcing us to live in this delightful vale of tears, and ... you can prove anything with surveys."

As for the challenge to long-time Chapel Hillians that this is a "cold" place for newcomers — well, I wonder. During my three-score years here I've heard it said as often that Chapel Hill is a very friendly, laid-back place as I have that it's just the opposite:

... You walk along the street and people you don't know won't greet you; some won't even respond to your own cordial greeting. Indeed, many will deliberately look at the ground as they pass, or turn their head as if preoccupied.

— Not so, the Chapel Hill-o-phile will counter. This is an unusually friendly place to live. He likes it, he says, because nobody is a stranger, because the townfolk do indeed go out of their way to give friend and stranger alike a friendly "hello."

Which is correct? Fact is, both are correct, but the negative view needn't be. There will be those who are deliberately and unfortunately stand-offish any place they live. However, most of the non-greeters are simply souls who are initially bashful — who think they don't want to make waves ...
(12/10/79)

A gracious greeting to one and all is always Chapel Hilly, I concluded, in spreading the gospel of "Hey, how yew?"

I was more inclined to "circle the wagons" a few weeks later when a Durham Morning Herald letter-to-the-editor writer started a literary war by accusing Chapel Hill folk of being snooty, while wanting Durham's water (because of the perennial water shortage in Chapel Hill in the summers):

... With a tinge of what we feel is pardonable cosmopolitan jingoism, we pridefully boast of our Carolina blue blood. So what kind of animals are we in "chic, romantic, sophisticated" Chapel Hill, as the critics have so delightfully labeled us? Okay, then. Let's hop on the analyst's couch and plumb the depths of our own psyche.
(9/5/77)

In an attempt to capture the essence of the "Chapel Hill chap" I modestly admitted that the unusual thing about us in Chapel Hill was "... we don't just **believe** this is a better place. The simple **fact** is, it just is."

... As a center of education we can teach and preach to the world, but we may not as effectively resolve our own problems. That is partially because of one thing that's different about Chapel Hill from almost all other communities: Constancy is their pride. In Chapel Hill the only constant is change ... But change is, and must be, the accepted, if confusing, constant in Chapel Hill. It makes us incomprehensible to outlanders. It causes us internal strife ... The newcomer has as much right, as much vested interest here, as the fellow who by accident of birth has spent his life here.

So all these conditions unite us under one single circumstance: When some durn fools from Durham or anywhere else start criticizing us.

(9/5/77)

With the rise of the "preppy" cult across the nation in recent years it became important to know what was "in." Our good and controversial arbiter of tolerable taste, The Durham Morning Herald, pulled through for us again, with a list of things held to be tacky, including therein "Bumper stickers that say 'I'd rather be in Chapel Hill.'" "Obviously," I pointed out, "Durham's understandable envy is showing." For the benefit of local preppies I included the following for Chapel Hill as tacky types:

Joggers who arrogantly, or even unconsciously, trespass in auto and pedestrian traffic; auto owners who leave political bumper stickers on their cars—particularly those of the losers (super tacky); spectators who leave the game early—or scream "sit down" the instant you stand to cheer a good play; and motorists who blow their horn in greeting to pedestrians (I always reply silently "Hello, car" to this salute from behind the veil of tinted glass).

Visually Tacky—Hiking boots or blue jeans as dress wear; Ivy League T-shirts; women who nurse their infants in public; roll-your-own garbage carts; and cars parked on sidewalks.

In The Tacky Pack—... Professors and deans who have their secretaries telephone and direct you to "Hold the line for Mr. Big."; Cambridge dieters and nouveau joggers who are singularly convinced they've uniquely discovered the key to the secrets of the universe; PhDs who affect big words and adjectives instead of plain English; and folks who pompously proclaim "I like Chapel Hill, but ..."

(11/15/82)

Further in the realm of categorizing Chapel Hill, I was obliged to take up the cudgel to determine what were our real colors, literally, or, "the hue of the Hill." It was easy to determine the proper color for Orange County. The University from its earliest days established blue and white. The Appearance Commission rewarded us with two-tone fire hydrants of "buff barrels and burnt umber caps." The Town of Chapel Hill had green and yellow dump trucks, traditionally some chocolate brown buses, and a new fleet of all-white beauties graced with a dashing waistband of two-tone orange and brown. Transportation Dept. Director Bob Godding insisted there was no special significance to the new bus colors, that they just felt the three-part stripe would be nice hues against the basic white:

... Despite that disclaimer the columnist points to subtle signs of a Great Compromise: The brown stripe is a nod to the present bus bodies, and orange, in deference to big daddy Orange County.

Through it all, however, you can look with pride to the rugged independence of the Chapel Hill Police Department. True to the tradition of the "boys in blue," the law enforcers' patrol cars have remained steadily blue in hue (though of varying shades) and white. The constancy is comforting amid the many-splendored colors of evolving official Chapel Hill.

(7/21/80)

National Public Radio on one of its newscasts invited listeners to describe in a short, "scent-uous" phrase, the unique aroma of their hometown. Responding to the challenging query, we came to speculate on the local "aroma barometer:" "What is the 'aroma' of Chapel Hill — or, to put it in more academic doggerel — 'the smell of the well?' ":

... To capture it all in a single fragrance boggles the imagination. Is the Essence of The Hill in "hops, hookahs, and hortatory?" Should we be characterized as an emerging blend of "bookworms reborn by dogwood blossoms?" Is our corporate olfactory sense properly described in a recipe of "simmering students and parboiled professors?"

(1/5/81)

The response of readers was inconclusive. One disillusioned soul who'd just endured a stroll down East Franklin St. said the obvious and only scent for Chapel Hill was "petrol." Another response was more visual than aromatic. The Scent of the Hill, said this one, was pure "blue jeans and old lace."

Again I read in a trendy national publication a reference to the 50 most livable cities and towns in the country. It didn't actually list those fabled sancutaries, which they called "safe places" to live. But the criteria for them gave pause to the Chapel Hill partisan:

... The desirable places are said to be where the "environments are clean, living standards high, and taxes low; where the people are friendly, school and hospitals are excellent, and crime almost non-existent."

If this doesn't condition you to leave Chapel Hill already, you might be more prepared to do so on learning that the 50 "Safe Places" have not experienced riots or racial tensions and score high in the authors' appraisal of their recreational, cultural, and educational facilities, community organizations, job opportunities, tax rates, newspapers, radio and TV stations, libraries, transportation, climate, and scenery ...

(8/23/72)

While Chapel Hill can score all right on some of those qualities, it surely has enough shortcomings to be potentially "unsafe." But would you rather be in Alamogordo, New Mexico, Fairhope, Alabama, or Farmington, Connec-- ticut, all of which were touted as being extraordinarily "safe?" Eden, it seemed, was a place that inevitably was somewhere else.

This same sort of challenge came to mind when a study showing that Morganton was the "healthiest place in the state to live" was publicized. Chapel Hill was ranked second.

... It is heartening to know that the hospitable hills of Burke County have by dint of some smart programmer's computer totals been found the healthiest hummocks about the Valley of Humility.

We shan't low rate Morganton. But for all its robust populace, its fertile fields, fine industry, scenic beauty, and state mental hospital, we'd not favor it over the Southern Part of Heaven. We may have to "try harder" in second place. But The Hill is quite healthy enough in that less than exalted position, thank you.

(3/24/78)

Milestones in the ongoing life of Chapel Hill have been marked by exotic innovations. Already mentioned is the Cadillac count, which by now surely has us up in the "metropolitan" category. Another "first" worth noting was our first escalator, an $85,000 wonder at N.C. Memorial Hospital, which brought me to recall in 1969 that "... it seems only a couple of years ago when there wasn't even a real live elevator in town. Of such changing fabric is the vanishing village being made over."

Then there was our first pet store (not until 1969), a coffee store (Southern Season, in 1975), closely followed by the Chapel Hill Smoked Fish Company, and in 1982:

... Two (firsts) are in Carrboro. The "Paris of the Piedmont" has truly come of age. Where formerly the main business block was anchored by a good-ole-boys sandwich shop and drugstore, there is now a real, live Chinese restaurant ... (Does this historic innovation change Carrboro to the "Peking of the Piedmont?")

Second is the opening of Chapel Hill-Carrboro's very own beer distributor's warehouse. How, you wonder, have we managed to become the legendary "Beer Drinking Capital of the World" with service only from wholesalers in metropolitan Durham and Raleigh? Now Chapel Hill (spelled Carrboro) has its very own beer wholesalership ...

(11/29/82)

The beer drinking title, while widely touted, is is in my judgment a false laurel. I investigated and calculated in 1978 when Daily Tar Heel reporter Ann-Marie Downey first heralded this as fact. According to her findings, based on beer wholesalers' purported Chapel Hill deliveries, local topers averaged drinking almost 88 gallons of beer per capita a year—"as compared to the West German annual average of just under 39 gallons a person and the US national average of 16 gallons."

... If true, what this means is that every man and woman-jack of us in this charming vale of tears (and beers) drinks an average of two and one-half (12-ounce) cans of brew for each of the 365 days of the year—and that in doing this we are imbibing at a rate five and one-half times the national average.

Of course we have always heard that Chapel Hill is an extraordinary place—that it was not in tune with the rest of the state and region. But we'd never imagined we were over five-fold more bloated in beer than the entire country around us.

... Is it really true that Chapel Hill's average beer consumption is more than quintuple the national average? Are we now the Sudsy Part of Heaven?

(11/10/78)

I really didn't believe the "beer drinking capital" finding then, nor now. But this final milestone, I can report from direct testimony to me:

It is a good day for the bidet. You will recall that as a measure of the soaring sophistication of the village we recently reported that there were some two-bidet homes in little old Chapel Hill.

Now the lily has been gilded, so to speak. A townsman calls to report that his family is delighted with their handyman-constructed combination bidet and toilet.

There is another report of a two-bidet bathroom in one home. And — what will they think of next, marvel of marvels? We have learned of a family that has one of these posh installations in their mobile home trailer. **(9/19/77)**

There are myriad more milestones in the endless life of Chapel Hill. But surely these include the most noteworthy.

Chapter 8

All Around the Town

... town government needs to remember that it's created strictly for service to citizens, and not as a worthy enterprise in its own right.

We elect our aldermen to exercise sound judgment – not to accommodate our whims ... May our Honorables spare us any additional blessings in the form of "more services" and additional bureaucracy.

It all started quite naturally, innocently, and un-intentionally – my personal interest in Chapel Hill local government. As a brand new correspondent for the Durham Morning Herald in 1950 I heard that a new Town Clerk had just been hired. It sounded like a modestly worth-while news story, so I went to the Town Manager's office to learn the facts. Manager Thomas D. Rose quietly said they did in fact have a new Town Clerk, but it didn't appear she was going to stick with the job – and did I know anybody who might be interested?

Indeed, I did, and went outside to fetch my wife who happened to be waiting in the car. A skilled office professional, she applied for the job on the spot, and was hired. As a result, both of us had to attend all Town Board meetings – she to officially record them for the Town, and I to un-officially report them for the newspaper. After six years of this, with an almost perfect attendance record, I came to believe I had about enough sense and knowledge of the Town to serve on that august body myself. I filed for office and was elected and ultimately served 12 years as an alderman, retiring in 1969.

Elective local office in the l950s, it seemed to me, was not much different from the job currently, except that all the numbers are much bigger today. A townsman once asked me if it wasn't a lot of bother being an alderman. Naturally I cited both the pros and cons of the job, but basically it always seemed to me that because I'd voluntarily sought the office, I had scant grounds for complaint. I kept a "little brown book" notepad of every conversation I had with anybody about Town business, primarily as a reminder. It was also an indicator of the great amount of un-official activity involved in aldermanic affairs—which were on the average, three or four contacts a day. My reaction to that:

... there are bound to be excesses of personal interest and persuasion, but the elected public servant generally appreciates the constituent's interest in his government. Any time a person brings a public problem or an opportunity to me for consideration of the Town, I appreciate it just as much as he may ...

(12/7/61)

It also occurred to me many years later, that town government needs to remember that it's created strictly for service to citizens, and not as a worthy enterprise in its own right. This came to mind when a reporter for The Chapel Hill Newspaper wrote in a survey story:

... (1) That the Town's general fund payroll has soared more than 50 pct. (an increase of over $1 million) in a scant three years, (2) that the Town of Chapel Hill has created 10 new administrative jobs in less than a year; and (3) that the administrators attribute this trend to **"citizens and aldermen who want more services."**

We can't dispute the fiscal facts. But we surely must correct the administrators' folly in declaring that the local citizens **"want more services."** This lowly columnist/taxpayer issues the following statement with equal authority: The citizens don't want more services. They just want to be left alone. They want efficient fundamental services—police, fire, streets, and sanitation. Then they want local government off their back.

There is no doubt that the **alderman** want more services. As elected political beings it is natural for them to want to increase the municipal fiefdom. This isn't to assail their integrity. It's just to honestly cite their natural inclination ...

... we elect our aldermen to exercise sound judgment—not to accommodate our whims ... May our Honorables spare us any additional blessings in the form of "more services" and additional bureaucracy.

(3/31/78)

I had another stump speech in the column, this one in defense of the Town Council. Most constituents imagine the board is a simple legislative body that deliberates, decides what local laws ought to be passed, and then acts accordingly. As a civics lesson of sorts, I wrote about this every now and then:

Have a care, dear friends, for the poor, beleagured Town of Chapel Hill – a paper tiger, involuntary Gulliver, and mouse that roars but meekly. – You thought that the Town with its 400-plus employees, ominscient Board of Aldermen, and $6 million budget was powerful, didn't you?

Well, the facts of life come home to roost occasionally. They reveal that the Town of Chapel Hill has only as much authority as one single person wants it to have. That person is a member of the local delegation in the State Legislature – good folks like Trish Hunt and Charles Vickery. What we constituents overlook is that the Town of Chapel Hill and every other municipal government in the state can do only what the Legislature specifically says it can do in its charter, and is barred from doing anything else.

So, when the town father people want some additional authority, as happens pretty regularly, they are granted this only at the pleasure of the local legislators, who, by protocol of their General Assembly colleagues, pass judgment on their home fiefdoms ...

(4/20/79)

It is not unusual for municipal governments to exceed their charter authority, often unintentionally. The idea of being absolutely prohibited from doing anything you're not specifically empowered to do takes some getting used to in this free-spirited society.

Neighborhood crises and special interest programs that come before the Town Council provide the best local government laboratories for the citizens. Personal involvement makes the difference:

... Fast fellowships are often formed among these neighborhood delegations that must rise up to protect their areas. One of the most practiced and artful of these was jokingly known as the East Rosemary Street Marching Society ... From the municipal administration's point of view, there is a fringe benefit to the citzenry's descending on Board meetings and watching the deliberations of the aldermen. It makes for a more compassionate constituency.

(3/13/68)

Many members of the Council have been spawned by such groups – the East Rosemary clan, as a case in point, having furnished at least two. The opinion of some regular observers has often been sought by the Council, and these worthies can be valuable resources at times.

A classic continuing controversy that's of much less monetary than theoretical significance is the issue of pay for members of the Council. Since the job is obviously intended as public rather than professional service (and certainly not as a regular salaried moonlighting job), the Council members are natural targets when they talk about how much money they ought to pay themselves. For years the only such job in town that was really "pure" in this regard was that of School Board member. Though that service is perhaps the most demanding, time-consuming, and controversial of all, it paid nothing for many years, and then only a symbolic $1 a year until 1982 when the lingering question was settled with a $25 per meeting fee per member.

Town Council members have never been so bashful. In the seven years from 1969 to 1976 they kited their annual "honorarium" more than 700 percent to $3,000 apiece. The rate hike for the mayor was even better — 800 percent. The quantitative effect of that was not lost on another municipal public service body, the Planning Board. The planners picked up on the idea and considered a resolution to ask the Town Council to give them $1,000 a year salary each for their noble service. That seemed such a good idea that they amended the motion to triple the figure to $3,000, same as for the Town Council, then added one dollar more on the rationale that they had more meetings than did the Council:

> ... The motion was about to pass handily, when George Spransy suggested that to better emphasize their concept of public service in their non-salaried appointive positions they might do as well to reject the motion — but deliver the message. Exactly that was done. ... And so the knife was twisted — and plunged straight to the heart of the issue ...
> (6/28/76)

Writing in the Notepad column that other appointive town boards could just as logically put in their claims for public service boodle, I concluded, in behalf of the great unwashed masses, that "... all of us as taxpayers do our bit every now and then, too, don't we? How about the times we take the garbage out to the curb, clean the street gutters ourselves, or don't ask for municipal services to which we're entitled? That's 'public service,' too. Perhaps we could simplify things by just deducting our 'salary' from our tax payments."

That idea brings up another classic and equally un-solvable issue — just how much "free" service does our municipal government "owe" us? Chapel Hill's back-yard garbage collection is illustrative. Many municipalities, Carrboro included, make this a citizen participatory process through "roll-your-own" garbage carts that must be left at the curb-side for pick-up.

Chapel Hill considered this, gave it a trial run in one neighborhood, and cited the money that would be saved by this system:

... Yea, we applaud the noble notion of public thrift. With the tax rate already doomed to an increase of almost 15 percent for the coming year, the citizenry will thank its corporate government for almost anything it can do to lighten the load. But not the garbage load.

That is one of the very few fundamental services that personally and directly benefit every taxpayer. Public opinion has been vocally expressed against this idea every time it's been broached, yet the spectre of publicly-propelled garbage keeps rearing its smelly head. What does it take to finally kill a bad idea?

(6/6/80)

The idea wasn't adopted then, but it came up for official consideration again the next year:

ROLL-YOUR-ONUS – Foul as the refuse it wheels, roll-your-own garbage keeps bubbling up as a municipal program for Chapel Hill. For the third time, the witless proponents of personal participation in Chapel Hill's garbage disposal service are reviving the idea ...

... if the Town really wants to save money, it could simply eliminate all garbage collection and the taxpayers be hanged; let 'em haul their own refuse out to the landfill and local government saves a million dollars a year in the Town budget.

... Economy in government, yes. But reduction of the Town's one truly unique and fundamental service that directly benefits everybody, never! Preserve the quality of GLICH! Let's wheel the roll-your-owners to oblivion – permanently this time!

(5/25/81)

The herd instinct being what it is, the general trend to "rolling" in garbage collection is no doubt a scourge whose time will come to Chapel Hill. The point is the principle: How much public service are we due from local government free, and how much by fee?

Such fundamentally-oriented thinking also deserves an exception to prove the rule. That's readily available in the Chapel Hill Public Library. An eight-year ad hoc campaign by local citizens for creation of a municipal library was climaxed by the aldermen's approval of this in 1958. Though not a fundamental necessity as a municipal program, it was widely desired by Chapel Hillians. As the time neared for opening of the tiny initial facility in a former West Franklin St. rooming house, an appeal went out for help.

First Chapel Hill Public Library, W. Franklin St., 1/20/62

*Noting the long-standing public support for the library idea, I wrote that "...
by donations of books, periodicals, suitable furnishings, building material,
and money, they can give concrete evidence of their support." A decade later,
when the permanent library building was opened, I suggested:*

... The really special thing about the library is that it's actually the first
major public facility (exclusive of necessary utility things like police and
fire stations) that Chapel Hill has ever planned and done on its own without
the fostering of its benevolent big brother, the University. Truly it is a
beautiful and functional building, and one which as a "first" will be an
everlasting credit to the community and a monument to the dogged volunteers who persevered in bringing it to fruition.:

(8/16/67)

That public support continued and grew:

One of the best success stories in the Town's continuing history is the
Chapel Hill Public Library. A recent story in The Newspaper notes that it
had the highest book circulation of any municipal library in the state last
year. There were 334,779 books checked out, which means the entire
collection of 55,000 volumes was turned over more than six times. It also
means, coincidentally, that everybody in this literate little community of
approximately 55,000 checked out slightly over six books during the year.

(3/12/79)

Thus, in a contradictory fashion that's typically Chapel Hilly, local citizens may be getting their best taxpaid value for a non-essential municipal service.

One of the most interesting analyses of the pro-rated cost of tax-supported services was the plaint of the good lads of the Delta Psi fraternity (St. Anthony Hall) over what they quaintly called their inordinately high "pillow tax." By dividing the fraternity's total annual tax bill into the number of members they had, they found they were paying $9.05 per member per month in local taxes, compared to the average of less than half that amount, $4.56, for all fraternities as a group.

... Over $9 a month in taxes is admittedly a right heavy sum for a college student to have to pay in return for the intangible value to him of local public services ... There is no suggestion by Delta Psi that its plush new fraternity house and lot aren't worth far more than the $69,555 tax valuation ...

... So while the fellows at Delta Psi admittedly have a big tax bill, they also have some mighty fancy living quarters, of which they are no doubt justifiably proud ... Delta Psi owns valuable property and is equitably assessed accordingly. — Somebody's got to pay the highest taxes "per pillow" and it just happens to be them.

(4/6/61)

That issue of fraternities paying taxes has created some curious situations. In the annual public advertisement of delinquent taxes, the Town of Chapel Hill used to list fraternities under a special heading. By the loose nature of their organization, many fraternities regularly ended up on the list, whereby it was stated legally that their property would be sold at the courthouse door for non-payment of taxes on a certain day. While that is a technical fact, it doesn't actually work out that way. But I remember one year a University professor turned up as the sole bidder at this theoretical sale and offered to pay the $1,300 owed by Chi Psi fraternity if he could have the property at that price, which, he admitted, was a bargain buy.

For many years the property tax system was unnecessarily complicated by a deceptive ratio formula. In Orange County until 1973 the amount of taxes a property owner would pay was controlled not only by the tax rate, but also by the ratio. Then, as now, all property was appraised by the tax assessor at market value. Then the county commissioners would set a percentage ratio of that market value at which the property would be listed on the tax books:

... The built-in deceit in tax rates is a set-up this reporter has opposed for many years. The taxpayer never really knows what to expect so long as local government can manipulate both the rate and ratio. Real and personal property ought to be listed and taxed on the basis of its market value. Then the tax rate – and comparative tax rates – would be meaningful and the poor taxpayer could understand them.

(7/6/66)

When Orange finally ended this unnecessary and confusing charade in 1973 the ratio was 70 percent. Since then it's been 100 percent, so that the appraised market value and the value for taxes has been the same. Under the old system, for instance, the tax bill on parcels of property of identical market value in two counties with the same tax rates could be widely different, subject to the percentage ratio applied to the listings in each county. The rate explained nothing until you mathematically factored in the ratio applied to your listed property.

The issue of tax-exempt property has special pertinence for Chapel Hill since its biggest business, the University, is not subject to taxation. Whether or not one government agency ought to have to pay taxes to another for its property is a chicken-or-egg sort of issue. The University, which supplies to itself most of the services that municipal and county governments supply to everybody else, pays no local taxes. But is it really gaining a "free ride" that's a drain on the taxpayers? A chamber of commerce survey made in Greensboro showed that the 10,000 college students there put $30 million a year into the local economy:

... If applicable in Chapel Hill, where our one university has 50 percent more students, you could calculate that UNC has a $45 million annual impact on this community ...

The Greensboro Chamber, in light of the findings in its survey, noted that "Education, a major industry of previously unknown proportions, is Greensboro's hidden treasury." – At the least ... UNC might be recognized as Chapel Hill's "un-appreciated treasury."

(10/18/67)

Of course not all University-related property is tax-exempt – specifically that owned by University students. A near majority of them have automobiles nowadays and few of those cars, which constitute the greatest share of students' taxable personal property, are listed annually as required by law for taxes in Orange County. The property, under law, must be listed for taxes in the county where it is located for the greater part of the year. That student-owned property, particularly their automobiles, aren't listed for taxes in Orange County costs local government uncounted millions of dollars in lost tax revenue. A State Legislature study commission proposed that this condition be remedied by requiring the owner to produce a receipt for payment of his local property taxes on the vehicle as a condition of buying his annual auto license sticker.

... Orange County is particularly vulnerable to this form of law evasion because of its extraordinarily high proportion of University student population ...

To appeal for enactment of an auto tax enforcement law is not to cry out "soak the students." It is simply to ask equalization of a rightful tax burden. There are undoubtedly many auto tax evaders other than students in Orange and the other 99 NC counties. But there is no legitimate ethical argument against the autos they own being as subject to tax payment as any other piece of property. Every evader is costing those of us who do list our property as we're obligated to do more money ...

(1/8/79)

The State Legislature still hasn't closed that loophole. There are two other tax laws I believe ought to be passed that would have particular benefits for Chapel Hill. This University town needs these particular sources of revenue because it has to offer town services to so many citizens who live and work here but aren't local citizens. One is a payroll tax, generally a one percent deduction for local government taken out of all pay checks issued in any given city:

... The intention of it is to extend the tax burden for municipal services to many who don't now pay – namely commuters who work but don't pay property taxes in a given municipality. It is also intended to relieve the overload on property taxes. If enacted as a permissive measure by the Legislature, so that a city could impose this if it wanted to, this could be a very attractive proposal for Chapel Hill.

(11/3/72)

Through 1985 the support for authorization of local payroll taxes has been growing in the Legislature.

The other proposal which Chapel Hill ought to seek as a legitimate and much needed source of revenue is an entertainment tax. I suggested this at the time the Town Council was considering asking the Legislature to let it enact a local hotel tax:

... Why not directly tax the luxury – the entertainment ticket – instead of the few hotel rooms that some out-of-town sports fans use a few days a year? The principle of taxing shelter, a necessity of life, instead of entertainment, an optional luxury, is questionable. It's also using a shotgun where a rifle is called for.

Entertainment taxes are well-established all over this country and the world. Let Chapel Hill, one of the entertainment spas of the region, take advantage of this by a local surcharge on tickets to sports and other entertainment events.

(7/16/82)

Such an entertainment tax could be simply structured to apply only to major spectator events, such as home football games by designation, or by a minimum auditorium/stadium size. Its special benefits would be:

A tax that would be paid primarily by NON-Chapel Hillians and would serve to repay what they cost us. ... Those of us who attend Carolina's away football games out of state occasionally pay this tax as a surcharge on our regular tickets for admission to games.

... More than a quarter-million out-of-towners come to these games annually. The price of the tickets has been hiked regularly to the present $11 tab, and the main complaint has been that there aren't enough tickets available.

The momentary doubling of Chapel Hill's "population" during the short 60 minutes of football game time costs the town government considerably in traffic and sanitation services. The University provides some help on that, but not a full repayment. For the Town to recoup some costs and derive legitimate revenue from a fair and untapped source like this is a proposal worth serious investigation.

... How about it, friends – for a change – a tax on THEM for US?

(11/19/82)

Chapel Hill town authorities have been generally favorable to this idea but the University has "stone-walled" on it, opposing anything that would increase the price of football tickets. The Town has not been willing to pursue the matter as a result. There is no question that the University benefits the community and the Town of Chapel Hill to an incredible degree – that the University in effect IS Chapel Hill. But that does not mean that the relationship cannot and should not be equitably improved – as the columnist suggests.

Chapter 9

Police and Crime

We live the "good life" in Chapel Hill by grace of some of its natural attributes and a certain spirit of appreciation for the value of each of us as an individual. Good law enforcement is an absolute necessity for any good community. The men like Ted Cole are responsible for this. And some of them pay the ultimate price for the rest of us.

For all the well-publicized problems that go with his (or her) career nowadays, the life of a policeman is seldom the ideal of today's children. The storied majesty and power that goes with the blue uniform is not very often even the figment of every young boy's imagination, as it once was.

I report this from the comfortable background of days of yore in Chapel Hill when the policeman was envisioned by all of us lads as a glamorous figure akin to Superman of more recent times. How well I recall, during his childhood, our Number Three Son proudly telling a playmate, "My daddy knows 'Hummon' Stone!," referring to the then revered policeman, now police chief.

Gaining a closer insight into the policeman's life while a newsman, I learned from Police Chief Bill Blake:

... the policeman has no social life outside his associates on the force and other police families. He's in no way prohibited from this, but as a matter of natural course he's generally "ostracized." His otherwise friends are reluctant to be seen tippling or engaging in any mild social activity which could put them the least bit under the suspicious eye of the law enforcement officer if he were on duty ...

(11/20/66)

This came up in a discussion when the Chief announced that members of the police force, some of whom had been working a full 40 hours a week moolighting in addition to their regular 48-hour duty week, would be prohibited from more than 20 hours a week extra work on their own. After a policeman was killed (the first such instance locally) by a grudge-bearing assailant, Chief Blake admitted that "more and more convicted persons nowadays threaten to 'get even' with the officers who arrest them — but we try not to dwell on that too much."

... Friends, every one of us lives under the pall of death from nuclear fallout, global war, or accident each day. But the citizen who carries out his sworn duty in a career to enforce our criminal laws is courting infinitely more danger than any of the rest of us, excluding combat soldiers and astronauts. We live the "good life" in Chapel Hill by grace of some of its natural attributes and a certain spirit of appreciation for the value of each of us as an individual. Good law enforcement is an absolute necessity for any good community. The men like Ted Cole are responsible for this. And some of them pay the ultimate price for the rest of us.

(6/11/69)

While the federal courts have more recently prohibited it except at higher pay, overtime duty was in the past taken for granted. Some years ago when violence flared on a picket line during a strike of workers at the University's student dining hall, local police were called in to do extra duty to preserve the peace. The Town subsequently awarded each policeman $100 apiece as compensation for that extra duty.

... The workers [at the dining hall] who were on strike for better working conditions, higher pay and improved benefits, could present a legitimate case for public outrage if their compensation was in any way as skimpy as this extra duty pay for police so far ...

(12/14/69)

During this era of nationwide student activism law enforcement officers suffered from a bad image under the epithet of "pigs." Earlier in the decade local police made more than 1,400 arrests during a two-year period of civil rights demonstrations. But they were generally aplauded by everybody in the community for the painstakingly careful and impartial way they carried out their duties. But by the end of the decade the trend caught up with Chapel Hill to the extent that uniforms were altered to defuse the supposed militaristic look that was said to offend some people and hamper the policemen's effectiveness:

... It is fine that the change to civvies is made to give the policeman himself more pride.

But it is pitiful that the change is made for a more significant reason – to reduce attacks on policemen and lessen the abrasive reaction the military uniform brings out in so many members of the public whom the law enforcement officers serve and protect ...

What a sad commentary on modern enlightened times in which the liberated soul of mankind is supposed to accept people as just people – all of them.

(9/30/70)

The over-reaction spread to the University's Faculty Council, which took up a resolution to restrict the wearing of weapons by campus police:

... Certainly any plan to up-grade the calibre and training of campus police is good and necessary. They are the official greeters to the campus, for instance, to more people daily than anybody else. Theirs is a job requiring infinitely more ability in dealing with the public then the issuance of parking tickets. But as a ... believer in the ultimate bedrock virtue of enforceable laws, I will feel much better having my sworn police patrolman reasonably armed at all times – for their protection and mine. If does not offend me in the slightest. Those whom it does offend are the ones who need additional education far more than police do.

(1/17/71)

About this time the Chapel Hill Police Department gained a real police station of its own when the entire 1938 Town Hall building was renovated for police use. After a tour of the new facilities I recalled that "It is thankfully a far cry from Chapel Hill's first police station," which I recalled as a lad. "That was an eight-by-12-foot cottage shack, built by the University and delivered in a dump truck to its mid-town corner location on one of the grass plots by the Texaco Station [Note: at the Franklin-Columbia corner]."

... one of the intangible qualities that have been added to Gracious Living in Chapel Hill has been the fact that it has traditionally had a good police department ...

... It should not be overlooked, either, that the Police Department is basically the only municipal operation in which racial integration is effectively practiced throughout – a fact which may account for the respect and effectiveness of that department ... in an era when it's more fashionable to say "pig" than "policeman," a good word for Chapel Hill's Finest.

(6/13/71)

A decade later, the beneficiary of a $1.2 million local bond referendum, the Department moved into its new "police facility," a state-of-the-art cement and glass structure overlooking the town from half-way up Mt. Bolus on Airport Road. After a tour of that new building, courtesy of Chief Stone, I wrote in high praise of its innovative facilities, and felt obliged to dub its stainless steel three-cell holding jail "a veritable Chapel Hilton."

It inevitably recalled my only personal experience in the old mid-town jail on Christmas day, 1964. One of the most bizarre murders in Chapel Hill's history was discovered the night before. Frank Rinaldi, a UNC graduate student English instructor, was charged with the suffocation slaying of his pregnant bride, though he claimed to have been out buying her Christmas presents all that day. On Christmas morning the Editor of the Daily Tar Heel called me to suggest we go the jailhouse and try to interview Rinaldi. To our surprise, he agreed, and we were admitted to his cell:

... Nonetheless, Frank Rinaldi was as cooperative to his questioners as the extraordinary predicament in which he found himself would seem to permit. He even seemed embarrassed at not being able to offer his guests a seat ... In a low voice he answered all questions without hesitation or outward reaction to the nature of the inquiry ...

... On past 30 minutes the interview continued ... It was apparent that the carefully-planned release of the reporters had gone awry for the moment.

There were lapses of awkward silence. The reporters yelled for the police. A hollow echo bounced back from the hallway and only the quiet murmur of prisoners in the adjoining cells was audible. Through the top of the outside cell window trucks and cars pulling up to the street corner could been seen and heard. They seemed miles away.

A few modest stabs at casual conversation were made. The subjects seemed incongruously inappropriate under the circumstances, and were dropped ...

... Finally, after 73 minutes of confinement ... the sergeant appeared at the window and opened the cell door. He apologetically explained the unavoidable circumstances that caused the delay in his return.

... Outside again each reporter simultaneously asked the other one the same question at the same time: "Do you think he's guilty?"

Neither could give a definite answer.

(1/2/64)

Rinaldi was freed on no probable cause, then re-arrested eight months later, tried and convicted. On appeal the NC Supreme Court freed him on the challenge that homosexual implications by the prosecution were not directly linked to the case and tended to prejudice Rinaldi's defense. That, however, did not end the case. A decade later I wrote:

... The evidence was sensational, coincidental, and extraordinary. Lucille Regina Begg, Rinaldi's hometown sweetheart in Waterbury, CT, was betrothed to him a year to the day before she died. They were married in August, she came to Chapel Hill to share his mid-town apartment, and she worked one day as a teacher in Guy B. Phillips School before abruptly returning to Waterbury. In December Rinaldi bought a $20,000 double-indemnity whole-life insurance policy on his bride from a friend. Lucille Rinaldi returned to Chapel Hill on Dec. 20. The insurance agent-friend and family joined the Rinaldis for dinner on Dec. 23. On Christmas Eve the agent and Rinaldi spent the day shopping, the death being reported by them to police late that afternoon. In the trial a local waiter said Rinaldi had tried to hire him to kill his wife—and even told him on that fatal Christmas Eve, "It's over, I did it."

But the web of circumstantial evidence failed to hold up beyond the necessary "reasonable doubt" in the jury's belief. Rinaldi, testifying in his own behalf, was finally found not guilty nearly 22 months after the Christmas Eve slaying...

(1/3/75)

The separate murders of two other women in Chapel Hill remain unsolved mysteries. A 21-year-old Carolina summer school student, Suellen Evans of Mooresville, was stabbed to death in Coker Arboretum on July 30, 1965. No motive was ever established, nor were any arrests made. Recalling that tragedy later, I wrote:

... Seldom, if ever, has there been such a major crime in Chapel Hill that seemed so senseless. The victim, a quiet, likeable young woman, had no known enemies and was not attacked in an obviously hazardous nor tempting place for an assailant. She was simply walking back from her morning classes to her dormitory to return home for the weekend. Though her screams drew help almost immediately, she died from two stab wounds within minutes, never able to utter an explanatory word. Not a single solid clue was ever turned up at the scene—despite an inch-by-inch combing of the entire Arboretum...

(8/4/80)

The Rachel Crook murder was even more mysterious, as I recalled 30 years later:

Crook's Corner—12/29/51

... The 71-year-old sharp-tongued spinster, daughter of a Confederate general, came to Chapel Hill to pursue a graduate degree at the University. She remodeled an old filling station at the Chapel Hill-Carrboro town line and sold remnants, fish, and pecans from the family's Alabama plantation. Crook's Corner also housed one of the town's earliest automatic laundry operations ...

(8/30/82)

Rachel Crook failed to keep an appointment with a dressmaker one summer night. The next day her body was found on an abandoned road near New Hope Church five miles north of town. She'd been raped and beaten to death. Ten days later Hobert Lee of Burlington, a road machinery operator, was arrested and charged with the killing on circumstantial evidence that was related by a dozen prosecution witnesses in his subsequent trial. The events and testimony of that trial, which I covered for the Durham Morning Herald, were as sensational as the murder itself, as I later wrote:

... The sheriff went to Lee at his jail cell in Durham ... [and] said Lee told him he was so drunk he could hardly remember what happened on the fatal night. One of the more incriminating statements put into the hearing testimony by the sheriff was this:

(Sheriff Latta): "Did you turn into that road (the New Hope Church Road off Highway 86 because you had helped build it and knew it?" Lee answered, "I reckon I did."

And this: "While you were there do you remember hitting her with anything other than your fist?" Lee answered, "I don't think so."

... The defendant, never taking the stand, won an acquittal after the jury deliberated 85 minutes ...

(3/15/62)

Perhaps the most intriguing facet of the trial was the testimony on Lee's alibi — that he'd been at a Durham "sporting house" on the fatal night. The madam of that carefully-described establishment allegedly told an SBI investigator she'd never seen Lee, but when subpoenaed to testify was reported to be ill in the hospital all that week:

... In his argument to the jury, Lee's chief defense counsel, Bonner Sawyer of Hillsborough, made quick work of the question of his client's alibi: "Ladies and gentlemen of the jury," Sawyer boomed, "You certainly don't expect a madam to admit she's in business!"

And that, was that ...

(3/22/62)

As a matter of information to comparative newcomers, the Crook's Corner Restaurant on W. Franklin St. is the site of Rachel Crook's personal establishment, and is so named commemorating her and the tragedy that ended her life.

Chapter 10

Tar Heels as a Species

There is much that needs improvement in this state. But what is different about North Carolina is that the rugged individualism of its citizenry prevents our glossing over these sins of omission and commission. Being the legendary Vale of Humility has done us no harm.

Just as there are distinct qualities about Chapel Hillians, so there are inherent traits that are distinctive to North Carolinians. Through the years I have been reminded many times of the state's Latin motto, "Esse quam videri"—to be, rather than to seem—as being coincidentally appropriate to its later-adopted nickname, "the vale of humility between two mountains of conceit." It's not that North Carolina is the home of the meek, but rather that its tradition is to be concerned with substance rather than just image.

The North Carolinian, the Tar Heel, if you please, does not fit into any neat box as a personality, for rugged individualism is definitely a traditional quality of this species. But as a Tar Heel watcher, as well as a Tar Heel citizen, I have speculated as to what is distinctive about us.

... —Indeed, what is the product of the mixture of this state of thwarted beginnings in the Lost Colony years before Jamestown was settled; a state for decades the most backward of the original 13; yea—the next to the last of the 13 to ratify the Constitution, and to secede from the Union; the state often labeled "a little bit of everything and nothing much of anything."
(11/5/59)

Many have gone before me in this. One who spoke well to this idea was the late State Senator Irving E. Carlyle, a long-time Winston-Salem attorney and respected public servant. In a civic club talk he discussed what he felt were the distinctive qualities of North Carolina and its people:

138

... "Being a neighbor of Virginia, South Carolina, and Tennessee has meant a lot to our state and not the least of the meaning is our difference from them and their difference from us," he diplomatically declared in prologue. Basically, native son Carlyle said in sincere self-flattery, "North Carolinians have shown repeatedly that they will do their own thinking ... and that as a state they are not afraid to go it alone."

Here are the four attitudes which he declares typify North Carolinians, and which have molded the character of the state:

(1) "The respect of its people for public office." Politician Carlyle amplified this in stating "It is inconceivable that the people of this state would elect a Bilbo ... Talmadge ... or Faubus to any public office."

Quality Number Two of the North Carolinian is that he "is different because of the respect of the people for education. "... Carlyle ... plugged hard for passage of North Carolina's Constitutional Amendments that provide for local option public school pupil assignment. And these laws have allowed token desegregation over the past three years while not a single public school has been closed, though legally they might be.

Quality Number Three: "North Carolina is different because of the respect of its people for law and order ... The day has now passed when a political campaign based on the racial or religious supremacy of any group can succeed in this state."

Finally, what makes the Tar Heel tick, says analyzer Carlyle, is "the respect of its people for the liberal tradition." To be a bit more specific on this innately un-specific facet, he re-labeled it as the North Carolinian's "emphasis on human rights in preference to property rights."

... All of this ... adds up to what North Carolina historian John Wheeler called in 1851 "a high moral feeling." ...

(11/5/59)

You could start an argument quickly today over whether North Carolinians have shown, a quarter-century after Carlyle's words, that they wouldn't elect a "Bilbo..or Talmadge," and that as a generality they truly respect the "liberal tradition." My own perspective is that Irving Carlyle's appraisal yet rings true. His message must be considered in the tenor of those times.

For instance, he spoke courageously and successfully to prevent North Carolina's public schools from being closed at a time when they were racially segregated. The schools of Chapel Hill were totally segregated then, too, and racial integration of them was a highly-controversial idea.

Though the Constitutional Amendment to permit local option pupil assignment was later voided by court edict, the course of history shows it served its temporary purpose.

Native son Charles Kuralt, an unparalleled Chapel Hill and North Carolina partisan, espoused the "feel" of Tar Heelia from a broader viewpoint:

Carolina's Charles Kuralt is so popular with all of us among the Great Unwashed for a simple reason. He is "just plain folks" in his view of us, and himself. Yea, we love to worship a father figure like Eisenhower sometimes, and we revere Cronkite. But Kuralt we can relate to directly, for his easygoing credibly humorous insight and absence of pomp.

At his talk here the other night he reiterated his belief in the "little people" he talks to all over the country as "the real America." He finds a wonderful humanness and growing decency as he criss-crosses the byways of this great land. For all the problems we have, he believes there is good reason for optimism. His upbeat faith is heartening, even as we turn back to realize the hard facts of "That's the way it is."

All the same, there is bound to be a lot of good in a TV idol who doesn't take himself too seriously. Charlie recalled an episode back during the bicentennial year. Moving around the country, he was honored in many different ways—made a Kentucky colonel, then an official member of an American Indian tribe. —Whereupon his cameraman, Izzy, remarked to him sardonically, "You're working your way up to Jew."

(2/17/78)

The august New York Times put its journalistic microscope on North Carolina some years ago in a syndicated story which seemed to me "quite a grab bag of material" intended to show this state as a sham of progressivism in the South. Naturally I reacted:

... No sir, I am not going to fall into the trap of being a Cornpone Defender. The Yankees and pre-judgers can write what they want about Down Home in North Carolina. To deny or demur would be to dignify.

That is not the point. There is much that needs improvement in this state. But what is different about North Carolina is that the rugged individualism of its citizenry prevents our glossing over these sins of omission and commission. Being the legendary Vale of Humility has done us no harm.

Indeed, we cannot be joyful over a bad "image." But in continuously prodding—often even plodding—we are making some worthwhile progress.

It is quite to the heart of the Tar Heel ethic that the State motto is "To be, rather than to seem." "Images" are for those who seek illusion rather than substance.

(2/24/78)

An increasing media obsession with the "image" of North Carolina finally gained the journalistic best of me:

More and more recently a gaggle of other durn fool columnists have taken up the cry. They berate North Carolina for falling from the grace of its earlier days — back when its cudgel was courage and Tar Heelia was patronized as the pioneer of the Old South. "Bad image" today, they declare — that the Old North State is no longer the bastion of "liberalism," the courageous leader within the yet benighted Confederacy.

I gag. "They" cite a mixed bag of buzz-words to "prove" their point: Wilmington 10, Joan Little, Ku Klux Klan, and HEW lawsuit against the University.

North Carolina has its faults today, just as it did in an earlier era when some of our visionary leaders led the quest for justice. That the issues are more complicated today, only makes it more compelling to pursue them. The real culprit now is our simplistic demand for instant gratification.

(2/24/78)

The literal "image" of North Carolina might have been the turtle — plodding, unimaginative dumb animal that he is. A state legislator announced some years ago that he planned to introduce a bill to declare the shell-backed animal the official state reptile. The News and Observer editorially opposed the idea, citing the less attractive qualities of the turtle and "warning that we'd be laughed at by witlings from elsewhere." I observed that the idea didn't seem to me one of the Great Issues of the time, but I was more impressed by the notion that "the turtle, slow but sure, typifies North Caroliona's steady progress — and eventual victory at the finish line." ...

(1/19/79)

It reminded me of an earlier decision on the symbol for one of Chapel Hill's most significant institutions:

Leave problems to the young, without adult interference, and they'll work 'em out all right. How true that seems, in the case of the Chapel Hill Senior High School student body's decision to adopt the tiger as its symbol, in place of the wildcat.

The issue came about as a result of the racial integration of the all-Negro Lincoln High School with Chapel Hill High. Nominally the previous traditions of Chapel Hill High were carried on. Most of those of Lincoln were lost, since the racial integration meant a physical move out of Lincoln. The issue having been deliberated by an official student government group this past summer, and being recommended by it but obviously with the votes of a good number of white students, the traditional Chapel Hill wildcat was dropped, and the former Lincoln tiger was chosen as the official symbol.

... I spent 12 years in the old wildcat school. But what is in that symbol of other days is not important. It is symbolized by the way in which the decision to change was reached.

(9/7/69)

Another beautiful illustration of how to resolve acrimony is typified in the very fundamental and natural manner of the late great Paul Green, Chapel Hill humanitarian and playwright. The story may or may not be true, but I have heard it for so many years, that it's touted as gospel, and makes a worthy point:

A recent newspaper story reported that Democratic senatorial nominee John Ingram had attacked Sen. Jesse Helms as a "spendthrift" over his multi-million dollar campaign war chest. Asked to comment on Ingram's charge, Helms was quoted as replying simply: "Bless John's heart. I know he feels that he must say something."

That brought to mind a reverse of the same message that has been reported as local legend for many years. Story is that Jesse, as a TV commentator, delivered a scathing attack on the views of Chapel Hill playwright Paul Green on some social issue. A local reporter telephoned Mr. Green for comment, reciting what Helms had said. "Did Jesse really say all that?" Mr. Green asked quietly. "Yes sir, Mr. Green," the reporter responded.

"Well bless old Jesse's heart," said Mr. Green. And that ended that.

Whether the Paul Green incident is true or not, both of the "blessings" neatly illustrate how perfectly a well-turned soft answer can totally upstage an attack.

— So what is new since The Master taught us all of this 2,000 years ago?

(7/31/78)

The State of North Carolina suffers from an identity crisis in the same way that South Carolina does from the fact that both call themselves "Carolina." Despite its potential for the accusation of chauvinism, there is some

'Whose Moon?'

Gator Bowl weekend ad in the
Jacksonville Journal – 1979

There is only
one CAROLINA · · ·
It's located in Columbia!

sponsored by a Gamecock

*historical validity in the idea that North Carolina is the "real" one, which I
cited in the column as applied to alma mater and published under the
headline "Name-Nappers:"*

We call it simply "Carolina" – our affectionate short name for the first
state university here in Chapel Hill. Trouble is that quite a faithful following
of the University of South Carolina folk call their institution by the same
name.

In response to a recent inquiry from a Carolina (Chapel Hill) alumnus, the
Alumni Office attempted to determine which is the **real** Carolina. The quest
brought forth some interesting rationale – and lack thereof.

There are broad implications in the issue. Terry Sanford – a loyal UNC-
Chapel Hill alumnus – was taken aback when at governors conferences back
in the early 60s he saw his South Carolina counterpart, Fritz Hollings, stand
up when the band played "Carolina Moon" and "Carolina in the Morning."
Hollings allowed he was naturally proud to stand and take a bow when "his"
state's songs were played.

Sanford dispatched then State Archivist H.G. Jones to research the matter
and find out which Carolina was really in the minds of the song writers.
They copped out and stood squarely on the fence. However, Jones (now
Curator of the University Library's North Carolina Collection) noted the

lyrically northward leaning of the words to the song itself. That line "Carolina moon, I'm **pining**" betrayed a transparent bow to the Land of the Long-Leaf Pine, rather than the Palmetto State, he pointed out.

Declared Jones, "The whole thing reeks with North Carolina moonlight—except for the last two lines, which raise doubt, since one shouldn't be 'blue and lonely' in North Carolina." To that, partisans of UNC-Chapel Hill might well counter that anything "blue" obviously referred to the popular belief hereabouts that "God is a Tar Heel," by his painting the sky in North Carolina's hue.

When a Charleston newspaper took up the issue some years ago, Jones as NC State Archivist told their reporter stoutly, "You've stolen half of our name, you have the lower half of our rivers, the end of our mountains, and now you want our songs." ...

(12/28/79)

Of course no amount of logic will convince Sandlapper state partisans that they're not just as much or more entitled to be the real Carolina. In a scientific approach to the problem I called the University of North Dakota to find out if they had a similar situation with the University of South Dakota. That proved no help as the spokesman said "There's none of that 'Carolina Moon' stuff here. It's too durn cold." He added that to his ken the people of neither state popularly called their state or its public university "Dakota."

I did establish as a matter of history, insofar as the Universities of North and South Carolina are concerned, that Chapel Hill had the potential to be called "Carolina" long before the institution in Columbia did. U.S.C. was chartered as South Carolina College in 1801 and went by various names until finally being changed to the University of South Carolina in 1887. At that time the name of the student newspaper was changed to "The Carolinian." My conclusion, thus, was that this suggested a beginning for USC as "Carolina" coincident with its new name, and at a time more than three score and 10 years after Hinton James trekked the long miles from Wilmington to become the first student at "Carolina" in Chapel Hill.

I also had to admit that all of this resounding logic was lost on my wife, a native of Union, SC, who both graduated from and taught at the University of South Carolina. She still harkens back to the good old days at her "Carolina."

Naturally, in an independent-minded state like Tar Heelia, there's bound to be some fearsome internal bickering on even fundamental points such as this. About the time all of the above was being discussed I spotted bumper *stickers declaring "The Only **real** Carolina Is East Carolina," and, closer to home, "Duke – THE University of North Carolina."*

Politics provides the greatest opportunities for both capitalizing on and tripping up on one's identity as a native son:

One of the most telling un-intended slip-ups we heard from the campaign trail lately came from a political meeting in a nearby county. The candidates had just finished their speeches and the floor was opened for questions. "How would you stand on a gun control law for North Carolina?" one was asked. "I wouldn't mind such a law at all. In **my** state we already have such a law," the hopeful vote-seeker responded, not realizing how he'd so readily reminded everybody of his carpetbagger status.

(8/23/76)

Our former Congressman Jim Gardner revealed in the following gaffe why he failed to cut a wider and longer swath in elective office: In his brief Congressional career to date our own Hon. Jim Gardner has shown quite a flair for positive public relations, and has utilized certain public issues and the press quite effectively to his advantage. Now he's come a cropper; stubbed a political toe on his own forte and apparently doesn't realize it. First off – if informed press reports are correct – Hon. Jim wants to hire a New York public relations firm, the one that accompanied Barry Goldwater to his disaster, to aid his quest for the governorship.

Secondly, he's fallen into the same pit as Dick Nixon did in his fateful swan song to the public three years ago – the time when he apologized to the press that they wouldn't "have old Nixon to kick around any more." Gardner did this in his pitiful plaint that he couldn't "seem to get a fair shake from the News and Observer and the Charlotte newspapers" – a statement dutifully front-paged in both of these offending journals. Maybe the foggy air of Washington is getting him down. Yankee public relations hawkers and blasts at the major daily papers aren't yet gambits accepted as part and parcel of the humble Tar Heel ethic.

(8/30/67)

Through the years you hear so many of the same stock statements by political hopefuls. It brought me to issue a brief translation of several of these:

… "We must have long-range planning for our community … " (translation: Since I don't know what's going on this is a good way to learn. And it sure beats action.)

"What we need in our government is more business sense ... " (Translation: Let the taxpayer beware.)

"I am not running against anybody else—just FOR myself ... " (Translation: There really isn't much you can say about me.)

"What we need in this town is closer cooperation between the University and municipal government ... " (Translation: The University ought to kick in more dough for the town budget.)

(1/27/66)

A political institution that's been honed to a fine science in Chapel Hill, and has spread throughout the state is the "coffee" as a campaign ploy. I analyzed it as an "often uptight social institution whereby candidates for local office are thrust upon hapless friends of the coffee-giver at that person's home:"

... The host/hostess is the real "patsy" in the "coffee" situation. He/she has to scrounge around to inveigle all manner of innocents to attend. They are invited to assemble in the parlor, eat finger sandwiches, sip a demitasse, and listen to the candidate inveigh on the salvation he'll bring to the Great Unwashed if they'll only elect him ...

... Everybody is always on their best behavior ... The guests inevitably give the office-seeker the feeling he's the greatest human being to grace their presence since the creation of the Australian ballot ...

The real effect of the "coffee" is not in what happens at the occasion, but the spin-off later. Everybody who attends is automatically an instant authority—indeed, a campaign confidante and advisor to this temporary political celebrity. The rumor mill begins to work its wiles. By one scale of values I have calculated that every "coffee" attendee is good for 14 votes, figuring an average of 10 days campaign time remaining until election day ...

Frankly, I am now hoping that by the next campaign somebody will make a social breakthrough and sponsor a neighborhood "liquor" or perhaps a modest "beer." These wouldn't likely end up as polite as the "coffees" do, but they'd surely be more tolerable to us hard-core topers.

(11/11/77)

The love-hate relationship of North Carolinians toward the First State University is a fragile thing. Some years ago when Jesse Helms was a TV commentator he attacked the University administration for its defense of an English instructor who assigned students to write a paper on what Helms simplistically called "a theme of seduction:"

Through the years the accusation has been the same – only the specific events have been different. The perennial cry is, "They're stirring up a mess down there at Chapel Hill."

Thirty years ago a University English professor drew disdainful taunts at Chapel Hill for fellowshipping with a controversial Negro political candidate in Durham. The students of the late 30s caused an uproar because of their movement in support of the Lincoln Brigade fighting against Franco's armies in Spain. Openly-avowed Communists on the campus here 1946-52 made Chapel Hill again the "hotbed."

The mere fact that some people called it a "Red nest" some years later was cause for horrified finger-wagging in the wake of the Gag Law's passage ...

Regularly as seasonal cycles there will be "incidents" at Chapel Hill. All the incident watcher has to do is fill in the blanks ...

Chancellor Sitterson, asked recently if crisis was necessary to the health and mission of a good university, replied that the University should indeed have a spirit of "involvement" in society. President William Friday has now spoken even more strongly to this point: ...

"I believe that controversy is fundamental to the existence of a good major university. We've been almost constantly in one during my 10 years as President. The University should be a place where the students and faculty can speak and act freely within the law, and the University should protect them."

President Friday realistically recognized that a university cannot effectively remain an ivory tower from history in the making ... We should keep his words in mind in Chapel Hill – and live within the vital spirit of them, immediately painful as it may be from time to time.

(10/26/66)

Controversy has in fact become a way of life in Chapel Hill, distinct from the pattern of harmony that citizens of the rest of the state seem to naturally seek:

There is no place that thrives on controversy the way Chapel Hill does. By the very nature of its reason for existence and the genus of human animals that live in it, the university community nurtures and naturally cultivates good controversy ...

... the community conscience has been aroused to choose up sides no less vigorously on anything from the cutting down of a single slender sapling to the mightiest issue argued before the United Nations. These have included the moral rightness of building home fallout shelters, the necessity of fraternities, corporal punishment in the public schools, dog control, and the late Great Hamburger War.

At a local civic club meeting some years ago spokesmen for the Arab and the Jewish points of view shared the after-dinner program. The two speakers disagreed sharply – almost violently. Each eloquently stated his position and vehemently denounced the other.

At the end of the meeting a number of members went up to one speaker or the other and some to both, to express their apologies and embarrassment over the "scene" that had been created.

They needn't have. It was one of the most informative, interesting, and stimulating programs ever presented before the group. And it was quite in keeping with the constructive spirit of controversy in this community.
(3/10/66)

That was a regular meeting of the Chapel Hill Rotary Club and the program chairman who arranged the controversial program was Edward G. ("Papa D") Danziger, the Viennesse candy-maker who came to Chapel Hill as a refugee after Hitler invaded Austria. At this particular meeting of the Rotary Club, while the other members were lined up to express their apologies to the two speakers I walked up to Papa D, standing all by himself, and told him it was the best program we'd had in months.

My commenting on our traditional Tar Heel traits brought on the well-intended ire of a reader once. I wrote about it under the heading "Too Uptight:"

"Aint that just like a Yankee!" we wrote in mock disdain of the breach of etiquette by Miss America. The beauty queen from New York had tactlessly turned down an offering of grits during a breakfast in Atlanta. But the Newspaper columnist's flippancy brought in the mail a demand for an apology from a self-proclaimed Yankee. "You wouldn't dream of saying 'Isn't that just like a black or Jew or Episcopalian,' the reader chastened. 'Wouldn't you bridle if I said 'Well isn't that just like a Southerner!'' "

Naturally I wrote her back and assured her I meant no real slight to anybody in the entire family of mortals. But as a fellow Yankee, I simply couldn't get all uptight over the little snippet of sarcasm I'd written about Miss America. That I was born in Fall River, Massachusetts, and was brought to Chapel Hill as an infant by my Yankee parents doesn't make me sensitive about my status as a Northerner, about my lifetime in these southern boondocks, nor the accident of birth and circumstances that led me to become a member of the white Presbyterian minority on this big blue marble.

We're all too sensitive, defensive, and humorless about our human foibles. To be able to recognize and accept jesting jibes about ourselves is a quality of grace that we sorely need. — Enough of the posture that makes us so stiff-spined we have to be constantly demanding our rights, guarding against even unintended slights, and preaching down to each other!!

Now I've said it all. — Aint that just like a newspaper columnist — playing god to everybody!

(9/29/75)

The conception of stereotypes is general. My good friend Jean Holcomb recalls her first trip to Chapel Hill in 1957 when she and her husband were considering moving here from Wisconsin. A delegation from Chapel Hill met them at Raleigh-Durham Airport for breakfast. The waitress brought everybody's breakfast order, but failed to put grits on Jean's plate. When she inquired, the waitress, acknowledging Jean's midwest accent by implication, simply explained "I didn't think you'd want any."

In that same spirit I recall that in my World War II army days I once went to the first sergeant of our infantry rifle company and asked him if I could go to jeep drivers school. He summarily told me go get out in what I figured was basic style for first sergeants. Two weeks later, while our company was on a training exercise out in the boondocks of Ft. Bragg, he sent for me and declared "Giduz, you're going to jeep drivers school — but it's not because you asked." Again I figured that was standard style for first sergeants — that he just didn't want to admit to doing anything nice for me.

Years later I met this New Jersey fellow at a reunion and recited the incident for him. He demurred. "You've got it all wrong. I knew all you southern boys had been driving tractors out in the fields from the time you were 10-years-old, so you'd be the best person for a jeep driver." — Thus was my previous lifetime in the academic community of Chapel Hill stylized by an honest Yankee first sergeant.

Chapter 11

Racial Issues and Their Solution

All must realize that there is no longer, nor should there be, any such thing as "our" university, country, and world, except insofar as it is that of all of us, black and white, any race, and regardless of race.

Two vignettes from some years ago poignantly illustrate both the simplicity and the complexity of racial issues. The simplicity was aptly revealed in a story about a white and a black congregation in Raleigh that swapped churches for a month each year. That is, during the month their ministers were on vacation, each body attended Sunday services with the other. As a result of the experience, at least one child made an "A" on integration:

... The white child's parents explained to her that for this reason they would be going to "the black church." After they returned from services there the mother asked her how she'd liked the black church. "It wasn't black at all," declared the youngster. "It was red." With such innocent wisdom coming from the mouths of babes, let us all go forth and think likewise.

(7/26/70)

The complexity of the issue was illustrated in a Chapel Hill situation. As a move to resolve a near riot over an alleged racial incident a meeting of the student body was held at Phillips Junior High School to air questions and complaints from students on all sides.

... Among those who arose to speak was one well-meaning lad with a sincere complaint. He declared that he was tired of having black students pushing and shoving in the hallways, and tired of having black students making uncalled-for remarks. In fact, he said it appeared to him that the black students were "trying to take over **our** school."

It took nearly 15 minutes to restore a semblance of order ...

(10/1/69)

That remark by the white student had a germ of historical accuracy at the time, but that, of course, is the pity of it all. This point, which seems so fundamental and simple today, was in the process of evolution just a few years ago. In writing about it, I concluded:

... There is a lesson to be learned and a responsibility to be accepted by parents and young people alike in this. All must realize that there is no longer, nor should there be, any such thing as "our" school, or "our" town, nor "our" university, country, and world, except insofar as it is that of all of us, black and white, any race, and regardless of race.

(10/1/69)

One of the difficulties was the lingering stigma attached to integration, even in supposedly sophisticated Chapel Hill, where the process was carried out without significant violence or litigation. A county-wide school construction bond referendum was held in 1966. The Chapel Hill School system was to be a major beneficiary, and receive $1.5 million for a new junior high school. The 15-year-old Lincoln High School building was to be abandoned, since a new fully integrated high school was being built north of town. It seemed to many of us the natural thing to do to simply convert the vacant Lincoln building, though located in the heart of a black neighborhood, to a junior high school:

... And the real underlying issue for Chapel Hill's end of the bond referendum is whether the people there want to support this official decision by borrowing $1.5 million for a new junior high school, while sacrificing a perfectly good existing junior high school building – plus another Negro school (Northside).

As The News editor put it – "We are going to have to pay for our prejudices as well as our school population growth."

(9/8/66)

The voters of the county did choose to "pay for their prejudices," having no other choice on the ballot. The abandoned Lincoln School building was converted to one of the most commodious administrative office buildings any

school system of only 5,000 pupils has ever had. And the new Culbreth
Junior High School was built for $1.5 million a mile south of it.

Many years later the legal issues involved in eliminating racial discrimination in the public schools here had been resolved. But Superintedent
Pamela Mayer spoke succinctly to the point in 1981 when she said "Schools
have been desegregated. Now they need to be integrated." — To which point
I wrote: "... what she said is that the law has been met, but minds and hearts
have not yet been altered sufficiently; that this will take positive effort."
(5/11/81)

While the community was acclimating itself to the law of the land on
integrating its public schools, public opinion was working against segrega-
tion in other realms. One of the earliest was in local movie theaters. The
strategy of the moderate element locally was to try to assure theater
operators they need not fear a loss of patronage if they opened their doors to
black spectators. In a poll conducted on campus the results overwhelmingly
favored the theaters' desegregation:

... A total of 1,800 of the 9,000 students enrolled were questioned in the
poll, thus it can probably be considered a fair cross-section of the student
body. Student patrons are the mainstay of the local movie houses, so if 87
per cent of them chose to act on their belief regarding the theaters'
desegregation by not patronizing them now, there'd be some mighty slim
houses ...
(3/23/61)

Discussion of the issue continued for many months before the inevitable
came about and the theaters were quietly opened to blacks. Citizens groups
picketed the movie houses, many meetings were held, and long lists of
people asking that the movies be desegregated were published in the local
newspapers. The press was criticized by theater managers for writing too
much about the issue:

... In the present situation of theater desegregation in Chapel Hill, the
people preaching for withholding of information are way behind the public
on the whole issue. Theater desegregation in Chapel Hill is a foregone
conclusion—not a matter of "if," but imminently "when." It is obvious that it
is going to come about soon, and the public knows this whether the public
generally likes it or not.
(12/21/61)

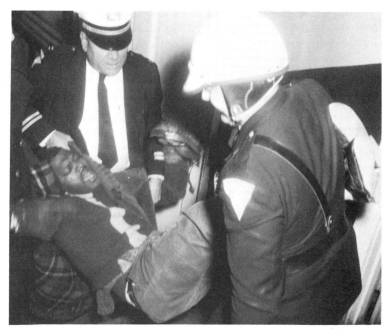

'Freedom demonstrator' Hilliard Caldwell, as passive resister, being taken into custody by Chapel Hill Policemen Coy Durham (left) and Lindy Pendergrass – 1963

The most significant and dramatic of Chapel Hill's struggles over civil rights issues occurred in the winter of 1964 during the campaign for passage of a local public accommodations ordinance. That era was marked by massive sit-ins, street and highway lie-ins, quasi-military intrigue, and endless conferences. The almost 1,500 trespass arrests clogged the court dockets for three years. The Chapel Hill Board of Aldermen considered but did not pass a local law barring racial discrimination in private business service. However, that was resolved on July 4, 1964, when Congress, as expected, passed a nationwide law to the same effect.

The campaign that evolved into the push for enactment of a local public accommodations ordinance began with a lie-in at the office of the Chapel Hill-Carrboro Merchants Association by an activist group of Lincoln High School students. Sensing a couple of days before that something was about to happen, I invited the activist leaders, Hilliard Caldwell and Harold Foster, to come to my home to talk things over along with my good friend and neighbor, Ed Tenney. The four of us had a frank, and, it seemed to me, a respectful discussion for several hours. But during the time it was apparent that the die was cast for what we learned the next day was the opening gun of the local civil rights campaign—the lie-in at the Merchants Association office.

Again, what seems a simple issue now did not so appear at that time. While all civic and governmental leadership was publicly united on the goal of eliminating all forms of racial discrimination, the issue at hand was more complicated than that. It was whether a precedent-setting local law for which the town had questionable authority should be passed as an inspiration to other communities, and not just the simple accomplishment of the purpose of such a law.

The Board of Aldermen became the focus of the issue, and as a reporter/ editor I was at the center of it all. My non-aligned position was exasperating for many people, and made life difficult for me. Quite simply, my stand was: (1) That accomplishment of the goal was more important than passing the local law; (2) That municipal government in North Carolina did not have the required state authority to pass such a law and, thus, was specifically prohibited from doing so; and (3) that the expected imminent passage of a nationwide civil rights law by Congress was the most appropriate means of carrying out this objective.

Those arguments palled on the sincerely zealous partisans of a local public accommodations law. Various civil rights groups, including the nationwide Congress of Racial Equality (CORE) focused their efforts on Chapel Hill. At one time there were nine separate committees in town all pressing for this law. There were almost daily parades, then called "demonstrations," massive acts of civil disobedience, not just against segregated businesses, but also against the local government for failing to pass the desired public accommodations law.

During a Board of Aldermen discussion of this issue I once stated that I would "not be affected in working toward this goal (the elimination of racial discrimination) by any and all extreme pressure tactics for the enactment of a public accommodations law. In short, I will not be intimidated or stampeded in any way to pass such a law." The "not be intimidated" part was picked up by the national press and brought me a flood of unneeded pro and con mail from all around the country. At the time it seemed to me that:

... the community is inflamed by the Pharisees who view the issue as such a simple one, solvable in a nonce by elementary steps: "Pass the law;" "Lock 'em all up;" "Turn down the law once and for all;" "Call a town

'Demonstrators' picketing W. Franklin St. dairy bar, 3/7/60

meeting and give the issue a good airing out;" or "Tell 'em you won't budge an inch until the outsiders leave." These are a few of the suggestions, many of them given in truly concerned sincerity, that come to the aldermen and those rightfully charged with leadership in the situation.

The best thinking and suggestions of all citizens are sorely needed, indeed. But the diligence and patience of one and all is even more necessary in the face of the opposite views of the "nay-sayers" and the "yes-now" militants. ...

(1/30/64)

All of this is not to be unduly critical of the activists of that era. Their lot was not easy. After attending a meeting to discuss the situation once, I wrote about the division within the group on a particular issue:

... It happened that almost all of the white persons in attendance voted one way on this motion, and the Negroes, the other. However, a scattering of Negroes stood up to vote with the white majority. At this point one of the Negro leaders ... declared with bitterness, "I'd like to get the names of all the Negroes who are standing now."

— Couldn't help being reminded of another incident a couple of weeks

beforehand. This same leader was standing before his fellow members of the Committee for Open Business as they sang songs of brotherhood and protest in front of the Chapel Hill jail where some of their number were at that moment imprisoned. With lusty voice and fervor befitting the occasion, he led the group in singing "Black and White Together."
(8/8/63)

Most moving of all the demonstrations was a lie-in of several weeks duration by a group of young activists who fasted on the flagpole grass in front of the downtown post office. Their goal, of course, was passage by the aldermen of the proposed public accommodations ordinance, and the extent of their conviction was impressive. While I could not agree to do their bidding, it seemed to me that "the price of life in a free society requires that the right of peaceful difference of opinion be preserved," and I further wrote:

... in historical perspective Chapel Hill may be shown to have been direlict in answering its obligation to the cause of brotherhood. It should have the humility to admit this as it plods the difficult path to bring about the justice for all and equality of opportunity that is the necessary and proper goal ...

The only thing the post office sitters-in have proven is that they want something very much—in short, that they are sincere. This, however, has never been basically in issue.
(4/2/64)

The campaign ended quietly on July 4 when Congress enacted the civil rights law, after which I noted:

... There can be no quarrel with the intent of the new civil rights law. People of good faith may differ as to its legality and effectiveness ... But there can be no quibbling about its existence and the business operations to which it applies ...

Every businessman in Orange County who is affected by the new law will be acting in his own self-interest, if not in the interests of the community and the spirit of Christian brotherhood, if he acts to comply with the law as expeditiously as possible.
(7/9/64)

While the civil right issue was then settled as a legal matter, the fall-out from it lingered for three years until:

The last of what amounted to nearly 1,500 court cases on civil rights-

'Freedom parade' in downtown Chapel Hill, 5/23/63

based charges brought against defendants in Orange County during 1963 and 1964 was finally resolved this week. The US Supreme Court in Washington upheld the appeal of Duke Zoology Prof. Peter Klopfer against a nol pros with leave verdict. It was left "hanging" over him a year after his case ended in a mistrial. Many other cases were terminated by nol pros with leave, but only Dr. Klopfer appealed. To allow the Orange County Superior Court's decision to stand, legally leaving his case open to prosecution at any time, was a denial of his right to a speedy trial under the sixth amendment to the Constitution, the high court unanimously held. – And so, it all began one chilly, drizzly winter evening with a sit-in at Watts Grill ... and ended in the hallowed halls of the US Supreme Court over four years later this week – the decision that guarantees a defendant the right to a speedy trial. **(3/15/67)**

Enactment of the various civil rights laws marked the end of a long crusade, but also the beginning of an era of suspicion that continues to some extent through to the present. The late Harry Golden, who in his Carolina Israelite had strongly supported the civil rights laws, was concerned that the spirit of confrontation was replacing conference:

... He may well be right about this. Our local, state, and federal governments have passed many just and fair laws in recent years which insure the constitutional rights of persons who have been illegally and unjustly discriminated against.

But perhaps we have indeed come to depend too much on the uncommunicative arm of the law in these matters. The laws require that we act in a certain manner. They do not require that we understand why the laws are just, nor do they necessarily bring previous antagonists closer to reconciliation.

It is axiomatic that anything we can naturally and successfully acccomplish without the fetters of laws is done better. But in this complex society we must, of course, have laws. And these, in part, bring on our dilemmas – and the lack of "dialogue" that Harry Golden sees.

(8/24/66)

... "Civil Rights Movement Is Dead" reads a headline in The Weekly, referring to opinions garnered in an interview with a University political scientist ... The populace should hope that this movement is dead because the need for it has been eliminated and racial discrimination ended – at the least, ended as government has authority to end it. Perhaps that is why the Mayor's Committee on Human Relations, a body set up six years ago by local ordinance, has been dead here in enlightened Chapel Hill. Unfortunately, in this realm, the local citizenry has been more concerned with cure than prevention.

(1/18/67)

As feared, the spirit of acrimony did increase in the wake of the new civil rights laws. After participating in a local church-sponsored "dialogue" meeting on the comparatively new phenomenon of "black power" I wrote:

... "whitey" was told, and he'd better believe it, too, that Black Power advocates will use any means to attain their end, which they state in occasionally gentler terms, is to get their piece of the action. Whitey was reminded time and again that his ancestors had enslaved the blacks for 300 years and had not yet granted them justice. The small progress made toward dropping the bonds have only made the black man more impatient because he has at last experienced a little of what he should be having.

... the place to start is by eliminating the lingering discrimination from which the dangerous racism of Black Power gains its nourishment One spokesman for this concept declared that it was necessary to inculcate into the black person the idea that "black is beautiful" because he had had no pride in himself as a person ...

I will agree with the initial premise. But the fatality of this notion in the spirit of the "master race" is that it will create a monster that cannot be controlled. Certainly the white race by its past historical action has laid the groundwork for today's reaction. But this is not a sin for which even our untaught children of today can be rightfully convicted even before they know the difference between races purely because they happen to be white. What is needed is less race pride by all, and the acceptance of any person as a unique human being ...

(3/17/68)

Feelings worsened during the succeeding year:

On campus Wednesday afternoon I heard Durham Negro militant Howard Fuller exhorting student listeners at the entrance of strike-bound Lenoir Hall. Moments before I'd heard excerpts on a radio news report of a statement by NC State Univ. Chancellor John T. Caldwell at a convocation of his institution in Raleigh. The contrast in attitudes of the two speakers, addressing similar audiences on basically the same topic, was timely and significant.

"You students are the real niggers on this campus," shouted Fuller. "How much do you have to say about how this University is run?"

Addressing himself to student militants, Chancellor Caldwell declared, "You young people of this great and promising generation have some important work to do while you have the time and energy and independence and idealism to get it done. The world can use your noisy impatience, your fearless insistence on a new scale of values, and your deep inside goodness. But it doesn't need from you or anybody else hate, or lawlessness, or vulgarity. And we don't deserve it here."

Again from Fuller: "It's supposedly hard to find the money to make this (the Lenoir Hall workers) raise, but they find the money to equip the 'pigs,' and they go out and pay some idiot $1,500 to lecture on something that doesn't make any sense."

"Stop being so disgustingly self-righteous," declared Chancellor Caldwell. "Self-righteousness is the most unbecoming, unproductive, and unenjoyable of all the sins in the catalogue ... If there's steam in your boiler, let's put it through the cylinders. If the cylinders can't take it, let's design some new ones ... This is the way to bring the new day you want, instead of a wreckage nobody wants."

With which speaker would you ally yourself?

3/9/69)

Another reaction to the progress of the civil rights movement was the occasional rise of the Ku Klux Klan around the state and even in Orange County. I followed this with interest, beginning with a rally of more than 2,500 masked and hooded Klansmen near Whiteville in 1951. Assigned to cover that occasion for the Durham Morning Herald, I briefly interviewed Grand Dragon Tom Hamilton, who assured me "This is a public meeting. You take your pictures and write up what you see." Many years later I recalled what happened next:

... Bulky Speed Graphic camera in hand, I took him at his word and flashed a shot of the hooded "knights" as they rode in on horseback. Instantly a corps of goons grabbed me and hauled me backstage. "Take me to your leader," I appealed. Finally they did, and he assured them it was okay for me to fire away. "These reporters are all right," he explained. "The newspapers just won't print what they write." (That was, by the way, one of the latter big hurrahs of the Klan before the State Legislature enacted an unmasking law.)

(12/8/75)

Occasionally in comparatively recent years there have been Klan rallies in Orange County. At one of these near Hillsborough I felt that I had:

... never witnessed a more venomous outpouring of racial poison than that delivered from the speaker's platform of the Klan rally in Orange County last Saturday night. Some statements, allegations, and supposed jokes are too indecent to be published. This is a free country, and freedom of speech, within the law, must apply to the Ku Klux Klan as well as to responsible organizations. But we shall certainly hope that this unhealthy spectacle is no more than a passing cycle again ...

(8/6/64)

One of the more graphic experiences I had in covering the Klan was the day it staged a rally in Raleigh just before the Rev. Martin Luther King spoke on the NC State University campus. His speech, as I later recalled it, was even more dramatic against the background of the earlier Klan rally:

... "I look to the day not of the white man nor of the Negro man—but of man as man," said Martin Luther King. The echo from Klan leader George Dorsett came back from an hour earlier: "... Let them know you're white people and they're niggers ... We're making history right now. All that is needed is dedicated white people, patriotic Americans."

Then Martin Luther King spoke again: "The Negro is freer in 1966, but

Ku Klux Klan rally near Whiteville, 8/18/51

he is not free. We now stand on the border of the promised land of integration. The only question is how costly the segregationist will make the funeral."

The Grand Dragon's wife had put it differently: "Today we're standing together for equal opportunity ... They holler for black power. It would be nice to have some white power."

Stronger yet, the Rev. Mr. King declared with fervor: "The doctrine of black superiority is as evil as the doctrine of white superiority ... The rise of black power is only in response to the failure of white power to give justice to the Negro."

The Klan leader had good words for North Carolina: "We've made it from a moderate state to Klansville USA. It's the greatest Klan state in the country."

Well, at least on that he found some accord with the message of the Coliseum speaker (Rev. King): "North Carolina has some good qualities and has been reasonable ... But it amazes me that a state which prides itself on being the most liberal in the South can also have the largest meetings of the Ku Klux Klan ..."

The challenges rang out on one side of town and the answers came back.

As the applause in the coliseum faded, one of the choral groups filing out of the hall put the question in a final hymn—"Which Side Are You On, Brother?"

(8/3/66)

Through the years I gained a passing acquaintanceship with some Klan leaders, including Grand Dragon Bob Jones. He consented to come to what he called "Communist Hill" for an interview I participated in on Station WCHL. Analyzing his ideas as expressed at that meeting later, I wrote:

... when he talks about Communism at Chapel Hill, he is not talking about the generally-accepted definition of this ideology—the kind that the blue-ribbon Gag Law Study Commission sought at Chapel Hill and couldn't find. He is talking about some things as basic to contemporary civiliization in the United States as public welfare, prohibitions against racial discrimination, and a sophisticated approach to global diplomacy—you know, "socialism." And these "radical" views are eloquently voiced in Chapel Hill.

(7/10/68)

The ideological nature of Chapel Hill is at least in part a matter of what's fashionable. While we may be gratified that the simplistic views of the Grand Dragon are not valid, we are too often less than tolerant of conservative views of any type here. Charlotte Observer Publisher Rolfe Neill once wrote that the conservative was the "leper of American society and is treated as if malignant and unspeakably backward in outlook." This seemed to me to apply to Chapel Hill:

... Here in intellectually sequestered, free-thinking Chapel Hill, we clasp liberal ideology to our community bosom. It is equated with "enlightened thinking," "progressive-minded," being compassionate and all those good things ...

The cold facts of political life in Chapel Hill are that dealing with and acceptance of the liberal psyche is necessary to progress, and even to continued healthy existence. Local history in the past decade proves that the scant exceptions to the rule were no more than passing fancies—amusing little dalliances to prove the comparative virtue of dominance by the liberal ideology.

... In a place such as Chapel Hill—dedicated to the development of young people and the spirit of change—it is natural that the conservative spirit is in a minority.

(9/7/79)

Chapter 12

Crusades

The freedom afforded a personal opinion columnist was heady wine. Inspiration for the issue of the moment frequently came from readers, but often as not from the day's news.

Editorial crusades for all manner of minor and major issues have occupied the Newsman's Notepad across the years. Some of these were local causes: For example, the idea of a railroad train instead of school buses to the new high school site, which was not even accessible by any existing road. This was a middling serious hometown issue intended to evoke both humor and a view of the massive scope of the Chapel Hill of the future. Another crusade was for fluoridation of the local water supply, an ultimately successful campaign that covered several years.

Of more general concern were, for instance, continuing crusades for telephone courtesy, sportsmanship, specific changes in election laws, and against automobile horn honking as a means of personal greeting. The freedom afforded a personal opinion columnist was heady wine. Inspiration for the issue of the moment frequently came from readers, but often as not from the day's news. Such an example was the construction of the Jordan Reservoir, which area environmentalists and local government vigorously opposed. It's an issue not yet settled, since professionals have been divided on the lake's quality as a public water supply:

... The greatest pollution of local streams is the product of the town's sewage treatment plants. Only we don't notice it—most of us— because it only befouls the New Hope Creek valley below us. And in an amazing contradiction of aims, some of the local opponents of the New Hope (Jordan) Reservoir complain that its construction will require Chapel Hill to go to great expense to further purify our sewage effluent.

The implied presumption is that we should have the right to pollute our neighbors downstream. Even more obvious should be the necessity of improving our sewage treatment regardless of the outcome of the New Hope project court lawsuit. Ecological piety downstream surely cannot be legitimate grounds for upstream pollution.

(9/22/71)

Of course the Town did significantly upgrade its sewage treatment facilities and the lawsuit against the project failed — though there's no doubt it has resulted in effective pressure for a more environmentally sound reservoir. But after "columnizing" in favor of the reservoir project for more than 25 years, I was ready to appreciate a humorous note injected into the dedication ceremonies for Jordan Dam on May 1, 1982. Congressman Ike Andrews, speaking at that occasion, recalled the last time he'd heard "Jordan Dam" mentioned on such an auspicious occasion. He said it was the night Carolina was playing Georgetown for the NCAA basketball title in 1981. Andrews was watching the game on TV in Washington:

... A group of Georgetown fans behind him were jubilant as the Hoyas continued to lead in the final minute of the game. Then Carolina freshman Michael Jordan started dribbling down the court. The clock showed less than 20 seconds left, the score 62-61 in favor of Georgetown. "Michael Jordan sent up a jump shot about 20 feet away from the basket. I couldn't look. I ducked my head. Then I heard the Georgetown guy behind me holler 'Jordan ... damn!' I knew it went in and we won."

(5/3/82)

Meantime, while opinion in the scientific community is still divided on the quality of Jordan Reservoir water, the lake's use for recreational and flood control purposes is achieving its intended objectives.

Consumer concerns were natural topics for more general crusades in the column. While the positive changes came not as a result of my written opinions, I was glad to utter a small voice over a period of many years in favor of the federal truth-in-lending, advertising, and packaging laws, against the un-solicited issuance of bank credit cards, and for common sense automobile construction. Some consumer protection measures now taken for granted took a long time to achieve:

... one of the finest boons in consumer protection is the brand new innovation of unit pricing in grocery supermarkets. I hope that the pressure of free enterprise competition will force this into all types of merchandising.

As a result of this revolutionary trend in the grocery world, the shopper can tell at a glance what can, bottle, or package is less expensive by the pound, ounce, or square foot. This gives him a simple basis for comparing prices on different brands. Otherwise we have to compute whether two "giant economy size" packages at 79 cents are actually a better buy than the "large" size at 43 cents ...

(5/30/71)

Free enterprise competition has also wrought a full circle of changes in credit practices in just 10 years:

Perhaps we haven't appreciated them enough – those literally free credit cards from the banks. How, we have often pondered, could BankAmericard and Master Charge issue their plastic charge tickets free when the other big boys in the credit business, such as American Express, charged an annual membership fee?

The answer, of course, was that most users didn't pay off their charges within the first month of billing, and thus incurred the 18 pct. annual rate of interest on later payments ...

Perhaps the fact that too many of us are paying off our credit card accounts within the first month to avoid the interest charges is responsible for the move by some Master Charge bank groups to sock their users with a service charge on current month payments. Small as this token bargain was, it was too good to last.

(6/25/76)

Today some nationally accepted credit cards are again being issued free and the monthly service charges on paid-in-full accounts have been ended – all of which indicates that the public must be paying its bills slower, so the banks can make their profit on the interest charged on installment payments, and drop the annual card fees. Evidence of this appeared in my mailbox one day:

... No thanks, though, to the otherwise fine folks at BankAmericard for the circumlocution they have included on this month's credit card statement. I quote to you the salient part:

"... Because of your prompt payment record you may skip the payment due on this statement, if you desire. Normal finance charges will apply." ...

I certainly realize that BankAmericard is not going to make as much money on me if I pay my bills promptly at no interest charge as they will if I accept their invitation for a less "prompt payment record" and pay them 18 pct. interest on my credit. But I don't appreciate their deliberate attempt to (unsuccessfully) deceive me and imply that they're giving us "prompt payers" a favorable concession.

Federal laws enacted in recent years have required truth-in-lending statements in the extension of credit. The law ought to apply to this deceptive promotional message, too ...

(7/18/77)

One of my fundamental crusades throughout the years of columnizing has been for common courtesy. It was gratifying several years ago to read that even the New York City taxi organizations are sponsoring courtesy schools for their drivers. Because our slavish devotion to automobiles is so often related to discourtesy, I've written about this every few years:

With the sunny season fast coming on us, and warmer weather yet in the offing, people are naturally taking to wearing dark glasses more and more. Often they howdy to you in passing—a neighborly thing to do, of course. What they need to realize is that they're not only shielded from the sun, but from recognition, too. Thus handicapped, we sometimes feel like responding, "Hello, person."

In a similar situation are drivers who beep their horns in greeting from passing cars. Tinted windshields also protect their identities. Windows closed for air-conditioning serve to further disguise them. We pedestrians wave in anonymous response, then say silently, "Hello, car." ...

(4/14/80)

Because my own profession depends on use of the telephone as much as it does a typewriter, I've written a great deal about telephone courtesy Thirty years ago the worst offenders, I felt, were the "phone goops" who opened their calls with the terse question "Who's this?"

... Safest reply, according to The Newsman's experimentation, is to give your own name and in the same sentence inquire "... and who are you, please?"

Or if you still want to keep the upper hand you can quite safely, if not as politely, ask the "Who's this-er"—"To whom do you wish to speak?" or— "Who wants to know?"

Most of the time the phone goop who uses this approach is doing so out of ignorance instead of arrogance. But he's certainly getting off to a bad start with the fellow on the other end of the line, and leaving himself open to some equally rude retorts.

(1/10/57)

The slickest response I ever heard in answer to the "who's this-er," although etiquette bans it, is: "Your voice sounds familiar, but I'm not certain who you are," or: "I don't know," and then hang up. We should certainly forgive frustrated victims of the phone goops once in a while:

... we like the one about the guy who won revenge one day when the operator answered "682-1200," and he asked for Mr. Carson. "Who's calling?" she returned. "563-0680," he answered with joyful heart.

(8/15/75)

In poetic terms the prize-winning response surely must be this one in Dear Abby's column:

> When calling Mr. Jones
> I find it most appalling
> To have his secretary ask,
> "May I tell him who is calling?"
> One of these days
> When I find it all too taxing,
> I'll come right back to her and say
> "May I ask you, WHO IS ASKING?"

(11/17/72)

Prime present-day candidates for phone gooping are those secretaries who unnecessarily run interference—as at one campus office where the receptionist first demands your name, then transfers the call to the secretary who again asks you the same thing:

... Now I am not wholly unsympathetic to this gambit, for the telephone caller should not have carte blanche to interrupt everybody. Even ruder is the exec who will permit every Tom, Dick and Harry telephone caller to butt in while he's in a conference with some guy who's talking to him in person by previous appointment. But a whole lot of this "Who's calling?" business by secretaries is simply personal curiousity and self-aggrandizement ...

(6/25/67)

In this same spirit:

... how is it that so many otherwise rational and generally thoughtful persons will abjectly permit a telephone call to invade and upset their logically well-ordered routine?

... I can understand why it is necessary for them to have their girl Friday telephone and ask you to hold the line for Mr. Big. But it is the grossest affront to the person you are calling to do this unless it is truly necessary. Doing this in effect tells the person being called that his time is not as valuable as yours, and that it is all right for you to wait on the line for him, but not vice versa ...

(3/12/72)

Since I practically live on the telephone at the office every day I try to make it habit to ask everybody I call if it is convenient to talk to them at that time — and am not offended when the person asks me to call back at a specific time, or volunteers to do so himself. When you're being conned by an overly curious secretary, it's almost forgivable to give a snappy reply to the "May I tell him who's calling?" person: "No, I'll tell him myself."

Another frustration is remembering telephone numbers. I use all manner of mnemonic devices for this, but one of the most effective when it happens to work out, is to simply remember the letters on the dial instead of the numbers. At one time, for instance, "WEE BEER" was the number of the U.N.C. Dean of Women — so you can see why I remember that.

The telephone has a noble heritage as an honorable business enterprise. It occurred to me many times that it was one of the most successful operations against the trend of modern times:

... Public posture toward honesty is an ambivalent thing. The national average for shoplifting from variety stores, for instance, runs about five per cent of the gross sales.

Yet in contrast to this, the profit of the world's biggest corporation — American Telephone and Telegraph Co. — is obtained in large part on a pure honor system. Except where the Distance Dialing system is now in effect, the telephone company depends completely on the honesty of the caller in making toll billings for long distance calls. No doubt there are cheaters in this business, too, and the toll rates absorb and reflect this dishonesty so that the honest callers have to pay for it ...

(7/30/64)

All of that was in the pre-computer days, back when we could use counter checks at the bank as easily as our personalized ones, and most stores had individual charge accounts. In summary, my point is that telephone courtesy ought to be both permanent and fundamental. — As simple as the old chestnut Jim Phipps loved to tell:

... That was about the man who wanted a "halo box" in his new home, as

he explained to the puzzled building contractor. The "halo box," he said, was the little box you put on the wall and picked up a handle to say "Hay-lo."
...

(6/27/63)

In this University community where big-time college sports is so significant to our social fabric, the issue of courtesy is closely tied to athletics:

... Mob psychology all too often takes over—though common courtesy and good sportsmanship can and should be the automatic rule for all spectators. But excesses occur most of the time simply because of a momentary vacuum of leadership. Any one of a number of responsible persons could almost instantly take care of, stop, or prevent these unsportsmanlike situations—the Chancellor, the PA announcer, the home team coach, head cheerleader and members of his squad, athletic directors, or head ushers and/or security officers ...

(1/13/71)

... Of course the referees can put a quick halt to all of this if they want to by simply invoking their authority to call technical fouls on the home team. Cheerleaders can aid and abet the cause of civility, too, if they will. But the real responsibility naturally lies with us as fans. We can help the Heels by hollering for 'em and respecting the enemy.

(2/13/73)

In recent years the conduct of Carolina fans has consistently improved through leadership of various persons cited above. One of the most effective tactics for squelching discourtesy has been deliberate silence by the home team spectators—a mass reaction that has occasionally been spontaneous and successful.

A successful long-running crusade was the one I carried on for fluoridation of the local public water supply. I professed no real knowledge of the benefits of this treatment but was impressed that the University dental faculty unanimously endorsed it, while the University, which owned the water supply, failed to heed this counsel. Finally, after my good friend Manning Simons instigated a lawsuit to further forestall the long-delayed action (which I labeled "The Great Fluoridation Procrastination"), several of us formed an ad hoc group, the Citizens Fluoridation Committee. With about a thousand dollars in contributions we intervened in the suit as a friend of the court, and, I believe speeded up the inevitable decision to fluoridate by several years.

On a broader scale was my continuing appeal in behalf of passenger railroad service, as the most intelligent and environmentally sound method of mass transportation. I carried on the appeal by riding on and then writing about the last passenger train out of Orange County in October, 1962, and by continuing the editorial crusade through and since the beginning of AMTRAK service in 1971:

... rail transport is the nation's safest — less than one per cent deaths per million passenger miles, versus three times as much for buses, twice for scheduled domestic airlines, and — 15 times as much for private automobiles ... Trains on a single railroad track can transport as many passengers per day as a 20-lane expressway, if fully utilized.

(1/17/73)

However, the competition that has brought about lower air fares, plus Americans' incurable addicition to the private passenger automobile, presently bode no optimism for the future of AMTRAK. Few travelers check first to see if more convenient and less expensive rail service is available. We may in due time see passenger trains primarily for excursion junkets, which offer:

... the heady pleasure of being there to hear the confident cry of "All 'board;'" waving at every passing car and spectator; the tasty picnic lunch you brought along; and a personal satisfaction in reliving a part of America's heritage ...

(6/18/82)

One of the greater frustrations in crusading has been in the continuing great debate on the effects of tobacco — not as a health issue, on which the harm of smoking is well established, but on the effect of a reasonable tax on cigarettes. The North Carolina General Assembly for many years has had legislative lockjaw on this. Twenty years ago, when increasing the sales tax from three to four percent was first proposed, I repeated the appeal:

... But how about taxing some un-tapped luxury sources before raising the levy on the necessities of life (Note: meaning food and clothing).

— Like a tax on cigarettes and tobacco products, especially; or, up to a point short of diminishing returns, whiskey; or the pay of non-resident workers ...

(6/29/66)

A token tax on cigarettes, the lowest in the nation, was adopted despite the tobacco partisans' lingering appeal that it would hurt tobacco farmers.

... the people of North Carolina—even those who chain smoke and who buy their beer and whiskey by the sack full—are way ahead of their political leaders in realizing the sham that epitomizes North Carolina on this issue; near the bottom of the list of states in so many measurements of its public education system; unable to "afford" higher appropriations for its schools; yet fearful of enacting a tax on tobacco products because of the potential political controversy it represents ...
(10/25/67)

Some false notions die hard. One of the rankest of these is the illusion that a reasonable tobacco and cigarette tax will hurt the interests of North Carolina tobacco farmers. It's now proven that the discriminatory warning from the US Surgeon General on each pack of smokes isn't reducing smoking. A reasonable increase in the nation's lowest cigarette tax won't do it, either.

But it will: (1) Be a fairly-placed levy on a luxury product; (2) Make up partially for funds that would be lost by removing the regressive sales tax on food; and (3) Go a long way toward eliminating the flagrantly profitable traffic in cigarette bootlegging from this state.
(3/7/75)

The false mystique of North Carolina's own concern for tobacco was illustrated in a finding about Chapel Hill that came out 15 years after the U.S. Surgeon General first issued his warning. An annual poll of all entering freshmen college students in the nation revealed in 1980 that only 6.6 percent of the first-year students at UNC-Chapel Hill would admit having smoked more than a single cigarette in the previous year, whereas the nationwide average percentage was 8.8 percent. So surprising did this seem for the state that is the cradle of the tobacco industry that I double-checked with the poll-taking American Council on Education, but the same general figures held true for two more years. This suggested that North Carolina youth have fewer illusions about smoking than their peers nationwide.

This state finally lost a special opportunity in 1981 and again the next year when it rejected a manufacturers tax on cigarettes—a penny a pack levy that would have made smokers everywhere pay more for North Carolina cigarettes.

If the federal tax on cigarettes is doubled by Congress, as appears likely now, it will harm the economy of this state to some extent yet unknown. More significantly, it will doom North Carolina's chances for really significant income from its own "national" tax on cigarettes in a manner that wouldn't have harmed it at all. That chance twice was presented to the State Legislature this past year in bills to impose a simple one-cent-per-pack tax on all cigarettes manufactured in this state. That token levy—which would be paid equally by smokers all over the country and world—would have given North Carolina a legitimate and permanent bonanza estimated at over $100 million a year ...

North Carolnians need to do as the multi-faceted tobacco manufacturers themselves have already done successfully—seek alternative livelihoods and stop their fruitless rear-guard war against higher taxes on cigarettes.
(7/26/82)

As expected, the federal tax on cigarettes was significantly increased, while North Carolina Congressional interests also waged their perennial losing battle on that front, too.

The frustration of those of us in The Great Unwashed who had nobody we wanted positively to vote FOR inspired a continuing crusade that I believe is more practical than ever in this age of computer-tabulated elections:

... In referenda on issues you are permitted to vote either for or against a proposal. But your choice is much narrower in candidate elections. You must either vote for a candidate or not vote at all.

If there were a "for" and an "against" box beside each candidate's name in contested races, the voter might be able, for his own good reasons if he were so inclined, to add a vote to that candidate's total by voting for him, or literally subtract a vote from his total by voting against him ... Thus the interests of truly representative government would be advanced by the outcome of the election more accurately reflecting the people's true feeling ...

(9/26/71)

Under this system it would theoretically be possible for the person who had the fewest negative votes to be elected, if enough people chose to "vote against." Inspiration for this idea occurred to me from the prospect of Ted Kennedy's candidacy for president. I took up the appeal again during the McGovern-Nixon campaign:

We aren't so much against either or both candidates personally. We're just full up to the skull with the shrillness of the campaign oratory ... Those who rant and rave about the high crimes and misdemeanors of the other side are trying to make up in volume what they lack in fact ...

Under the circumstances I am ready to trot out my favorite proposed amendment to the Constitution – the right to vote against candidates. This would be the ideal election for this sacred right. Those who don't especially like either nominee would not have to be trapped into voting FOR the one they disliked the least ... If the Constitution would permit it, we could actually vote AGAINST the candidate we disliked the most ...

(11/1/72)

An additional benefit, as I wrote the following year, would be "in showing the victor the extent of his support – whether he had a positive mandate from the people as Nixon in his landslide 1972 victory mistakenly thought, or, whether he was simply the beneficiary of votes 'against' the other candidate ..."

(10/4/73)

Scaled-down versions of this idea have been suggested by other writers and politicians. Laws to permit a "none of the above" ballot have been proposed and passed in some places.

My editorial support of another Constitutional amendment had wider nationwide backing but is yet unsuccessful. This was the drive for the Equal Rights Amendment – a proposal that seemed to me purely symbolic and certainly harmless, since its effect was already being observed in every court interpretation of the existing Constitution:

Tomorrow, we are told, the NC House of Representatives will vote on the Equal Rights Amendment to the US Constitution. For all the folderol over these few redundant words, we'll be well advised to approve this highly-overrated phrase of would-be deliverance and be done with it. The era of ERA has unqualifiedly arrived. Legally removing the burden of sexism from our backs won't practically make us any purer of heart. But it will eliminate an unnecessary issue in contemporary Americana.

(4/14/75)

In that and subsequent votes, North Carolina and a required number of other states have failed to endorse ERA, and the perennial campaign continues in times of ebb and flow:

... Laws written in an earlier American Victorian spirit are going to have to be cleaned off the books – with or without the Equal Rights Amendment. But anybody with a grain of political insight can see that its enactment is forthcoming. We may not like everything about government by consent of the governed, but at least it still beats every other system.

(2/11/77)

... Two fundamentals remain unchanged: (1) Equal rights, as a matter of literal fact, are already provided in the Constitution, so the hassle is essentially a moot issue. (2) The holy crusade for passage of ERA is going to continue under any circumstances until this amendment is passed ... We'll be blessed in the sweet by-and-by when this bootless battle is over and the victory won.

(5/19/78)

A companion of the eventuality of ERA, I predict, will be the extension of national service in times of such need to women as well as men. During the great debate on ERA I also suggested that "integrating women into the defense effort of this country is both a rational and a legitimate part of their obligation as 'liberated' American citizens. That all people are not created equal in a physical sense does not mean they can't all serve their country in equally necessary ways ..."

Chapter 13

Favorites

... not necessarily the best-crafted writing. ... just items I like and feel good about ... They include family recollections, tributes to certain Chapel Hillians, and a potpourri of incidental snippets.

Some events, some people, and certain subjects claim a special spot in the mind's eye. The products of these subjects are not necessarily the best-crafted writing, nor the most popular column topics or particularly significant ones. For me they are just items I like and feel good about.

Of such are the "favorites," many of which are pretty personal, but still favorites. They include family recollections, tributes to certain Chapel Hillians, and a potpourri of incidental snippets. One of these was about Carrboro, our sister community where I spent a decade of intense involvement as a local newspaper editor. Another writer's kindred feeling about Carrboro struck a chord with me, also:

News and Observer columnist Jack Aulis showed an instant understanding of the village when he wrote that "Carrboro is a town with its feet in two different worlds, like a country gal who has had to move to the city, but is not yet willing to quit wearing field shoes, poke bonnet, and apron."

Long may it prevail, too. Carrboro has forever been an appropriate complement to its twin community across the track, Chapel Hill. Many's the time when we've said "Thank God for Carrboro!" and also "Thank you, Carrboro." but if it continues to become more of a "Chapel Hill bedroom" all that will vanish. Poke bonnet, apron and all, we like her best like that.

(9/26/75)

In that spirit of personal honesty, too, is this gem that the renown Carolina football alumnus, Charlie Justice, once recalled:

Charlie Justice told it on himself at a Carolina alumni meeting in Wilson the other night. — About the time when he was a celebrated football player for the Tar Heels and the graduating class at Belhaven High School asked him to speak at their junior-senior banquet. Charlie checked with Coach Carl Snavely, who said it would be all right, and called the young lady to accept. She hesitated and then asked what he'd charge. Charlie said he'd be glad to do it for free. "That's great," the girl rejoined. "Then we'll have more money for entertainment!"

(9/19/75)

Self-acceptance is a quality that has carried me through many a rough period to the tender age of three-score. Without considering myself an "expert" on the subject, I have nevertheless written several times, when the subject has come up, about how to get along in the US Army. This was the product of World War II experience in an infantry rifle company:

... As the ranking Private Second Class in all of Orange County (27 months at that rank, 1943-45), The Newsman absorbed and was subjected to considerable authority from above. In fact, just about everybody was above this yard bird ...

(1) Keep your mouth shut; (2) Do as you're told; (3) Never volunteer; and (4) Never, never worry — you can't do a thing about it.

You may scoff and jeer. You may indeed point a finger and properly declare that the great free enterprise system and the might and glory that is America is not built of such stuff.

Of course it isn't, and thank goodness for that.

But the Army is. And the system works wondrously for the Army.

Let all young fellows about to enter the service read and remember these four points. Follow this four-point creed and you'll get along all right in the Army. And the defenses of Uncle Sam will be none the worse for your wearing of the uniform.

(10/8/64)

As a postscript, I wrote on another occasion:

... The system might not work to the benefit of capitalistic private enterprise. But its acceptance by the average civilian-oriented GI Joe is the only way the US Army has managed to function as effectively as it has ...

(9/6/70)

I still believe as firmly in those simplistic-sounding rules and would press them upon anybody entering even today's armed forces.

A "favorite" that's not just my own is about a drink that originated in Chapel Hill and has merited widespread growing popularity, surprising as the mixture of ingredients may sound:

"Carolina Morning" is an amazing and simply-concocted punch that has become a tradition for some Carolina alumni affairs since its invention by the hometown alumni chapter four years ago. In response to several inquiries, we give the recipe here for those who may wish to try it as a New Year's Eve concoction. Part of the "beauty" of it is in the easy manner that it can be mixed quickly in two-quart "batches" right in the punch bowl – as follows: Pour these ingredients over ice cubes – one pint of whiskey sour mix, one pint of vodka, and one quart of beer; "season" to taste with a dash of lemon or lime juice, and serve. – Sounds like an incredible mixture, we'll admit, but it is a really tasty and "effective" punch.

"Carolina Morning" won a $2,000 first prize award for UNC alumni in a 1971 contest with Duke alumni. Smirnoff sponsored the competition for the best football party drink between major gridiron rivals across the country. **(12/26/75)**

As a matter of historical record it should be noted that Carolina Morning was the invention of Chapel Hillian Edwin Tenney Jr., then the local alumni chapter chairman. He credits Mark Sumner with helping develop this product during several evenings of trial and error mixing and tasting. One local civic club still serves up several bowls of it before each week's meeting.

It is inevitable for any parent that certain family stories will be their classic favorites. This one came from the period of massive civil rights "demonstrations" in Chapel Hill:

... The youngsters were getting dressed for Sunday School, while this oldster lay sick abed with a momentary case of the seasonal misery.

One of the trio – no doubt it was the 11-year-old, groused about going to Sunday School and suggested they stage a sit-in protest against it. The idea was accepted with enthusiasm by the two younger brothers.

As soon as all were slickered up and ready to go, they planted themselves in good TV style blocking the hallway, declaring for all to hear that they were staging a 'demonstration' and would not go to Sunday School ... To get the idea across more firmly the lads issued frequent verbal bulletins calling attention to their plans at passive revolt.

Three times their mother called them routinely to come along with her to

Sunday School. The reply was then total silence. At this, the ailing Newsman/parent rared out of bed and stalked down the hall. Honest, he didn't utter a word, just walked along with hand outstretched in flat palm style.

Well sir, The Newsman doesn't claim that he has a magic formula, but for what it's worth to any reader, the demonstration evaporated forthwith. The 11-year-old and the seven-year-old got tangled up in each other's legs as they dashed for the door, and the nine-year-old nearly bowled 'em over as he followed.

Let the family counselors or psychiatrists make of it what they wish. So far as we were concerned, it was simply another of many crises nipped in the bud.

(4/9/64)

Such gems of family life must come up spontaneously:

No question about it, in the realm of family milestones this was an auspicious occasion. The candle-lighted cake was brought to the table after supper last Thursday, and set down before mom. "Make a wish before you blow 'em out," prompted the three boys.

"What'll I wish for?" asked mom curiously.

From the four-year-old: "For a horse." From the seven-year-old: "That everything I like will be in the refrigerator." From the 10-year-old, bless him: "For us kids to be good."

(5/3/62)

And this one, finally, which was a harbinger of this youngster's natural financial acumen:

"Buy me a Coke, please," pleaded the 11-year-old. It was during an unguarded moment after church services last Sunday.

The Newsman, flat broke, pleaded poverty and invited the youngster to search his pockets. The boy did so promptly and verified the fact. Immediately he renewed his plea. "But you can see I don't have a cent," The Newsman said.

"I know," came the cajoling reply, "but you could borrow the money from me."

(9/14/66)

Two columns that I personally felt strongest about also related to the children — at least, Number One Son — on special occasions for him, and so, for me, also. First was on the occasion of his 21st birthday:

... What happened to those years that brought the youngster to this monumental day, from that Good Friday, April 12, 1952, when he was born? Surely that couldn't have been a score of years ago, plus one. ... Now he writes from France, on his junior year in college abroad.

The latest letter, hastily penned as he waits in Paris for a train to reminds us that he'll be with college friends in Germany on April 12. —Does that date "ring any bells?" he asks ...

And what a great occasion this year of his majority has been for him, we reflect. He's certainly wrought every potential instant of three-dimensional experience from it. Europe is his oyster. With characteristic unabashed mobility and vitality, he's been and done everything possible to make this the truly historic epoch of his life that it should be.

How wonderful to accept life with such good grace, as this lad does, for all the positive things that it has to offer. And how refreshing, too, to see one at peace with himself, yet with such a zest for living—yea, for accepting the inevitable disappointment and rebuff simply as a normal pattern of life, and even a challenge.

So often nowadays the young fancy the need for a chip on the shoulder. As though it were fashionable, some take shelter in feeling "oppressed by the establishment." How heartening, then, to realize that here's one who doesn't seem to discern that he might be in any way victimized by contemporary society. Optimistic self-reliance, somehow, just seemed to evolve.

And so you daydream, philosophizing as only an indulgent parent may, on that historic day that you share with a beloved first-born, 3,000 miles away. Happy Birthday, Bill.

(4/17/73)

The other occasion needs no introduction:

Thank goodness one long-standing wedding tradition was shattered. Calm, self-assured as he could be, the bridegroom gave his own vows with no prompting from the minister. He said them with feeling, just as the bride declared them with utter charm and grace.

I knew this better than anybody else because I was standing up for him Saturday afternoon when No. One Son plighted his troth. Today's youth may have their human frailties, but at least for these two, their decision was as positive as it was joyful. The stereotype of quaking bridegroom and tenderly nervous bride—recollections no doubt familiar to almost all parents— seemingly never existed. They knew what they were about and were richer for it.

Perhaps there was a key to it in a casual fillip he let drop the night before at the rehearsal party. It was part of a toast to his parents — "who had the good sense to liberate me 10 years ago." And what a rewarding, retroactive bit of instruction that provided: That we must do our parenting early and thoroughly, and then release them — "for better or for worse," as the vows declare. But for our sake, and for theirs, release them — in deepest love — we must.

(4/6/81)

Across the years I enjoyed writing personal tributes to various home-
towners, sometimes at their death, or whenever the notion prompted it:

The death of Paul Eubanks recalls memories of the cordial poker-faced fellow who greeted and served thousands of customers and friends through the years from his handy mid-town window-on-the-world in Eubanks Drugstore. His establishment was accepted and used as much as a public institution as it was a place of business. Everybody arbitrarily and automatically took squatters rights on Eubanks' as a public thoroughfare, meeting place, free weight or parcel pick-up station. They also bought things from the drugstore.

Paul Eubanks took it all philosophically, viewing the passing pandemonium with the perspective of passive years on the scene. He had a subtle wit and close insight. Nuances of the big and little things that comprised the hometown scene were never lost on him. While his thrift was legendary, Paul accepted jibes about the habit in good grace ...

(5/10/67)

It is a blessing if each of us has at least one school teacher who specially
helped us, and rare if we have more than one. At her death I felt obliged to
write about one in Chapel Hill:

There ought to be a special medal presented to school teachers who have as many as 1,000 personal alumni. Such a person was Miss Lettie Glass, a gentle matriarch of the first grade at the Chapel Hill Elementary School for 37 of her 75 years. Miss Glass, who died last week, retired from teaching and left Chapel Hill some years ago — long enough that no children in the Chapel Hill public schools today were ever taught by her. But there are well over a thousand of us who are her former pupils and who started our formal educational careers at the knee of this kind-hearted and gracious school marm.

... A tall, white-haired woman, she won the love of her tiny charges by a remarkably incisive gentleness. It is difficult to imagine her ever raising her voice. Yet somehow, she never seemed to have any problem of control. For all the refinements that the brains of educational research have wrought in public education, there'll never be any substitute nor improvement on that one-in-a-million find, the natural-born first grade teacher that Miss Glass epitomized.

(12/30/69)

No book about significant Chapel Hill personalities could be complete, either, without a tribute to Helen Miller (Mrs. William H.) Peacock, who resigned from her many years of high school librarianship here in 1971:

... But that isn't what causes the deep regret ... It is rather that Chapel Hill High School, with her departure, is losing its finest living example of a once-revered quality that was the keystone of public education. That is discipline, with all the other traits that it nurtures, such as self-respect, dignity, security, unselfishness, and courtesy, to name only a few. And, we used to believe, it was also the foundation for learning and in later life making good use of it.

That Library, may the saints be praised, has been a domain inviolate. Mrs. Peacock in her Library was constant proof of the fact that the setting of definite standards of excellence, the application and appreciation of hard work, plain talk, in equal measure with dedication to duty and a love of young people, was the way to really accomplish the mission of the public schools.

... Her husband, UNC Professor Bill Peacock, epitomized those same qualities of sternness, mixed with devotion to profession when he was our high school coach and principal. He met his wife when both were on the school faculty and they were married 30 years ago this month.

At the time of the Great Armistice Day Riot in the school year before last, some pupils ran rampant throughout the building – but not in the Library ...

"I'm not running a popularity contest. I'm here to do a job," she'd say to many a boy and girl in insisting that they abide by rules and adopt the trappings of civility when they crossed her threshold. These are standards she not only imposed, but lived by herself. Sad it is, then, that we have come to the day when this is no longer "relevant," and a great teacher must depart. The alternative satisfaction is, of course, that we've had the benefit of this extraordinary woman in our schools for so many years.

(6/20/71)

Two other great ladies of Chapel Hill come to mind for the gentle force of

their personalities as wives of well-known local men, UNC Dean of the
School of Journalism Oscar (Skipper) Coffin, and Orange County Repre-
sentative John W. Umstead Jr.:

Mrs. Oscar J. Coffin, who died this past week, was a gracious lady who made her husband more lovable. There was a complementary contrast between "Miss Gertrude" and her spouse, the plain-spoken "Skipper" who shepherded so many students into their journalistic careers. She knew, was interested in, kept up with them when they left Chapel Hill, and always made them welcome when they returned. While Skipper was the professional journalist, Miss Gertrude had quite a bit of creativity, too. She'll be remembered especially for re-naming The Shack, then operated by Brack Creel, "The Iron Lung." It seemed, she sighed philosophically, that Skipper couldn't breathe outside of it.

Another great and gracious lady of this community who preceded Mrs. Coffin in dying recently was her neighbor, Mrs. John Umstead. Surely there has never been anybody to whom God gave more compassion and love of humanity for its own sake than "Miss Sallie." She loved the beauty of nature and her household and yard was filled with its bounty, cultivated by her own hand. But most noticeable of all was the natural grace which she fairly radiated constantly. Hate, you felt, was impossible for her. The community personality of Chapel Hill, for so many of its good qualities, has been drawn from persons of such abiding strength of character through the years as Miss Gertrude and Miss Sallie.

(10/11/70)

This one is primarily personal, but I must cite another lady who meant so
much to me by her love and gracious manner. Mrs. J. Ira ("Aunt Mae")
Mann is remembered by legions of local school alumni more as the music
teacher at Carrboro Elementary School, but to me from another perspec-
tive:

She had no children of her own, but she always called me her boy and lavished her love on me as a real son. —Why she was so dear, yea, so foolish about me, I'll never know. It all started with the newspaper. We were both reporters—she, the Carrboro correspondent for The News of Orange County, and I, the staff writer.

Mae Mann took her duties as the neighborhood columnist seriously, and had naught but good words for everybody she wrote about. That was in the good old days before objective journalism was strangling us. Many's the hour back then and in the warm wonderful years since that we visited. And

'Aunt Mae' Mann – 1974; Ed Lanier (left) and Donald Stanford, winners of second primary nominations for county commissioner, 6/23/56

however her heart and body may have ached as it did in the final painful months, the radiance of her perennial smile restored the soul ...

(9/3/76)

Another death I felt very keenly was that of a hometown contemporary, Donald M. Stanford. A dairy farmer who continued a family tradition of public service, he'd been an Orange County commissioner and representative in the General Assembly when he died, following a lengthy illness, on his 44th birthday:

... Here was a rare home-grown product, a person who was always destined for the role of leadership he accepted with zeal, in continuing a family tradition. One who willingly and willfully enters public life and politics as a way of life must realize the sacrifices it requires. Don Stanford chose this course and zestfully began a life of service to his community and his government as soon as he finished college.

His interests and accomplishments are evident in his participating in so many facets of our community life. Always he was abetted and encouraged by his wife, a model of courage and determination through his final moments. We mourn his passing and are grateful for his dedicated years as a good friend, and one who labored long and well for the betterment of the community he loved.

(5/10/70)

His widow, the Hon. Patricia Stanford Hunt, succeeded him as Orange County representative in the General Assembly, serving there until she was named to a local district court judgeship.

A man whom I revered for his fundamental qualities of greatness was Dr. Arthur London, a Pittsboro native who in his 45 years as a pediatrician in Durham came to treat third generation patients. My reverence for him was not as much in admiration of his professional skill in ministering to his patients as to their mothers. At his death I wrote:

... Thousands of parents would nod their heads knowingly and say "Amen" if they read these lines. Dr. London was unique. Not only was he the best "baby doctor" around, but he was also the best for their mothers. Many times his colleagues have admitted that distraught but thankful mothers too often confused him with God.

He had an extraordinary, quiet, but firm way with all youngsters. – They'd talk back to their parents, sass their playmates, and defy other doctors. But when Arthur London quietly told them to do something, they somehow always did it – instantly, and not fearfully. They just did it.

I never confused him with God, but I dearly loved him, too – not just as a pediatrician for our children. But every now and then through the years when things seemed a bit grim for the Woman At My House, for any reason at all, I'd tell her seriously, "What you need is to go have a talk with Dr. London. He'll fix you up."

There are many fine physicians in general practice and specialties hereabouts today, just as in the revered past. But Arthur London certainly epitomized that phrase, "the good doctor," for parents and children alike.
(4/30/76)

The "Grand Old Man" of the University at Chapel Hill, Librarian and Kenan Prof. Emeritus Louis Round Wilson, was also a good neighbor of mine for over 40 years. I fancied a kindred feeling with him because he was the original Editor of The Alumni Review magazine in 1912, and I served in this same post 55 years later. In his waning years before his death at age 102 in 1979 he was naturally called upon for the tradition of giving advice – a practice he deliberately shunned. He relented only at a centennial banquet in his honor to the extent of urging all who'd listen: "Get all you can out of life in your early years. Don't put off." It seemed to me especially appropriate that Dr. Wilson as the University's senior alumnus and rightfully-honored long-time servant lived such a full life:

... There is something majestic about living to be 100. The President of the United States sends you a birthday card every year. Everybody defers to you. You may ache and pain a good deal – and you probably can't dance a jig. But the liberty, the license of doing as you please has some precious rewards, too.

In Chapel Hill this is a two-way thing. The good health and long life of Louis Round Wilson gives us a special person to love and appreciate.
(12/30/77)

Among the most extraordinary people I have ever known was the late Allard K. Lowenstein, a post-World War II classmate at UNC-Chapel Hill who was assassinated at the peak of his activist career in 1980. After a memorial service for him in Chapel Hill I wrote:

... During the three decades since he left here (Chapel Hill) to become literally a citizen of the world, he remained deliberately tied to his Tar Heel roots. (So strong was that feeling that for some years he literally retained his legal citizenship in a Chapel Hill voting precinct.) How strange, and how fitting, too, we sensed, that a teen-age Jewish lad from Scarsdale, NY, became such a thoroughgoing product of the lofty ideals of the First State University.

... Most succinctly, pointed out one speaker, "You were not always **with** Al, but you were always **for** Al." All too often he was our conscience, and we were properly uncomfortable about it ...

I was particularly struck by examples of that quality pointed out by one of the speakers – his classmate, former US Assistant Postmaster General Dick Murphy of Washington. Noting that everybody had his differences with Al, Dick pointed out about his friend that Al also strongly supported his country's role in World War II; rallied young people in support of President Truman's opposition to North Korean aggression; had singularly powerful influence in bringing about US withdrawal from the Vietnam War, yet served two years in the Army (years earlier) himself; fervently opposed the Communist-dominated International Union of Students (while National Student Association President), but had to defend himself against charges that he was a Communist; fought courageously for civil rights in behalf of blacks and "with the same devotion against black racism;" and "while devoted to peace with freedom, always cautioned that violent demonstrations for peace were a betrayal of the cause."
(4/25/80)

Of all the people who helped mold me as an adult, I expect the one who most influenced me was UNC Student Aid Director Edwin S. Lanier during his five years as Mayor of Chapel Hill, 1949-54. I didn't write about him in the newspaper column at that time, since I was then a beginning reporter for the Durham Morning Herald and Sun in Chapel Hill and later for the Chapel Hill Weekly. Later, at his appointment to a Council of State office, I recalled:

Orange County has provided the State a great guardian of the public interest in the person of Insurance Commissioner Edwin S. Lanier.

As Mayor of the Town of Chapel Hill, Orange County Commissioner, and State Senator, Ed had a plodding, deliberate way of searching out ALL the facts and issues on any matter at hand. Often after things seemed clear, he would repeat the problem, write down the reasoning on all sides, and publicly struggle toward the logic of the right answer ...

(7/28/66)

Humble, gracious to a fault, and a deeply-concerned Baptist layman, Ed Lanier passionately believed in the importance of effective local government. He imbued me with this same feeling and left as a legacy many of the fundamental qualities that make the Town of Chapel Hill "go" to this day.

Chapter 14

Pet Peeves

—the opposite of the qualities that make for Gracious Living in Chapel Hill—

Less significant than crusades, not matters of worldly import, but little things that frustrate the good life—the opposite of the qualities that make for Gracious Living in Chapel Hill— are the day to day pet peeves. As self-appointed spokesman for those masses I called "the wailing rabble" or "the great unwashed" I frequently bemoaned our lot through complaints such as the following:

... You naturally start the local list with arrogant Duke and State partisans. Their clones are the clods who wave hands to distract Carolina basketball players at the foul line. In the same mold are the opponents' cheering sections. They are boisterously gauche when their team is ahead— as compared to the highly commendable enthusiasm of Carolina partisans when we're cheering our squad.

There are others, both town and gown: The pedestrians who surge across the street in defiance of the "wait" signals when you are so obediently standing at the curb; motorists who park for "just a minute" in front of the downtown post office mail boxes; the guy who beat you out—and can't seem to follow the computer directions—at the bank's sidewalk money machine; pigsty habitues who litter the "beer drinking capital of the world" with proof of their prowess; and professors who presume that their PhDs qualify them as ranking authorities on everything.

As ranking members of the Great Unwashed, we're also put off by surly

postal clerks, supercilious secretaries, the gratuitous "Hold the line for Mr. Big" telephone introducers; and officious public officials (who may not be purely a local scourge).
(2/2/81)

Reacting against the thoughtless souls who park in front of the curb-side mailbox to dash inside the downtown post office for "just a second," I once urged a contest among readers for punishment to fit the crime:

... Those more daring and of like mien to the offenders might quickly let the air out of one of the guy's car tires and go call the cops. You could stick a toothpick in his horn and then beat it; or sit down on your own horn if you think you're big enough to take his physical measure when he comes back. All of these are infantile reactions. But there should be some appropriate way that a law-abiding citizen could effectively deal with these clods on the spot ...
(11/24/71)

In that same column I again took up the editorial cudgel against windbag speakers, recalling an offender who went 20 minutes overtime in his talk to a large audience locally:

... The crime he was committing was that of wasting the time of almost 400 other persons. Thus he wasted over 130 man hours in those 20 minutes. Or, to put it a different way, every time the guy spoke one minute he was tying up six hours cumulative time of those 400 deathly-bored turned-off listeners. Willful windbag speakers should be sentenced to die by the boredom of having to listen to their own words thrice repeated, then cooked in their own hot air.
(11/24/71)

A kindred tyranny is the business of forcing unrequested services upon hapless citizens. I was reminded of this during a group tour in Italy, where the "Loo Lous," as I tagged them, plied their petty trade:

... These are the ladies stationed in women's public bathrooms who hand you a tissue or assist you in some minor fashion, whether you wish their services or not. Woe betide the woman who does not have at least a 100 lira coin or note to hand the Loo Lou as she departs. I've heard of some ladies being literally trapped for want of this rip-off payoff.

Even some men's restrooms in this country are subject to this scourge. Grand Central Station in New York City, where the facilities are definitely not worth the price, has a couple of old retainers strategically stationed to give you un-requested services and extort your coin.

This is all leading up to the Women's Lib crusades: They have in various states successfully lobbied to outlaw pay toilets on the grounds that women have to use the coin-opened booths while men don't. I urge the Libbers to add to their campaign calendar the outlawing of Loo Lous or anybody who would in bathrooms give you un-requested services for payment.

(6/13/77)

I am not at all unsympathetic to the appeals of salesmen. Theirs is an honorable calling on which the wheels of commerce roll forward. But the mass appeal long distance phone call pitch is not in that category:

... Salesperson from Golden Acres in Myrtle Beach is reading from a skillfully written, time-tested script and is anxious to establish rapport with you before he/she lets fly the hooker about your "free vacation" and "free prize" to come investigate their time share villas.

If you're really interested in time share stuff, magazine subscriptions or subterranean real estate — or if you're flat-out lonesome for a telephone call from just anybody, it's advisable to go ahead with the conversation. As for me, I come to the point quickly. "Friend," I gently interrupt, "if you are selling something, let me help you out. I have been a salesman myself, and I know it's a hard life. I will do you a favor and tell you to simply draw a line through my name on your list and move on to the next prospect, because I am not interested in buying anything at all." The invariable and desired result is an instant click.

(8/9/82)

In a less serious spirit, but yet in puzzled provocation, I wondered some years ago about a practice that's steadily grown since I first noted it back then:

One give-away symptom by which we prove we're really denizens of the SOUTHERN Part is our unfailing penchant for cancelling everything at the first drop of a snowflake. — Like that delightful little three-incher yesterday. Although the snowfall stopped by mid-morning and the weather turned the warmest in a week, almost all normal organized activities for the day had already been cancelled. — How come we all streak sheep-like for shelter, unthinking? Where's our curiosity, our pioneer spirit, our interest in enjoying nature in some of its more versatile forms?

(2/3/78)

While griping is one of our most sacred and pleasured rights, it has occurred to me that there are in our midst some "pleasers" as well as "peevers." The latter are the oft-unsung souls who brighten our day by their inherent codes of personal conduct:

... Efficient and helpful long-distance telephone operators – those who listen carefully and are alert to your first carefully-pronounced directions; courteous drivers – and there really are some – such as those who automatically yield the right of way, stay out of tailgate range, and graciously signal you good wishes; waitresses who are pleasant and attentive to your needs – but discerningly respect your privacy; and office receptionists who go out of their way to be helpful, instead of defensive and officious.

(5/7/79)

The "good guys" also won out in the end on another occasion when I complained in the column about the design of another consumer product – the newly-printed standard deposit slip at NC National Bank. Local bank officials explained that the new form was set up for use in computers which they weren't yet employing. So far as the customer trying to use it was concerned, the new form was as functional as that mythical animal designed by a committee, having miniscule spaces for listing checks and columns that you had to sub-total and add up from right to left. To my surprise I soon received a personal letter from the bank's vice president in charge of public relations at its Charlotte headquarters. Arthur H. Jones (who soon thereafter retired to Chapel Hill) wrote:

... As a direct result of your comments, we took a sampling of reaction by other customers, found that your views had much support, and therefore a re-study is now being made with two things in mind: (1) The needs of the customer first, and (2) The needs of the computer second.

When this is done, and it should be soon, we would like to invite you to a gourmet lunch where you can order the best the menu affords while watching us eat a dish of stewed crow, with Tony Gobbel and Bill Cherry (Note: local bank officials) as witnesses ...

(12/23/63)

Increasing competition in the credit card field since that time has no doubt held down the annual fee that all the credit card companies now charge – except for the new free "rebate" entry, Citibank's Choice card. This situation has also forced some of the card companies to resort to deceptive gimmickry. One of them regularly includes a computer-generated message on its bills to the effect that because of your prompt payment record you may skip a month's payments if you wish—though regular interest charges will still apply. The translation of that message is that the company can't make any money off of you if you pay promptly, so they wish you'd skip a month and pay them 18 pct. (or more) for the privilege.

A practice I labeled "Credit Card Cop-Out" cited what I felt was an especially tasteless practice by a local restaurant:

... A delightful new eatery in town carries a note at the end of its menu: "No gratuities on credit cards, please." On inquiry a hostess gave the obvious explanation—that management doesn't want to pay the three percent commission to the credit card company on tips that would go to employees.

A customer's response: (1) Why honor credit cards in the first place, then? (2) How cheap can you get—being willing to pay the commission on your 100 percent of the food and beverage charges, but unwilling to pay a paltry sum more on your employees' 15-20 percent tips. (3) If you must (though it's still a poor idea at best), why not have a private understanding with employees that you'll deduct the three percent from their credit card tips, or suggest to credit card users that they add three percent extra on gratuities to cover VISA or MC commissions?

—We use credit cards instead of cash for their convenience. Otherwise we'd pay both the tab and tip in cash. (4) Finally—what an un-gracious put-down this is to your own employees, Mr. Employer—to openly announce that they're not worth a piddling three percent extra portion of their tips for their service to **you** in pleasing us customers.

(9/14/79)

Was it only coincidence that this restaurant went out of business about three months later?

Everybody must experience kindred feelings about dentists from time to time. Dentistry is one of those necessary evils for existence, like life insurance, which we know is good and necessary, but none the less dislikable. Out of the stream of consciousness that must occur to all of us while we're strapped in that contoured chair, I recalled things I don't like about some dentists:

The jokers who ask you questions while they're poking their fingers or a high-speed augur in your mouth ... and who leave OLD copies (or even new copies) of mags like The Rotarian and The Dental Journal around the waiting room. ... or who sock it to you without warning when you have some high-priced work done, on the bogus theory that talking money would be unprofessional ... and especially the super-clinical types who gleefully tell you that your trouble is "a very interesting case" ... and whose bills for services rendered are a bunch of hen-scratching except for the figures at the bottom of the sheet.

Actually, I don't know any dentists in Chapel Hill who bring these pet peeves to mind. But since there's a dental school here, I thought some professor just might like to have these non-professional observations to pass on to his students, or as the subject of a paper before a learned society or for a doctoral dissertation.

(8/16/70)

In the spirit of "equal time" I note these "things I like about dentists," which I cited some years later:

When they (1) Are cordial but get right down to business; (2) Keep you informed about how they're coming along (and when the results verify it); (3) Don't ask you chatty questions while their fingers are in your mouth; (4) Warn you when they're about to hit a tender spot; (5) Have good, current popular magazines in their waiting rooms; (6) Are so prompt in meeting appointments that you don't have time to read the magazines; and (7) Are reasonable in their charges. These thoughts occurred to me while in my own dentist's chair, and they're all assets to his (and any other) dentist's professional proficiency.

(8/23/76)

The diminishing bounty of our natural resources has in recent years spawned a breed of people I have labeled "super-ecologists"—those who believe that they, and not God, invented the tree:

... Many of us who have been greatly concerned with conservation of natural resources for long years before ecology became a household word are, we believe, rightfully wary of some of the frenzy being whipped up in the name of saving our civilization from drowning in our own cesspools— tomorrow.

In this spirit we share with the new breed of instant super-ecologists a vital concern that intelligent self-interest be exercised in our stewardship over the dwindling un-spoiled surface of the earth. But we feel an equal obligation to question and even challenge, on proper authority, many of the headlines and reckless charges ...

Of immediate concern hereabouts is the New Hope (Jordan) Reservoir project. I will march to Zion with those who want to assure that this development will preserve and even enhance our natural resources. But there is continuing contradiction within the fraternity of those professionally qualified to pass judgment on the ecological aspects of New Hope Lake. That a lawsuit to halt the project has been filed does not prove in any way that the New Hope Lake is either an unsound or an illegal project. The courts will have to decide on that in due time.

(8/15/71)

The courts did decide the fate of that project and upheld construction of the reservoir. It is now generally agreed that the over-all quality of the Jordan Reservoir is good and that it has high potential as a public water supply. In that same season I issued a plea that stemmed from another peeve that is just as timely today:

Just for instance, I would like to see one of the major petroleum firms that easily has the resources to do the job right, design a service station that would be a real asset to the looks of the community. Could they propose an attractive but functional and low-key building that would not cry out in the harsh tradition of massive plate glass and garish colors? Could they not carefully but usefully lay out the service area so that there would be shrubbery, flowers, and trees around the bays of gas pumps, instead of a flat sea of asphalt, cement, and towering totem-like mercury vapor lights? ...

(10/3/71)

The work of the Chapel Hill Appearance Commission has somewhat modified this corporate mindset in some recent Chapel Hill business construction. But I remember many years ago when Ted Danziger offered Esso his choice lot at the corner of Airport Rd. and Hillsborough St., conditioned on their agreeing to a non-standard design that exhibited some Chapel Hill ambience. Esso insisted it couldn't be done, but after three years of Ted's stubborn insistence they went along 100 percent. Since then the original use of the property has been changed but the looks of the building have not been completely spoiled.

A long-time peeve that has been remedied is in our courts system. The creation of county jury commissions and laws that more fairly regulate jury service have ended many long-standing abuses and made citizen service in the courts a more positive experience. After being called for jury duty for the fifth time in 14 years, I wrote:

... The judge and court officials are inordinately deferential to those of us drawn by lot for this mandatory judgment on our peers. Time was when the lowly juror had to wait endlessly in abject ignorance for the call from the bench. He deigned not ask the high and mighty of the court what was going on, or if he might be excused for some matter. The phrase "contempt of court" was oft-bred in the juror's bosom by his wastefully unpleasant experience in the court. Not so, has been our experience in the last two of the five times I've been called for service. The constructive change reaps its own reward in citizen appreciation of the system, since jury service is most people's only experience in the courts.

(1/23/76)

The parking problem is one pet peeve that the inevitably increasing laziness of the human race decrees shall never be resolved:

While people elsewhere worry about too much cholesterol, over-population, dandruff, and the high cost of living, we in Chapel Hill are preoccupied with the parking problem. The crush this fall, particularly on campus, is awesome to behold. Where there are four times as many cars entitled to park as there are spaces for them, the sight of a vacant space maketh maniacs of those normally mild-mannered ...

(9/27/69)

The campus parking problem was shared by visitors as well as local people and students. Noting the increasing plague of parkers on the University grounds by football game visitors, I wrote:

The psyche of the contemporary college football spectator is an awesome thing to behold in action. Apparently he presumes that his purchase of an eight-dollar pasteboard also entitles him to trespass on public property with his automobile.

... So the visitors casually appropriate an un-given right to pick out a spot in the middle of the campus grounds, tailgate their lunch, lock the car and leave for the game. The ranks of ingrate trespassers are growing by the natural process of imitation. The logic: "Others are doing it, so why shouldn't I?"

At some place a halt will have to be called. If not, the Silent Sam and Caldwell monuments in the middle of McCorkle Place — the most hallowed historic grounds on campus — will be endangered ere long by motorists in search of a vacant plot of grass to park on.

For all the congestion there's never been a football Saturday in this town when sufficient parking was not available **on public streets** within 15 minutes WALK of the stadium ...

(10/6/78)

Blessedly, the University soon thereafter forcibly halted this wanton invasion by blocking off the old campus grounds and posting guards there on game days to direct visitors to appropriate parking areas.

Akin to the thoughtless autombile parking trespassers are many cigarette smokers. They are normal, civilized human beings in so many other ways, but:

... how is it that people who are otherwise thoughtful will habitually toss a cigarette but on the ground and crush it out? They wouldn't similarly cast aside the whole cigarette package or a paper cup, for instance. But the paper-wrapped butt is no less litter.

In the Army we Dogfaces were taught to pull open the cigarette butts and scatter the remaining tobacco on the ground whence it originated. Then we were to dispose of the remaining waste paper in a trash receptacle.

The problem would be resolved today if the Surgeon General would direct that an additional warning be imprinted on the cigarette package: "Throwing Cigarette Butts on the Ground Is Harmful To Your Visual Environment."

(6/9/75)

To be peevish about this sort of thing is quixotic in this Age of the Discard Society, but the urge persists.

In the days before the mid-town Rosemary Square parking and commercial project was proposed, some less sophisticated ideas were being discussed, one of which I cited under the heading, "To Park A Car:"

That has become our most important prerequisite to carrying out our workaday activities in this sophisticated Space Age. Now comes the Town of Chapel Hill with a bold plan to build a bond-financed four-level brick-faced parking garage, replete with landscaping plaza above the existing municipal lot behind downtown stores.

Cost of the project, which would basically be repaid by user fees, is estimated at $1.6 million. This figures out to about $3,500 apiece for each of the little-bitty cubicles in which 446 cars will be accommodated ...

Dear friends, we protest not. Parking space – sad to admit – is the essence of civilized economic life on this mortal coil in the fading decade of the Seventies. But what a price to pay! ...

(9/14/79)

That project was included in a bond referendum package that local voters rejected, and the more recent public/private partnership business development evolved as the next idea.

Chapter 15

In the Chuckular Vein

A Southern Democrat is a person who if he lived in any other region would be a conservative Republican—only not that liberal.

It's said there've been no really new jokes since the time of Shakespeare. Perhaps so, but the re-birth of some of them is as fresh as tomorrow's news to anybody who hasn't heard a certain one previously. For many years I ended the column with a sometimes-appropriate chestnut. —Or perhaps it was just the latest one I'd heard. "In The Chuckular Vein" seemed a fitting title for capping the column.

While a majority of these are dated in the second half of the decade of the sixties (when I was writing the column for two different local newspapers), most of them came from the personal clipping file I've kept since I first started the column in the early fifties. Naturally a number of them are on subjects related to the lot of a newsman—politics, put-downs, and the courtroom. Credit should be given to a variety of sources from which some were lifted, such as The State Magazine, and the former professor of political science at Duke, Hodge O'Neal, who published a delightful anthology of political humor. But, in deference to Shakespeare, these jokes probably weren't original with my immediate sources. My personal favorites among the dozens published in The Newsman's Notepad are several which I'd call high humor, though not belly-laugh types:

The young Yankee tourist visiting England for the first time walked into the lobby of his hotel and pushed the button for the elevator. "The lift will be down presently, sir," said the hotel clerk. "The lift? Oh, you mean the elevator," corrected the American. "No sir, I mean the lift."

"I guess I should know what it's called," boasted the American. "Somebody from the United States invented the elevator."

"Quite so, sir," returned the hotel clerk, "but somebody from England invented the language."

(8/14/66)

The three referees were swapping lies at the bar after a game. "I call 'em like I see 'em," said the first. "Well, I call 'em like they are," upstaged the second one. "You boys may be pretty good," allowed the third, "but they aren't anything until I call 'em!"

(2/21/75)

Regional orientation for outlanders and newcomers:

A Southern Democrat is a person who if he lived in any other region would be a conservative Republican — only not that liberal.

A Southern Republican is a person who feels he didn't get enough attention when he was a Southern Democrat.

A Yankee is a northerner.

A Damyankee is a northerner who moved South.

A carpetbagger is a Damyankee who moved South and became successful.

A good ole boy is a native son — no matter how young or how bad — who does not act uppity.

A good old girl is a well-behaved female hunting dog.

(5/7/76)

Politics is a fertile field for "chuckulars," not necessarily from its practitioners, but about them:

Nelson Rockefeller tells it on himself from his 1958 campaign in New York. Making the rounds in Manhattan, he dropped into a delicatessen to greet the customers. As he extended a hand to one old gentleman the guy simply turned away and went over to a corner. An accompanying newspaper reporter followed him and asked "Don't you want to shake hands and say 'hello' to the candidate?"

" — I should put 'hello' in the bank?" the guy replied laconically.

(10/27/66)

The effusive Congressman was making his campaign rounds at the county fair. Coming up to an old acquaintance he hadn't seen in several years, he greeted him, "Well, hello Joe, it's good to see you. How's your father?" To this Joe replied, "I'm sorry to say he died last year."

The politician continued his handshaking of the multitudes until he again came upon Joe. "It's good to see you, Joe," he said afresh. "And how's your father?" To which Joe replied blankly "Still dead."
(4/26/67)

In the backwash of the hotly-contested general elections of 1966 when Republican Jim Gardner ousted our veteran Democratic Congressman Harold Cooley, I was reminded of the handy rationale of politicians:

The political science student asked his father to explain what a "traitor" was in politics. "Any man who leaves our party and goes over to the other one is a traitor, son," the father explained.

"Well, then, what is a man who leaves his party and comes over to yours?" the lad pursued.

"He'd be a convert, son, a real convert."
(11/13/66)

After several minutes of ingratiating himself, the candidate finally asked the farmer directly for his support.

"Nope, can't give it to you," said the farmer. "I've already promised to vote for your opponent."

"Well, in politics, promising and doing are two different things," the politician pursued.

"In that case," the farmer replied, "I'll be happy to promise to vote for you."
(6/30/68)

"You'll be happy to know that you're now my second choice," the voter said to the candidate for the Town Council as he entered the polls.

"Thanks," said the candidate. "By the way, who's your first choice?"
"Anybody else," replied the voter.
(5/7/72)

Talking with the politician who was complaining of the critical treatment he'd been given in the newspaper, the reporter responded "I don't see why you're unhappy. You're getting a lot of free publicity, and we've spelled your hame correctly."

"Yeah," replied the politician, "but half of those lies you've been printing about me aren't true anyhow."
(6/30/68)

"There are 100 jails in this state, and I'm proud to say that no member of

my family has ever been in one of them," announced the candidate on the stump. "Yeah?" asked a listener. "Which one is that?"
(11/3/72)

The Republican ward heeler was pumping up a staunch party supporter during a heated election campaign. The voter allowed he'd always voted Republican, his dad had, and so had his grandfather. "Then I suppose you'll vote Republican this election, too," the old pol suggested. "Oh, no," the voter corrected. "There comes a time when you just have to cast principles aside and do what's right."
(11/19/67)

Like the three guys arguing over whose profession was the first established on earth: "Mine was," said the surgeon. "The Bible says that Eve was made by carving a rib from Adam." "Not at all," interrupted the engineer. "An engineering job came before that. In six days the earth was created out of chaos. That was an engineer's job." "Sure it was," topped the politician. "But who created that chaos?!"
(11/5/67)

They tell the one about the late Illinois Sen. Everett Dirksen who had just had a telephone installed in his car and wanted to impress President Johnson with that fact. He dialed Lyndon one day on their car-to-car hook-up and said "Lyndon, I was just thinking about something so I thought I'd call you on this new telephone I've just had installed in my car—" "Excuse me, Everett," interrupted the President from his own limousine. "I got to answer a call on the other line."
(11/17/72)

This one came up during Jim Hunt's first campaign for Governor of North Carolina:

Lt. Gov. Hunt, House Speaker Jimmy Green, and East Carolina Univ. Chancellor Leo Jenkins were chatting informally at a Democratic party clambake. Hunt announced that he'd had an extraordinary revelation the night before in which the Lord urged him to run for Governor. "Funny coincidence," chimed in Green. "I had an experience just like that." "Funny about that, indeed," said Jenkins. "I don't remember speaking to either of you."
(9/22/75)

An apocryphal story has it that an ambitious young Greek once asked

Demosthenes how to become a politician. "Just fill your mouth with marbles," said Demosthenes, "and spit them out one at a time as you talk. When you've lost all your marbles, then you'll be a politician."
(11/3/75)

Put-downs, for their simple glory in puncturing the spirit of pomposity, provide some of the best jokes of all:

The slick operator gave his best wolf whistle and a seductive "Helloooo" as the good looking gal passed by. When she turned and gave him a frigid look he quickly retorted, "Excuse me. I thought you were my mother." "I couldn't be your mother," the doll replied, "I'm married."
(3/3/66)

"I'll be frank with you," declared the young casanova as he relaxed his embrace. "You're not the first girl I've kissed."

"In that case I'll be frank with you, too," she replied, "and tell you that you've got a heck of a lot to learn."
(10/6/66)

The hometown Romeo noticed a beautiful girl sitting by herself in a hotel lobby. Infinitely confident, he registered "Mr. and Mrs. So-and-So," then strolled over to make her acquaintance.

Two days later the desk clerk handed him a bill for $900. "What's the idea?" he sputtered. "I've only been here two days." "That's right," the clerk replied smoothly, "but your wife's been here almost three weeks."
(7/6/66)

Two Carolina classmates, meeting at their 10-year reunion, eyed each other. One was much fatter and the other skinnier than when they were in college. "From the looks of you there must have been a famine in your area," said the fat one. "Yeah," returned the skinny one, "and from your looks, you must have caused it."
(11/15/67)

At the same reunion one classmate greeted another: "You're looking well," he said. "I wish I could say the same for you," the friend tartly replied. "You could," said the first one, "if you were as big a liar as I am."
(7/14/68)

A young writer was being torn to shreds in absentia by a group of self-styled literary critics in the presence of a well-known author. "It isn't right to talk of him that way," said the good-natured celebrity. "I like him a great

deal." "What's so good about him?" asked a critic. "I'll tell you," answered the author. "He doesn't show off. And that's quite unusual for a man with so little talent."
(4/20/69)

The prime survivor of the the put-down was this one, attributed to the hardy traveling salesman:

The new salesman was chatting with an old-timer on the road, who asked him how he was doing.

"Not so good," said the new drummer. "Every place I go, it seems the prospective customer insults me."

"That's funny," said the old-timer. "I've been traveling this area for over 20 years. I've had my samples pitched out, been ushered out of offices, had the door slammed in my face, and was even socked in the nose once—but I've never been insulted."
(10/13/66)

Although the mores of women's liberation are changing the humor of domestic jokes, some survivors hold up well:

A shy little office worker was frightened of his boss. One day he told a fellow worker he was sick, but afraid to go home for fear the boss would fire him. "Don't be silly. He'll never know. He's not even here today," his comrade reassured. Finally the man went home. As he walked up the front pathway, he looked through the window and saw his boss kissing his wife. He raced all the way back to the office. "A fine friend you are," he exclaimed to his advisor. "I almost got caught!"
(1/20/66)

A gentleman who loved his pet cat had to go to Europe, so entrusted care of the animal to his brother, George. In Europe he missed the cat and telephoned George to find out how pussy was doing.

"Oh, the cat died," George said bluntly. Heartbroken, the brother hung up. Two weeks later when the traveling brother had to call home again he criticized George for his un-feeling report. "Why couldn't you have told me slowly? You could have first said 'The cat's caught up on the roof.' The next day you could have phoned me and said 'The cat fell and was taken to the hospital with internal injuries.' Finally you could have called me and said 'The cat died in his sleep last night.' That would have been much better." George was remorseful. "I just wasn't thinking," he said apologetically.

The brother then asked, "By the way, how's mom doing?"

George thought for a moment, then stammered "Well, uh, you see, mom's caught up on the roof."
(7/10/66)

Talking with his wife's doctor, the husband asked the physician how she was, in general. The doctor replied, "She's not sick. She just thinks she's sick."

Several days later when the man happened to see the doctor again, the physician asked the man how his wife was coming along.

"Much worse," the husband replied. "Now she thinks she's dead."
(2/8/73)

The Carolina married student was discussing his home life with a new neighbor. "Man, for about six months after we were married we nearly went broke trying to feed and entertain all the relatives that kept dropping in on us."

"I'm having the same problem," said the neighbor. "How'd you take care of it?" "Simple, when I figured it out. I just loaned money to the poor relatives, and borrowed money from the rich ones. We haven't been bothered by visits from any of 'em since."
(7/20/66)

At the side of the road a woman looked helplessly at the flat tire on her car. A passing motorist stopped to help out. After he'd changed the tire the woman thanked him and cautioned "Please let the jack down easy, sir. My husband is sleeping in the back seat."
(8/4/66)

A woman walking across a shopping center parking lot saw a driverless car slowly rolling toward her. With unusual agility she sprinted toward it, jerked open the door, hopped in and pulled it to a halt with the emergency brake. As she got out a man in coveralls was among the fast-gathering crowd that approached her. "Well, I stopped it," she announced to the assemblage. "Yeah, I know, lady. I was pushing it," the coveralls guy returned acidly.
(7/5/70)

The wife of a lush invaded his favorite stag bar where he was toying with his Scotch on the rocks. She grabbed it, took a swallow and almost gagged. "How can you stand to drink that awful stuff?" she asked. "See, I keep telling you," he countered. "And you think I'm here just having fun!"
(7/9/67)

Lady in the supermarket says to the manager: "Give me a pound of those turnip greens. My husband is so fond of them. —And have they been sprayed with any kind of poison?" "No lady," the grocer replied. "You'll have to buy that at the drugstore."

(7/16/67)

Woman in the supermarket to another clerk: "How much are your eggs?" "Eighty-four cents a dozen, lady." "That certainly is high—seven cents an egg. That's ridiculous," the lady countered. "It may be ridiculous to you, lady," the clerk replied, "but it's a full day's work for the hen."

(7/16/67)

The "switch"—the unexpected turn—is the key to the point of the garden variety general run of jokes:

A so-so artist in Chapel Hill wasn't doing well until a wealthy young hometown woman called to offer him a commission to paint her. She insisted that he paint the portrait in the nude. "But madam, I can't do that," the artist protested. "I have my ethics." She offered $2,500 for the job but he still refused, insisting "I don't know about that nude business. I'm just getting started and I'd hate to jeopardize my future." When the woman jumped the offer to $5,000 he gave in. "I'll do it on one condition," he relented. "I'll do the portrait in the nude, but I insist on keeping my socks on. I gotta have somewhere to stick my brushes."

(7/3/66)

One of the hometown policemen was recalling a downtown accident he checked on a while back. A man passing by stopped and was looking over the injured person when a woman rushed up, shoved him aside, and started applying first aid. The man looked on for a minute, then leaned over to the lady and said quietly, "When you get to the part about calling a doctor, I'm already here."

(7/28/66)

The patient seemed worried and wanted to question the diagnosis of the doctor. "Are you sure it's pneumonia, doctor?" he asked. "I've heard of cases where a doctor treated a patient for pneumonia and he ended up dying of typhoid fever."

"No worry about that," the doctor replied. "When I treat a patient for pneumonia, he dies of pneumonia."

(9/21/66)

Whenever I hear that one it reminds of the truly tasteless one about the woman patient who thought she had only a minor illness and was shocked when the doctor informed her that his treatment would cost her $2,000. "I want a second opinion," the woman complained. "Okay, then. You're ugly, too," the doctor added.

The gray-haired woman, entering the elevator, saw a man facing her and keeping his hat on. "Young man, don't you know you should remove your hat in the presence of a lady?" she reprimanded. "I always do," the man replied gallantly, "in the presence of **elderly** ladies."
(8/14/66)

The hometown boy, a successful TV star, ran into an old friend during a visit back home. "How are things going for you?" asked the actor. "Well, since you ask, I'll tell you," said the old friend. "My wife's in the hospital. I just lost my job. My mother's sick, and I'm behind on the rent. I sure could use a loan." The TV star stalled around for a few minutes, explaining his own problems, then finally said "No." "There's one thing I'll say for you," the hometowner continued. "Success sure hasn't changed you a bit."
(5/28/67)

A group of young intellectuals on the Carolina campus had as a rule at their Monday evening meetings that anyone who asked a question he couldn't answer himself had to pay a $5 fine. One evening a member asked "Why doesn't a ground squirrel leave any dirt around the top of his hole when he digs it?" After some deliberation he was challenged to answer his own question. "That's easy," he explained. "He starts at the bottom and digs up." "Very nice," countered another member, "but how does the squirrel get to the bottom?" "That's your question," retorted the wise guy.
(4/16/67)

The blue collar worker, testifying before a committee of efficiency experts, was asked to identify himself. "I'm an executive with the East Side Sanitation Company," he explained. "Tell us about your work," the committee spokesman said.

"Well, we clean out more septic tanks than anybody in this region," the worker replied.

"But how does that qualify you as an executive?" the questioner pursued. "Well, it's like this. All us men that work off the truck go out on the job each morning and drive to a septic tank. Then I gets down in the tank and dips up a bucketful of the material, and I hands it to Woodrow, and Woodrow hands it to Elmer, and Elmer hands it to Mose and he dumps it in the truck."

"But I don't understand how that makes you an executive," the committee spokesman pursued. "Of course I'm an executive," the worker replied. "Don't you see? I don't take nothin' from nobody."

(5/21/67)

Fred Friendly, the TV producer was talking with Walter Lippman and recalled that he'd seen a college girl carrying a sign, "Make Love, Not War," at a campus demonstration. In his day, Friendly said, no respectable girl would have carried such a sign, since the "make" phrase would have meant "making out" rather than "making peace."

"That's interesting," said Lippman, "but tell me, Fred. What does 'making out' mean?" Friendly was so taken aback that he told his family about it that night. All were amused that the columnist didn't know the meaning of the common phrase, except for Friendly's teen-age daughter. She knew what "making out" meant, she said, but added quizzically, "Tell me, who's Walter Lippman?"

(6/19/68)

"How do you spell Mississippi?"

" — The river, or the state?"

(11/27/68)

The proud new father was passing out cigars at his office. "Boy or girl?" asked the boss. "It's a boy — named John," responded the beaming father. " — Why'd you name him John?" countered the boss. "Don't you know that every Tom, Dick, and Harry is named John!"

(11/27/68)

That calls to mind the one about the guy who handed a friend a cigar and also lit one himself. "How do you like these two for a quarter cigars?" he asked the friend. "You must have the 23-cent one," the friend replied.

(10/8/69)

The town busybody spied a youngster sitting on the curb, smoking a cigarette and drinking a bottle of beer at 9 o'clock in the morning. "Why aren't you in school, young man?" she chastised. "Hell, lady," the child replied defensively, "I'm only five years old."

(10/8/72)

It must be my experience as a private second class "yardbird" in the infantry that accounts for my appreciation of army jokes:

The new squad of draftees was awakened to their first morning in the Army by a burly sergeant who strode into the barracks, snapped on the lights, and roared, "All right, you guys, it's 4:30!"

"Four-thirty!" gasped a sleepy voice. "You better get to bed. Tomorrow's gonna be a big day!"

(7/21/66)

The bartender in the officers club served a Scotch and soda to a brusque and taciturn full colonel. The officer tossed down his drink and dropped a five-dollar bill on the counter as he left. The bartender walked over, picked up the bill, and muttered to his waiter, "Now aint that just like a bloody colonel—leave a five-dollar tip and skip without paying!"

(9/15/66)

The dogface, standing in line for his discharge from the Army, was confronted by his tough sergeant, who seemed more charitable at this final occasion. "I suppose," the sergeant said, "that many years from now after I'm dead and buried you'll want to come and spit on my grave." "No, sergeant," the delighted draftee replied. "I've already promised myself that after I get out of this Army I'll never stand in a line again as long as I live."

(7/30/67)

—And finally, some of the gems that come from the courtroom:

The drunk was picked up and brought before the judge. "I got into bad company, your honor," said the defendant. "I had a quart of whiskey and the two guys with me didn't drink."

(8/25/66)

The highway patrolman on the witness stand failed to say that the defendant he'd charged with drunken driving was actually intoxicated. "Was he drunk when you saw him in his car?" the prosecutor asked. "No, I can't say he was," replied the officer. "Well, then, would you say he was sober?" "No, I can't say he was sober," the officer insisted. "Well then," the exasperated prosecutor continued, "just what was his condition?" There was a long silence—so long that everybody in court began to wonder if the officer was going to reply, when he said "I'd say he was just right."

(6/9/68)

The badly bruised woman was telling the judge her story: "Your honor, he gets up every morning and starts knocking me around the bedroom. He hits me in the head with his fist. Sometimes he uses a shoe. If I don't fix his meals to suit him, he throws the dishes at me. If I complain he clouts me with his beer bottle. Your honor, he ought to be in jail." Looking at the defendant the judge asked "What do you have to say about this?" "I say you can't believe a word she says, your honor. She's punch drunk."

(9/18/66)

"Were you covered by anything during this performance?" the court prosecutor asked the strip teaser being tried for indecent exposure. "I certainly was," the young lady replied haughtily. "What specifically, then?" the prosecutor pursued. After a brief pause the witness announced triumphantly: "Workmen's compensation."

(12/11/66)

The defendant was being tried for using obscene language, specifically calling a policeman a jackass. After the judge questioned him about it, the defendant admitted the offense. The court let him off with a reprimand. As he turned to leave, the defendant stopped and asked the judge if it would be all right to call a jackass a policeman. The judge pondered that a moment, then said "I suppose that would be all right." As the man reached the door of the courtroom he met the officer who'd arrested him. "Hello policeman," he greeted the bluecoat.

(3/27/69)

The judge was explaining to an elderly indigent defendant how to pick a court-appointed lawyer. "You may choose any of the five lawyers sitting over there on that bench," the judge explained, "or another who is downstairs at the moment." The defendant perused the five barristers thoughtfully, then told the judge, "If it's all the same, your honor, I believe I'll take the one downstairs."

(5/7/72)

Index of Names